Explanations

GWYNN NETTLER

The University of Alberta

McGRAW-HILL BOOK COMPANY

New York   *San Francisco*   *St. Louis*   *Düsseldorf*
London   *Mexico*   *Panama*   *Sydney*   *Toronto*

This book was set in Linofilm Garamond Number 3 and Spartan Book by Applied Typographic Systems, and printed on permanent paper and bound by Vail-Ballou Press, Inc. The editor was Ronald D. Kissack.

Printed in the United States of America.

Library of Congress catalog card number: 71-11451

1234567890 VBVB 7876543210

46291

IN SUMMARY

How do men explain their behavior?

They do so by attempting to clarify the symbols with which they interpret themselves and others. They give definitions.

They do so also by telling stories that offer "good reasons" for action. These tales employ conventions that would make us feel as the man-to-be-explained must have felt when he behaved as he did. The conventions vary, but their satisfaction as explanations results from their ability to make us "feel-in-with" the actor. They build empathy.

As one moves from explaining an individual to explaining social events, he graduates from the simpler arts of evoking empathy to the grander stories that organize experience. These fictions may still rest, in places, upon shared sentiments and "good reasons," but they are tales that weave empathy with myth and moral judgment. Men group themselves in the names of these grander visions of the world that describe what succeeds and fails, what "it all means," and what "needs to be done." Men explain matters with ideologies.

Men also try to explain their behaviors by *knowing* something, as distinct from feeling and believing. They attempt to order observations as declarative statements called "facts." They attempt to build facts that have generality—that apply, not only to the particular action described, but also to classes of acts deemed similar. Then they seek to relate one generalization to another and to construct tales that tell how patterns might be discerned among the facts of varied generality.

This kind of story about human behavior aspires to meet a demanding set of requirements. It satisfies as an explanation when the event to be explained can be shown to be an instance of a general rule that has been invented in terms of the desiderata. There is an assortment of such general, empirical rules. The distinctive test of rule-fulness is the provision of a more accurate map than is given by folk knowledge. With such rules, one would expect to be able to guide his conduct, and that of others, so that he receives fewer surprises in wending his way through the maze of human situations. The stories that tell these rules are scientific explanations.

Although an accurate tally has not been made, it seems that most explanations men offer each other appeal to empathy and ideology. Scientific explanation of human conduct is difficult. It is rarely achieved, and it is both lauded and condemned.

The term "science" has become an honorific because of the success of this thoughtway when applied to the physical world. Thus encouraged, men have attempted to apply similar procedures in thinking about themselves. They have not failed entirely; techniques for controlling observations, for enlarging their scope, for classifying, counting, and correlating behaviors have been developed that improve upon folk knowledge. But the cachet of science has been borrowed by men whose explanations scarcely meet the desiderata and tests of a science. This becomes more true as the putative scientist advances from explaining individuals to explaining collectivities, and from explaining with counts and correlations to explaining with causes and interpretations. Here ideology masquerades as science.

To call studies of economies, governments, personalities, and societies "sciences" is to express either aspiration or arrogance. Individuals and governments that would purchase such "science" are advised to consume it with caution.

An additional advice to be drawn is that it is wiser to count continuities than to await revelations and ill-advised to use as guides of personal or political policy men whose explanatory skill is keen at hindsight and myopic in foresight.

If this counsel seems trivial, there are yet men who neither know it nor take it.

Thinking about it has been a privilege granted me by the taxpayers of the Province of Alberta who have built a fine university in which I have enjoyed teaching some of them and some of their children. This privilege, the luxury of study and contemplation, is not taken for granted and my appreciation is due those who have supported its exercise. I am also grateful to the Canada Council for financial assistance in the prosecution of my inquiry.

GWYNN NETTLER

ACKNOWLEDGEMENTS

A bibliographic index, alphabetized by author, begins on page 215. Appreciation is due many of these writers and their publishers for permission to reproduce their thoughts at some length. In addition, specific recognition is accorded the following copyright holders who kindly consented to citation:

The American Scholar for permission to reprint excerpts from Daniel Bell. Copyright © 1966 by the United Chapters of Phi Beta Kappa.

Basic Books, Inc., for citation privileges from A. Michotte (1963), Lazarsfeld, Sewell, and Wilensky (1967), K. Popper (1959, 1963, 1965), and L. S. Feuer (1963).

Beacon Press for allowing quotations from B. Moore, copyright © 1967.

Mrs. A. C. Benjamin for permission to publish excerpts from the late Professor Benjamin's *Operationism* (1955).

The British Psychological Society for reprint rights to portions of papers by D. B. Bromley (1968) and Wilson and Patterson (1969).

Cambridge University Press for permission to quote M. Oakeshott (1933).

The University of Chicago Press for the privilege of citing T. Abel (1954), W. Bell (1969), S. C. Dodd (1943), F. A. Hayek (1967), C. W. Mills (1946), E. van den Haag (1968), and M. Zonis (1969).

Commentary for quotation rights from B. Berger (1962), M. Friedman (1969), and R. Heilbroner (1967). Copyright © by the American Jewish Committee.

Harcourt, Brace, and World, Inc. for permission to quote from Cohen and Nagel (1934), Gerth and Mills (1953), G. Homans (1961, 1967), K. Mannheim (1941), E. Nagel (1961), and L. Wirth (1936).

Life for the privilege of quoting L. Wainwright (1968). Copyright © 1968 Time, Inc.

The Macmillan Company for permission to cite from G. Bergmann (1968), M. Brodbeck (1968), A. Koestler (1941), D. P. Moynihan (1969), F. S. C. Northrop (1947), G. Ryle (1966), and H. Simon (1968). Copyrights © as of the dates indicated.

G. & C. Merriam Company for permission to quote from *Webster's New International Dictionary*, Second Edition, © 1959 by G. & C. Merriam Co., Publishers of the Merriam-Webster Dictionaries.

The New Yorker for citation rights to excerpts from N. Bliven (1969) and R. Rovere (1968).

Princeton University Press for authorization to quote from J. Douglas (1967). Copyright © 1967 by the Princeton University Press.

Science for rights to reprint portions of papers by L. A. DuBridge (1968), N. E. Miller (1969), R. C. Nichols (1966), D. K. Price (1969), M. B. Smith (1969), and J. A. Wheeler (1968). Copyrights © on the dates noted by the American Association for the Advancement of Science.

Scientific American, Inc. for permission to cite from M. Gardner (1968) and R. R. Sokal (1966). Copyright © by Scientific American, Inc. All rights reserved.

The Society for the Study of Social Problems for permission to quote from their journal, *Social Problems*, excerpts from T. Hirschi and H. C. Selvin (1966) and G. Nettler (1967).

Time for citation rights from "The Diary of a Vandalized Car," February 28, 1969. Copyright © 1969 Time, Inc.

The Viking Press, Inc. for rights to reproduce from *Between Past and Future*, copyright © 1967 by Hannah Arendt. All rights reserved. Originally appeared in *The New Yorker*. And for reprint permission for excerpts from *The Portable Nietzsche* edited and translated by Walter Kaufmann. Copyright © 1954 by the Viking Press, Inc.

CONTENTS

Contents

CHAPTER ONE

QUESTIONS AND ANSWERS

Explaining is something we do to each other, and for ourselves. What we attempt to explain, and how, are functions of familiarity and strangeness, of expectation and surprise, of purpose, and of the customs of thinking that are embedded in language.

We do not attempt to explain everything. In each culture, only certain kinds of behaviors and situations are felt to require those verbalizations called "explanations." And we are accustomed to different sorts of explanations for different situations. For example, we in the Western world usually employ a different set of concepts in the explanation of animate and inanimate behavior or approved and disapproved conduct (Evans, 1968; Leifer, 1964; Schiffman and Wynne, 1963).

We can explain explanation by noting that man, like his simian cousins, is curious. We may say, then, that *explanations are manipulations of symbols performed in an attempt to satisfy curiosity.*

1

The arousal of curiosity varies with individual temper; some persons are more curious about some kinds of things. Our curiosity varies, too, with social stimulation. Whatever we take most for granted, we are least likely to try to explain. Taking-for-granted is learned in a cultural climate. This means, conversely, that there are questions in every culture that require answers only because men have learned to think with the concepts that carry the question. What is love of God? is such a question. Today's consensus calls this inquiry meaningful in Canada but not in the Soviet Union.

Explanations, then, are addressed to questions. A first step in the art of explanation is to examine the question to ascertain what it asks — that is, what would satisfy it. In doing this we determine whether the question is "answerable."[1] The comforts of our language are such that we assume some questions to be proper and others improper, although we have difficulty specifying the criteria that distinguish a silly question from a sensible one.[2]

How many angels can dance on the head of a pin?

What color is justice?

These questions arrange words in correct grammatical form, yet most moderns assume them to be unanswerable. The culture of literate North Americans is not congenial to the description of the behavior of reified, transcendental abstractions or to the attribution of colors to principles. Other times and other places have found such questions answerable; they aroused curiosity, and the arousal was satisfied.

If the arousal of curiosity and its satisfaction are cultural, then the "correct answer" to questions rests upon consensus, so that, if most people who ask the question *feel* satisfied, *their* question is answered. This means that even "silly questions" — those whose answers are beyond the tests we prefer — even these questions may be "answered" if the question-raiser has learned a convention such that, upon its invocation, *he* feels satisfied.

We respond to many "profound" questions with this style of reply — questions such as:

What is the purpose of life?

Why did this have to happen to me?

Why *my* child?

The art of response to such questions is to seek the conditioned linguistic conventions that allay the curiosity of the interrogator. The reply need not be provable or true.[3] It needs only to have been habituated to satisfaction.

It is a prejudice to hold that only the other man's thoughtways contain silly questions and ridiculous answers. Every system of symbols with which man interprets his environment and himself carries the hazard of inquiry deemed fruitless from some other system's logic. We "know" much that gratifies us because we live in an agreeable social atmosphere, an atmosphere in which other men, like us, "know" the same kinds of things. The empirical validity of this comfortable knowledge ranges from the confirmed to the untestable.

A philosophic approach to debates about explanations asks what it is we seek to effect when we "use our heads" in symbol manipulation. Sometimes this question reveals a lack of purpose, other than gratification from the play with words. At other times the continuing disputes about the image of man can be shown to result from differing tests of the accuracy of the picture that our congenial conventions allow. From within one culture, some examples illustrate the failure of minds to meet because of the varieties of purpose in taking thought and the varieties of assumption about how to explain human action.[4]

THE GROUP-THERAPY SESSION

Alpha: Why do you need to be so neat?

Beta: If I like to be neat, what makes you think I "need to be"?

Alpha: We are trying to help you understand the sources of your behavior.

Beta: But what is it you wish me to search for when you ask me "why I need to"?

Alpha: Well, there must be some reason for your behavior.

Beta: Yes, but there are "reasons" and "reasons." Which do you want to hear and how will we know when I've given the "right" reason?

THE NOVELIST AND THE PSYCHOLOGIST

(Abstracts from a debate between Miss Kathleen Nott and Professor H. J. Eysenck. Nott, 1964)

Miss Nott: The kind of Behaviorist psychology I am discussing is an "anti-subjectivist" ideology. [It denies] . . . a place for "value" and "choice" — strikingly subjective notions.

A "therapy" must claim to help or heal human beings. Doesn't it also imply something about what is a human being and what you might mean by human development? There might still be much to learn from those who have spent their life and work in thinking about this: for instance, some artists, some scientists, some moral thinkers. Or some patients. One here or there might try to mumble to you what he really wants and so give you a slant on the "moral future of mankind." (September, pp. 62-63)

Dr. Eysenck: The very notion that we can study human conduct scientifically seems to appall and upset many people. They cry out in spiritual agony that this is a "mechanistic device" for denying freedom-of-the-will and for treating men as if they were machines. (October, p. 53)

Miss Nott: In all systems of (psycho-)therapy, the patient is at a disadvantage. The therapist is often trying . . . to impose a "norm." Even if he isn't, the patient can't help thinking that the therapist somehow represents such a concept. (September, p. 63)

Dr. Eysenck: Here is a boy of sixteen who is suffering from encopresis — in other words, he is constantly defecating into his trousers, has done so for many years and continues to do so in spite of all that orthodox psychiatry can do for him. Is a therapist trying to impose a "norm" on him when he tries to cure him of this? Perhaps, but even more certainly the *patient* has no doubt at all in his mind that he wants to overcome this debility. . . . (October, p. 55, emphasis in the original)

Miss Nott: . . . the boy with encopresis . . . while I can see that his habit made him unhappy because of his social unacceptability, I also think that he developed the habit because he was unhappy in the first place. For "neurosis" in the quotation from Professor Eysenck, read "unhappiness" and we may get somewhere, both semantically and psychologically. (November, p. 91)

Dr. Eysenck: (. . . "unhappy in the first place"?) Well, he wasn't. (*Ibid.*, p. 92)

Miss Nott: The guiding idea seems to be that man is *merely* a social animal: and that "symptoms" are nothing but a sign of difficulty in conforming to whatever the current social demands may be. They *could* be, on the other hand, a form of obscure social criticism, not stupid at that, and needing interpretation. (*Ibid.*, p. 91, emphasis in the original)

Dr. Eysenck: Perhaps she is right in thinking that our patients' symptoms "can be a form of obscure social criticism." From what I have seen this seems to me wildly improbable, but again, if Miss Nott would like to produce a proper criterion and carry out an empirical study on a few hundred cases, I should be very happy to consider her results. My motor car may miss on one cylinder because it is unhappy, or as an obscure criticism of my driving, but if I can cure it by cleaning the spark plugs I shall feel that I need some substantial evidence before considering such esoteric hypotheses. (*Ibid.*, p. 92)

Miss Nott: What matters . . . is Dr. Eysenck's implication that the "symptoms" don't *mean* something important and therefore don't need the fullest understanding and interpretation, especially of what they mean to the person who suffers them.

Whatever you do in the emergency treatment of "symptoms" should you not, as a philosopher or theoretician of human nature, be aware that you have to take the possibility and the value of personal freedom . . . into some kind of account? (*Ibid.*, p. 91, emphasis in the original)

Letter to the Editor 1: The question raised by Miss Nott . . . was that of the validity of a method of treatment of emotional and intellectual disorders which does not recognize the existence of the disorders underlying the manifest symptoms . . . . (December, p. 94)

Letter to the Editor 2: How do you know there is a "disorder underlying" the behavior you wish to correct? How do you know when a behavior is a "symptom" of other events? How do you know when a method of treatment is "valid"? (Unpublished)

THE SCHOOL COUNSELOR, THE BEHAVIORIST, AND THE MOTHER OF THE RICH, BAD BOY

Counsel: Dr. X is highly recommended. You and Bill might want to see him.
Mother: But we've been to two psychiatrists already. And a psychologist.
Counsel: Dr. X is a specialist in problems of adolescence. He ought to be able to find out what's troubling the boy.
Behaviorist: Bill doesn't like school and doesn't study. He yells at his mother. He lies, fights, and steals a little. You, Mr. Counselor, interpret this behavior as a *result* of "something troubling the boy." This is an assumption. How do you defend it?

Disagreements such as these are representative of the variety of descriptive language used, the multiplicity of "things looked at," and the assortment of assumptions made, when one offers an explanation of human behavior. The study of these styles of understanding may be facilitated if modern attempts to explain human conduct are grouped as:

(1) Explanations by definition
(2) Explanations by empathy-building
(3) Scientific explanations: those stories that would explain by referring the particular to some regularity of occurrence
(4) Ideological explanations: those stories that falsify in order to justify an interest

This grouping is not free of overlap. When people tell their explanatory tales, they may use a mix of these thoughtways. And each of these modes is, in turn, full of a variety that moves with the concepts employed, the logic preferred, and the conditions and events cited as explanatory variables.

Before describing these types of "explainway,"[5] it should be clear that many explanations — perhaps all — are fictions; they describe events, put them together, *as if* the descriptions were complete, uniquely accurate, and the relationships the only patterns discernible. It should be clear, too, that fictions work — some better than others, of course — and that there is no one correct way to explain human action *if* it is agreed that explanations are encouraged to satisfy diverse purposes. It should surprise no student that explanations that satisfy one man's curiosity or another man's morality or the third man's urge for action may fail the fourth man's desire to predict. It will be seen that some explanations are not merely irrelevant to prediction, but actually obscurant. Conversely, other explainways that seem to assist one in making forecasts do not satisfy some investigators' "need to know why."

NOTES

[1] More correctly, in interpersonal relations we are trying to answer the question-asker rather than the question.

[2] One philosopher, at least, has come to the frustrating conclusion that it is impossible to specify principles by which one separates sense from nonsense. Wittgenstein's *Tractatus* (1922) argues, in Ryle's words (1966:5), that:

To try to tell what makes the difference between significant and nonsensical talk is itself to cross the divide between significant and nonsensical talk. . . . the rules and conventions of map-making (cannot) themselves be mapped.

So Wittgenstein argued . . . that the philosopher or logician is debarred from saying what it is that makes things said significant or nonsensical. He can show it, but not tell it.

This point of view contrasts with that of von Mises (1956) who offers a lucid exposition of means of discriminating "meaningful" from "nonsensical" questions, particularly in his Chapters 3, 4, and 6.

[3]"Provable" here means "amenable to empirical test." "True" refers to the satisfaction of some consensual empirical test.

[4]All examples—all cases, conversations, illustrations, and correspondence—paraphrased or verbatim, here and on following pages, are actual.

[5]This neologism is justified by our intention to regard explanations of human action as styles of stories employed with varying success toward many ends. Hereafter, the coined word will be used without the apology of quotation marks.

Dictionaries tell us that "to explain" is "to make things clear, understandable." The word derives from Latin roots meaning "to flatten, to make plain."

Since men perceive their worlds through a veil of symbols, it is felt that making the symbols clear is a necessary step to making reality plainer. And since men talk to each other about their worlds, they face the problem of comprehension. For both types of problem — knowing the world and comprehending the sentences uttered about it — a "semantic" explanation may be devised (Kaplan, 1964:327). Such explanation is directed toward the clarification of meaning, and it proceeds by translation.

The translation that is supposed "to make things plain" usually consists of definitions. The kinds of definition offered and their effectiveness in "making clear" depend upon the linguistic tools of the translator and the repertoire of learned symbolic associations available to the auditor. The symbolic instrumentation on both sides of this conversation — the auditor's and the translator's — is limited; there are, then, breakdowns in semantic explanation and "communications experts" are today concerned with repairing these lines. The repair is considered satisfactory when signs are given that the auditor is responding appropriately to the translator.

Explanation by definition involves only an exchange of symbols.[1] The exchange is deemed "an explanation" when foreign symbols are converted into familiar ones. Upon this transfer, curiosity rests.

The utility of semantic explanation, apart from its resolution of curiosity, is another question. As will be seen, it remains moot to what extent "knowing the world" requires clear symbols. A stronger use lies in the clarification of sentences for interpersonal purposes.

Since symbols vary in their denotative power, level of abstraction, and connotative range, translations vary in their ability to appease curiosity and they may remain at levels of abstraction remote from physical consequence. The exchange of symbols that characterizes most definitions is purely "intensional," as the semanticist calls it; one word is substituted for another without any effect upon experience, other than that called "satisfaction of curiosity." For example, when Alpha tells Omega what he means by "human dignity," "justice," or "freedom," the consequences of the translation may be nothing more than Omega's thinking, "Ah-ha, so that's what he means." Depending on how it is done, the clarification of meaning may or may not bring us "closer to experience." Other translations, however, have more immediate application to a range of nonverbal observables. This occurs, in particular, when a definition gives an instruction, as in a recipe.

Definitions are devised by several procedures, each of which has advantages and disadvantages that are functions of the kind of question asked, the conditional learning of the auditor, and the uses to which translator and auditor put the symbolic transaction.

One may attempt to define by (1) citing synonyms, (2) enumerating, (3) giving examples, (4) classifying, (5) stating or demonstrating "operations."

(1) *Citing synonyms*

Curiosity rests in this technique upon our ability to find a familiar verbal coin of the same or similar value as the word to be defined. The synonym may or may not bring us "closer to reality." It tells us how terms are being used by placing the definiendum, the symbol to be defined, in a context of familiar words.

(2) *Enumerating*

A symbol can be defined by listing the words to which it refers collectively.

Spices are cinnamon, cloves, paprika, and ginger.

Crimes are robbery, burglary, assault, and homicide.

As opposed to some other definitional procedures (classifying, for example), defining by enumerating and by giving examples is often recommended to bring a classifying term "down the abstraction ladder" so that the events referred to are made more certain.

(3) *Giving examples*

We may define by showing samples of the sort of thing to which the word refers. This primitive form of definition is useful with children and foreigners. We point to a goat and utter its common name. We trust that, as we show "goats" and utter names, our auditors will, as they do, learn the differentiae that distinguish these animals from sheep.

Defining in this way has the advantage of saving one from the definition of fictions. It is difficult to point to a ghost.

(4) *Classifying*

To define by classifying is to give meaning to a term by subsuming it under a type or class.

Autocracy is a form of government in which . . .

Crime is behavior that . . .

The advantage of definition by classification is that, given the prior conditioned attachments of meaning to the symbols by which elements are grouped in a "class," classifying tells "what it is." It also tells how we regard it.

Classifying is the principal thought-mode by which sensation is organized and, in this sense, given "meaning." It is a first step in any science, where taxonomies are invented self-consciously, and it is, in science, but a reasoned extension of what man has done less consciously — that is, to collect experiences and notions under rubrics that permit, and channel, the perception of similarity and dissimilarity, continuity and change, and the everyday prediction of what others are apt to do under certain circumstances.

It is convenient to distinguish the classifying terms that have "grown naturally" from those that man has invented more purposefully. The crescive ideas may be called "concepts" to distinguish them from the enacted labels, "constructs." The definition of a concept is "lexical," that is, a "dictionary definition" reporting how, historically, some people have used a word (Robinson, 1950). By contrast, the definition of a construct is "stipulative." It legislates meaning. The stipulative definition is the scientist's, the logician's, Humpty-Dumpty's, and Adam's:

> "When I use a word," Humpty Dumpty said, in a rather scornful tone, "it means just what I choose it to mean — neither more nor less."

> Whatsoever Adam called every living creature, that was the name thereof.

Concepts and constructs impose order. They battle chaos by abstracting and generalizing. Their description of differences and similarities tells what to expect when.

To classify is, then, to state a rule. One evaluates taxonomies, as a *scientist,* in terms of the ordering properties of competing systems of classification. Classifications that "tell more," that predict more with fewer exceptions, are preferred for scientific purposes. (There are, to repeat, other reasons for taking thought). But most rules, particularly nontrivial rules about human behavior, have exceptions. Our classifications of men and their acts are imperfect; there are fuzzy edges and overlaps. To this knowledge-problem, there are two popular responses, both wrong. The one is to "neutralize" the exception by holding that it "proves the rule true." This is nonsense, of course, and a mistranslation of the Latin slogan, *exceptio probat regulam.* Exceptions *test* rules; they do not corroborate them.

A converse response, equally erroneous, is to talk as though there were no rules. "Every man is individual," some say. But to utter this truism is neither to believe it nor to act upon it. To follow the cliché faithfully would reduce us to silence about ourselves and others, and to inaction. With everything exceptional, there is nothing to be known. With nothing to be known, there is no question to be asked and no advice to be given.

But we do not practice this preachment about everyone's being unique. Man is a categorizing animal. His categories change, but he does not abandon the principle.

In short, we call each other names, common names, and we know each other by them. The continuing question is only how well they apply. We defend our generalizations against the other fellow's by noting the exceptions to *his* categories. In turn, we categorize his unpleasant classification schema by calling him, or his taxonomy, names. If we are sociologists, we call offensive categories "stereotypes" in contrast to our organizing constructs that are "ideal" or "constructed" types.[2] The other man reifies; we postulate; and we classify each other with moral conjugations:

I am dedicated.

You are dogmatic.

He is a bigot.

In the clash of material interests and world-views, there is always a ready label with which to categorize classification systems as odious or preferred: "racist," "historicist," "anarchist," "bourgeois," "deviationist," and on through the endless clean and dirty names we call each other and our beliefs for a multiplicity of purposes.

These varied purposes seem to generate different preferences in the test of a classifying system.[3] In the forums of everyday debate and political commerce, where we are set to win arguments, the test of conceptual utility is added power-over-people. When, on the other hand, the inquirer seeks "better understanding," the concept's efficiency becomes a matter of vogue (how many significant others use it), how much "sense" it adds to his story, and, hence, of the satisfactions felt with its invocation. As the thinker becomes scientific, his test is "resolving power": how much data can be organized by the taxonomy with what improvement in contingent predictive accuracy.

In the scientific use of classification, the definition is an aid to generalization tested by prediction and, sometimes, control. The definition is not itself considered as an explanation because the scientist thinks of explanations as logically consistent stories that tell which things go together and *how* things come about. He is not interested in "what things *really* are," nor is he interested in *why* things occur as they do, *unless* "why" means "how."

In contrast, some professional thinkers and most laymen *are* interested in the "what-is-it's" and in the "why's" considered, not as "how's," but as first causes or the "ends of action" ("the purposes behind the events").

Existentialist: What is man?

Christian minister₁: What is the purpose of life?

Christian minister₂: Where do my morals come from?

Student: Why are there wars?

Making things intelligible by classifying them, by telling-what-they-are, follows the Aristotelian tradition and is still satisfying. The intellectual satisfaction need not depend on any increase in forecast ability or control, nor even upon any *interest* in these consequences.

The explainway that illuminates events by assigning them their "proper concept" may impose the classifying term as much by the consequences of events as by their causes. Philosophers of history, for example, consciously employ "unifying concepts" like "revolution" or "economic depression" with which to weave that "significant narrative" that is the historian's distinctive product (Walsh, 1951). This process of binding disparate facts with meaning-giving concepts Walsh calls "colligation under appropriate conceptions." The justification of *this* binding rather than *that* one — the warrant for the appropriate use of a concept that makes sense out of matters — may be events that *followed* the happening to be explained as well as those that preceded it. A "revolution" may be identified by what comes after it as well as what went before.

Clarifying human actions by defining them, and defining them by classifying them, are perennial processes. Taxonomy — however engaged and whether discovered or invented, conditioned into habit or self-consciously constructed — is a foundation of thought. It is molded into morals — "good" and "evil" are among the earliest definitions of actions — and it is the first step in any science.

To mention disadvantages of this explanatory mode is, then, to remind ourselves that knowing is difficult. Summarily, at least these three problems may arise as one clarifies by classifying:

(*a*) Classifications can be constructed on levels of abstraction distant from experience. Incubi can be defined in terms of other spirits and much can be "made clear" that has no empirical referent.

(*b*) Applying a label may be confused with describing how:

What accounts for the way in which man and other animals developed?

That's evolution.

Rubrics may be shorthand references to processes that *can* be specified. But the risk is that, as concepts become familiar, they quiet curiosity whether or not they stand for specifiable events.

(*c*) Every taxonomy is open to challenge. The challenge feeds, as usual, on the different uses of thought and explanation. The classification that satisfies curiosity or that assists in the assignment of blame may have little value for mapping the world. And, even *within* one of these objectives, there are constant questions about the validity of this schema over that one. (See note 2.)

(5) *Stating or demonstrating "operations"*

Defining by indicating examples is one type of operational definition. There are other forms of operation by which one attempts to delimit the reference of a symbol, but they have in common that operational definitions tell or show what to do in order to experience the events to which the word refers.

An operational definition is often a construct. As such, it is stipulative rather than lexical and, therefore, a source of discomfort. The father of modern operational definition, P. W. Bridgman, came to abhor the term because it smacked of dogma, or a philosophy, where what he had intended was an attitude (1954:75). Bridgman's idea was only that . . . it is better, because it takes us further, to analyze into doings or happenings rather than into objects or entities.

For scientists, the experiential reference of operational definition is an advantage. Such definitions tend to be clear and certain. The clarity and certainty gained by this mode of definition are a result of both its empirical base and its referential restriction: The term shall be used to refer to what this test tests and nothing more.

Dodd (1943:482) has suggested that there are *degrees* to which a definition may be "operational" and has listed two criteria of "operationality": A definition is operational . . . to the extent that the definer (a) specifies the procedure . . . for identifying or generating the definiendum and (b) finds high reliability . . . for the definition.

Hart and others (1953) have described measures of these criteria and, in so doing, have demonstrated again the need for reliability in definition.[4]

As with most efforts to know, however, each procedural gain carries its price, and the advantages of an operational definition are sometimes seen to incur charges upon other ends of knowledge.

The alleged costs of operational definition can be summarized as seven intertwined disadvantages.[5] These are that the operational mode (*a*) may not satisfy curiosity, (*b*) is vague, (*c*) destroys comfortable (or necessary) ambiguity, (*d*) conduces to nonsensical measurement, (*e*) is circular, (*f*) cannot handle "rich concepts," and (*g*) may reduce predictive power.

(*a*) *Unsatisfied curiosity.* The first price is illustrated by the persistent manner in which inquirers, told that "the doing *is* the definition," continue to feel unsatisfied. The definiens may be clear; it seems certain. But curious man, confined within the straits of operations, often feels that "something has been left out" or that significant meanings have been confounded.

(*b*) *Vague operations.* Since men define concepts and create explanations in the service of different objectives and out of different histories of word-association, it is no surprise that a mode of definition invented to make abstractions more clear should be charged with obscurity.

Scriven (1966*a*), for example, calls the operational style "self-refuting" since no operational definition of an operational definition is possible, and Israel (1945) asks if a construct derives its meaning exclusively from a set of operations, how can we establish the equivalence *within* a construct of two or more different modes of measurement? Is measuring length by tape a definition of the same construct as measuring length by triangulation?

Some operationists respond to Scriven by ignoring him. For their purposes, an operational definition of an operational definition is unnecessary. Others offer a variety of "operations" that define "operational definition," including the "operation" of pointing to examples (Hart, 1953).

They answer Israel by saying, if one needs *that* degree of clarity, then, yes, constructs should be known by their different modes of measurement and length$_1$ is not length$_2$. How much "equivalence" obtains between these measures is a matter of observation (that is, of correlation) rather than logomachy.

Questions persist, however, concerning just what is to count as an "operation." Bridgman himself (1938) has proposed several kinds of operation, including "mental" or symbolic operations which may get one back into the very indefiniteness that operationists sought to escape.

This debate may be resolved, without being settled, if the *intent* of the operationist is kept in mind; namely, that the terms talked about shall have a greater degree of intersubjective repeatability and a more clear specification of the connection between a theoretic construct and the publicly observed attributes referred to by that term. Toward this objective, the operational definition makes a contribution.

(*c*) *The comforts of ambiguity.* Quite the opposite dissatisfaction with operational definition is implied by attack from another quarter. This criticism expresses the disquiet felt before a word-master who is overstrict and whose punctilio smothers spontaneity.

There are comforts in ambiguity. It is difficult to be proved wrong when one is vague. The exactness that makes proof possible carries with it the risk of disproof. But arguments based on complex assumptions and fuzzy concepts can be constructed to give "everyone a little of what he came to hear," as the politician must do. The familiarity and the ambiguity of the terms simultaneously make them appealing and immune to fact.

EFFICIENT AMBIGUITY IN POLITICS

(Tullock, 1967:103-104)

The politician, in making up programs to appeal to rationally ignorant voters, would be attracted by fairly complex programs which have a concentrated beneficial effect on a small group of voters and a highly dispersed injurious effect on a large group of voters.

Note that at least some complexity is necessary. . . . If . . . the politician can work out a complex arrangement for doing the same thing [redistributing income] . . . in a less clear way, he may have a winning issue. . . . The simple fact that the program has the "right" degree of complexity means that the politician proposing it can feel fairly safe in assuming that the people who will gain by the program will know about it and, thus, have their vote affected by it, while those who will be injured will not.

It may, of course, be possible to introduce a completely artificial degree of complexity.

CONCEPTS AS HISTORICAL CAUSES

(Gardiner, 1959:266-267)

While general terms like "civilization," "culture," "class," "race," "productive forces," "national spirit" and so forth have played a central role in the development of speculative theories of history, they have at the same time been employed uncritically and without being assigned a clear and unambiguous sense. In consequence, there has been a tendency to exploit the vagueness that surrounds them in unjustifiable ways; to treat them, for instance, as the names of autonomous agencies standing in some unexplained way behind the phenomena of history and producing or directing the flow of events. And even where hypostatization and personification of this kind have not taken place, the words in question have often been used so elastically as to make the "laws" formulated in terms of them void of empirical content.

We are consoled by ambiguity when, as is usual, we express sentiments along with facts. It will be argued in succeeding sections that the bulk of what passes for explanation of human behavior is an amalgam of hortatory, prescriptive, and descriptive feeling-sentences. In such explainways narrow symbols are confining and we prefer the broad symbol with a range of connotation that allows poetic resonance. Such overtones yield "understanding" or "correct feeling" without the sadness of test.

(d) *Operationism as nonsense-generating.* This charge is cousin to the criticism that the operational definition is in bondage to an empiricism that leads to meaningless measures. Put another way, it is held that the neatness of this style of definition may tempt investigators to the invention of nonsensical definitions of no relevance to any inquirer's questions.

Thus Benjamin (1955:75), following the suggestion of Hempel (1952:46), proposes an operational measure given by multiplying a man's height by his age, . . . getting a number which I then call his *hage*. This is operationally defined, but does it have any reference to reality? Possibly. But now let me take the square root of the logarithm of this number. This is operationally defined. Does it have any reference to reality? One would find it hard to say. In fact, it looks suspiciously like some of the verbal concepts which the operationists hoped to eliminate by their new method.

This *reductio ad absurdum* is meant to illustrate that empirically based definitions may be meaningless. True enough — but the answer to Benjamin's proposal is, of course, that any definition, including his measure of *hage*, is "sensible" or not depending upon what the inquirer can do with it in the service of his curiosity. In scientific theories of deductive form, this curiosity is guided by the postulates of the theory.

To take fright from Benjamin's stricture against the possibility of senseless operations is to close the door to the invention of constructs. It is to prejudge the utility of new conceptual combinations — whether of symbolic counters or kinds of acts. For example, it is conceivable that, with or without "axiomated theory," even such seemingly "meaningless measures" as *hage* might gain meaning, and utility, if the "hage score" were found to correlate discriminatingly with a complex of behaviors of interest to us. Imagine, wildly, that the distribution of male *hage* is highly correlated with a weighted index of "air pilot competence." One need not know "why" this association holds, or even how enduring it might be, in order to use *hage* as part of a pilot-screening procedure.

The "reference to reality" about which Benjamin inquires is answered by what the measure *does* in the service of question-answering. If Benjamin and other philosophers will not have this "reference to reality," they become suspect of "essentialism," of looking for what is "really real." In this Platonic search, scientists cannot join.

A related criticism holds that devotion to operationism draws attention away from the definitions used by the people whom we study. This argument maintains that concern with neat "scientific definitions" leads to a satisfaction with operational concepts that inadequately describe how people are and what they do. Deutscher (1967:7) puts the point this way:

> A concept is synonymous not with a corresponding set of operations, but with the recurring, empirically observable phenomena of everyday life to which it refers, which it identifies, and which it distinguishes from unlike phenomena and relates to like phenomena.
>
> The scientific definition of concepts is unimportant relative to the definitions employed by the people we are interested in learning about.

The work of the student of social behavior includes the invention of constructs that abstract in some useful way categories of acts to be attended to. When we try to do this, "meaningfully" as Deutscher urges, by categorizing the "recurrent, empirically observable phenomena of everyday life," we run again into the problem of how to certify our categories and how to report our constructs to others.

The history of such inventions in the behavioral studies indicates forcefully how invented concepts run away from their referents. Give a complex of behaviors and beliefs a name and watch the connotation spread. Meanings are added until the label becomes an umbrella that covers so much it "de-fines" little—thus "alienation and anomy," "exploitation," "prejudice and discrimination," and a host of similar rubrics that burst the bounds of definition under the pressure of their evaluative use.[6]

THE ANOMIC STATE OF ANOMIE

(Excerpts from a critique. Nettler, 1965)

The authors (McClosky and Schaar, 1965) . . . add to the persistent confusion between the Durkheimian "anomie," referring to a *societal* state, and the allegedly related *personal* states called "alienation," "anomia," and, now, "anomy." They call feelings, persons, *and* societies "anomic."

This usage is unfortunate because it leads from the idea of societal norm-lessness to the assumption that disaffected people are also normless. Calling deviant norms non-norms is inadequate sociological description. It also denies authenticity to the disgruntled.

How things really are "out there," how one feels them to be, and how one feels himself to be — regulated or purposeless — are disparate conditions; giving them the same name implies an equation that needs to be ascertained, not assumed.

I should like to propose an alternative view of the interesting reports by McClosky and Schaar, Srole, and others who have written about "anomic" persons. These people are simply down-and-out, run over by life, "invisible," joyless, miserable, quietly desperate . . . .

Srole's anomia and the present anomy scales are measures of despair.

If we are *not* content with vague concepts whose meanings we feel but are unable reliably to communicate, then we are returned full circle to specifying some kind of "operation" that identifies what we are talking about.

(*e*) *Operationism as tautological.* A related criticism of the operational mode holds such definition to be circular. Thus Popper (1959:440, emphasis in the original):

As to the doctrine of operationalism — which demands that scientific terms, such as length, or solubility, should be defined in terms of the appropriate experimental procedure — it can be shown quite easily that all so-called oper-ational definitions will be circular. I may show this briefly in the case of "soluble."

The experiments by which we test whether a substance such as sugar is *soluble in water* involve such tests as the recovery of dissolved sugar from the solution. . . . Clearly, it is necessary to identify the recovered substance, that is to say, to find out whether it has the same properties as sugar. Among these properties, *solubility in water* is one. Thus in order to define "x as soluble in water" by the standard operational test, we should at least have to say some-thing like this:

x is soluble in water if and only if (a) when x is put into water then it (neces-sarily) disappears, and (b) when after the water evaporates, a substance is (necessarily) recovered which, again, is *soluble in water*.

The fundamental reason for the circularity of this kind of definition is very simple: Experiments are never conclusive; and they must, in their turn, be *test-able by further experiments*.

Popper goes on to argue that this circularity inheres in the impossibility of drawing a sharp dividing line between an "empirical language" and a "theoretical language." "We are," he says, "theorizing all the time." In short, inference is built into observation, whether we "know" it or not.

A positivist response to Popper's criticism is to acknowledge that, at some point, "all science is a grand tautology." If the operational definition suffers from circularity, so, too, does every other style of setting limits to terms. If all attempts to know can be viewed as redundant at some remove ("explaining the unfamiliar by the familiar"), neither the operational definition nor any of the other types of semantic explanation will free us of this metaphysical limitation.

But the intention of those who resort to operations is to make symbols more definite, to increase intersubjective reliability in concept-handling. The operational definition remains one way to clarify meaning which, as with any other mode of defining, carries advantages and disadvantages. The net worth of these costs and gains can only be assessed in terms of the inquirer's reasons for taking thought. Where well-knit theory has been developed, it informs these reasons.

In this light, one can ask Popper why a test of "soluble in water" as part of the description of something called "sugar" need require its recovery after solution?

Much of Popper's problem is "philosophic" in the worst sense. That is, it proposes what men might do, but don't. Men do not always go around in circles, as Popper's criticism suggests, because most of their questions are satisfied at some point short of endless regression. If one is concerned with the properties of sugar, and "soluble in water" is held to be one part of the definiens, then this test, without recovery, suffices, and the question-raiser is saved the pain of thinking in circles.

(*f*) *Operationism and the impoverishment of rich terms.* Operational definitions often appear unsatisfying and circular because they seem to denude "rich concepts." When we begin to translate a many-splendored term into procedures for observing what it refers to, we run the risk of obscuring significant qualities.

For example, consider the idea of "accuracy in judging people." In a review of the problems of measuring interperson perception, Gage and Cronbach (1955) show that a simple operational score based on predictions about the other person may be variously derived. The same operation may mean different things. A judge may be accurate in "predicting the other" because he assumes others to be like himself, in which case his "accuracy" is "nothing but" projection.[7] This process of judgment may be qualitatively different from that involved in accurately forecasting how others will behave when we assume them to be different from ourselves.

Gage and Cronbach ask: If the judge predicts correctly, is he accurate? Or does he assume similarity? Obviously, these questions are operationally identical.

In this case, as in others where "rich concepts" seem to have been impoverished by their reduction to observables, the resolution of the problem depends, as always, upon the investigator's purposes. Gage and Cronbach wish to distinguish predictions by projection from predictions that are accurate whether or not the target person really is similar to his judge and whether or not the judge is making assumptions of similarity or dissimilarity.

These purposes may be one investigator's and not another's. However, one way of resolving this kind of problem that derives from the "thinness" of operational definition is to manipulate the scores derived from initial operations so that "second-order" operational definitions can be extracted. That is, one can observe ratios between scores of operational referent such that subtypes ("qualities") of the initial score can be discerned.[8]

These manipulations will not, of course, satisfy every thinker and, again, we are left with the possibility that "something is left out" of the operational definition. This "something" is often the range of connotation to which the symbol-user has been conditioned. In thinking about emotionalized topics it is this gamut of connotation that carries meaning and that accounts for the satisfaction, or its lack, gained from a "verbal massage."

Some philosophers of science put this problem in a different manner. Northrop (1947) argues that scientific theories operate with "concepts by postulation" and that the meanings postulated are inferred and theory-linked. He distinguishes such postulated meanings from "concepts by intuition," where the latter meaning is completely given . . . by something which can be immediately apprehended. The "concept by intuition" refers to "immediately apprehended knowledge" or to "pure fact." These immediately experienced data are subjective and interpersonally variable. Further, . . . we can say nothing about pure fact, since the moment we put in words what it is, we have *described* fact rather than merely *observed* fact. (P. 40, emphasis his)

Order is imposed on this subjective and varied world of sensation through the invention of concepts by postulation. As individuals who would know public, objective worlds, as well as our private, aesthetic ones, we are forever in the dilemma that . . . tests of hypotheses are made in one language; our thinking is done in another. (Blalock, 1968:10)

The task of the scientist is to devise and test modes of linking the two "languages."[9] These linkages Northrop calls "epistemic correlations," a relationship . . . joining an unobserved component of anything designated by a concept by postulation to its directly inspected component denoted by a concept by intuition. Thus an epistemic correlation joins a thing known in the one way to what is in some sense that same thing known in a different way. (P. 119)

Every attempt to order the world, to make sense of it, involves a testing of epistemic bonds. Mentally, we run back and forth between our postulations and our experiences. Our theories of the world, whether commonsensical or scientific, inevitably contain concepts by postulation so that with Einstein, we know the public world — the reliable and objective world — "only by speculative means."

The operations we employ in coming to know the world scientifically are operations whose meanings are given by our speculations. Without an embedding in theory, the operations may become as senseless as Benjamin construction of *hage*. On the other hand, theories without operations become so flexible as to defy falsification. Operation-free, they can be stretched to explain anything that happens — after the event.

Such unfalsifiable world-views gratify many men. They are called "faiths" to distinguish them, by degree, from those theories that permit a test of the epistemic bond against observable events. The advantage of faiths is that they order and gratify. Their disadvantage is that, devoid of operational meaning, they are immune to disproof and useless for prediction.

(g) *Operationism and the reduction of predictive power.* If prediction requires some specification, it may also suffer from an excess of denotation.

The problem here is entangled with the dispute about the "logic of discovery." Is this logic deductive or inductive?

If predictions were solely propositions deduced from theory, then the symbols through which we appreciate our worlds could be defined with clarity and certainty and knowing the future would be merely a logical exercise. However, it seems doubtful that events conform to the deductive logic with which we might hope to understand them. Nor does the invention of a transcendental Nature composed of Universal Truths arranged in syllogistic form seem to aid our forecasts.

We are left with the probability that the "logic of anticipation," as Benjamin calls it (p. 111), . . . is not deductive but inductive. And this means that it can give us neither a high degree of certainty nor a high degree of clarity; it must be venturesome, involving risks and guesses, and requiring us to supplement the satisfying knowledge provided by things which are given to us through our senses by vague and uncertain theories.

If Benjamin is correct, then the experiential referent of the operational definition, which we often regard as its principal advantage, becomes a disadvantage. The certainty gained through the description of operations is a result of referential restriction, it has been held, but this limitation in scope of reference may militate against the use of those less rigorous hypotheses which some philosophers of science hold to be a requirement of prediction.

Benjamin goes on to argue that (p. 112): If we prefer certainty and clarity, throwing out all conjecture and vague ideas, our knowledge will necessarily remain highly restricted in extent, and we shall have available no technique by which it may be extended. On the other hand, if we prefer knowledge of the widest possible scope, we shall be provided with a method by which this may be achieved, but we shall be forced to admit into the area of knowledge many ideas which are vague and many propositions which are conjectural. We can have certainty and clarity without predictability, or we can have predictability without certainty and clarity; but we cannot have both.

There is justice to Benjamin's warning. We may forever be torn among the purposes of our taking thought, so that the symbol-manipulations that serve one end defeat another. However, despite this possibility, scientists will continue to try to make their concepts more clear. For we distinguish between "prophecy" and "prediction" by saying that the former foretells without knowing how, whereas a prediction is based upon inference from publicly observable events and procedures. Prophecy works best when vague. Prediction seeks to work with cleaner tools.

The charge made by Benjamin and others that the use of operational definitions reduces predictive power is settled for the pragmatist not by debating the logic of prediction, but by testing the relative contribution of broad and narrow, fuzzy and precise, concepts to the solution of a forecast problem.

Some men have opted for clarity, against Benjamin's warning, because the history of science is read as the abandonment of hypostatization. Control over events—one test of our "understanding" them—seems to increase as we give up constructs that lack empirical referent. "Phlogiston" is no longer invoked to explain combustion, and "protoplasm" may go the way of other spirits (Hardin, 1956).

Relinquishing reification is a struggle insofar as we have learned to be comforted by terms that can never be referred to observables. In such cases an anxiety is induced lest "something be left out" of our picture of the world by the refusal to employ traditional verbal stimuli. Curiosity will rest here when one rings the appropriate Pavlovian bell.

The explanation by definition that makes things clear in this sense, however, may have no explanatory value in other senses. The rhetorical transfer that occurs in most definitions need tell nothing of "causes" or continuities and need have no predictive value. Indeed, an accusation leveled at the nonoperational forms of definition, particularly those by classification or synonym, is that they lend support to the use of terms without observable reference and hence are obstacles to the development of instruments that facilitate interpersonal communication and control of the environment. It only *sounds* paradoxical to say that some definitions that explain matters prevent us from knowing how things are.[10]

Delusions are comforting. They make things clear. And they are frequently defended by definitions.

In sum, explanations by definition are useful if the problem to which they are addressed is one of making meanings clear through some mode of translation. Definitions "make things finite." They "point to" that which someone intends as he invokes symbols, including, at times, only other symbols. But, as clarifying instruments, definitions have limitations that can be summarized as resulting from:

(1) *Restrictions on the range of associated symbols*

While the Greeks may have had a word for everything, most moderns live with limited vocabularies. Any purely semantic explanation, then, runs at some point to the end of words.

(2) *Variations in familiarity with a language, or portions thereof*

If satisfaction of curiosity is in some part conditional—learned by association—then one man's satisfaction, a function of familiarity, is another man's discomfort.

(3) *Variations in preferred style of definition*

To the intensionally oriented, the word-bound, an operational definition is an alien vocabulary.

(4) *Translations of symbols at one level of abstraction into symbols on another level*

Such translation often loses connotation or "emotional resonance." The auditor feels that "it lacks something," as would a concrete definition of "freedom" for the revolutionary or "love" for Juliet. If words can enliven feelings, they can also deaden them. "Clarification" is an emotional matter as well as an intellectual one and, for this reason, words alone may not illuminate.

(5) *Promissory inflation of the effects of explanation by definition*

Since definitions make some things clear, it is incorrectly assumed that all "unclear things" (and some unwanted events) may be made plain, or explained away, through adequate statements of meaning. Such hope is one source of word-magic (Chase, 1938; Hayakawa, 1939). Word-magic maintains residence in the confusion about what any explanation by definition does do and can do. The risk of taking excessive promise from symbol-manipulation is illustrated in such popular and questionable beliefs as the notions that:

(*a*) *Finding the word will evoke the idea.* This is sometimes true, but often false. Foreign words, even those in our own language, seldom stimulate ideas.

(*b*) *People can have ideas, but be unable to express them.* "Having an idea" remains an ambiguous concept. It usually refers to the ability to symbolize. It follows, then, that an "inexpressible idea" is not an "idea."[11] Whatever neural processes precede those expressions recognizable as ideas are, thus far, assumed and poorly described. Those who defend the importance of postulating an "idea" or "the intention of saying a thing" *preliminary* to the expression in symbols have difficulty denoting the intention. William James (1890, v.1:253) can only refer to the "premonitory views of schemes of thought" that precede the communicated idea, felt introspectively and dissipated upon expression:

And has the reader never asked himself what kind of a mental fact is his *intention of saying a thing* before he has said it? It is an entirely definite intention . . . an absolutely distinct state of consciousness . . . ; and yet how much of it consists of definite sensorial images, either of words or of things? Hardly anything. . . . Yet what can we say about it without using words that belong to the later mental facts that replace it? The intention *to say so and so* is the only name it can receive. One may admit that a good third of our psychic life consists in these rapid premonitory perspective views of schemes of thought not yet articulate.

Similarly Koestler (1967:39) wants to distinguish between the feeling-for-what-one-means and any utterance:

And while it is true that the idea or "intention of saying a thing" precedes the actual process of verbalization, it is also true that ideas are often airy nothings until they crystallize into verbal concepts and acquire tangible shape. . . . Thus our lecturer sometimes knows what he means, but cannot formulate it; whereas at other times he can only find out what exactly he means by explicit, precise verbal formulations.

To give more precise meaning to Koestler would require that there be independent signs of "knowing what he means" and "airy nothings," and that the hedging qualifiers, "often" and "sometimes," be given their contingencies.

Until then, it seems more accurate, as well as parsimonious, to translate such a sentence as I know what I want to say, but can't say it to Being unable to say it means you don't "know" it.[12]

Alice in her Wonderland expressed it better: How can I know what I think till I see what I say?

(*c*) *Explanation of the semantic sort (what-is-meant-by) leads to "understanding."* If "understanding" refers only to "ability to translate properly," there can be no quarrel. The sentence is a definition of explanation by definition. However, the possibility that "understanding" may be obfuscated by definition is also a possibility, and one that has not been adequately tested. Since "understanding" is a function of purpose and of familiarity with the symbolic currency, definition may diminish, as well as enhance, "understanding."

Thurman Arnold (1937:180), a lawyer, and hence a professional attendant of words, is yet able to advise us of "the traps which lie in definitions":

Definition is ordinarily supposed to produce clarity in thinking. It is not generally recognized that the more we define our terms the less descriptive they become and the more difficulty we have in using them. The reason for this paradox is that we never attempt to define words which obtain a proper emotional response from our listeners. Logical definition enters when we are using words which we are sure "ought" to mean something, but none of us can put our finger on just what that meaning is. In such situations priestly minded men believe that definition will make the meaning clearer.

As illustration of Arnold's point, it is notable that some of the "simplest" terms are the most difficult to define, and that, as we ask men to define what they mean by "I love you," we become more uncomfortable with their answers.

Louis Armstrong put this well in his famous reply to the "intellectual" who asked him for a definition of jazz: Man, if you got to ask "what is it?" you ain't ever gonna get to know.

Add to this questionable assumption, Semantic explanation leads to understanding, a second dubious notion, Conflict is caused by misunderstanding, and produce a popular and erroneous conclusion: Therefore, semantic explanation is a way of reducing conflict.

The student of semantics will recognize that this pacific syllogism may violate the canon of singularity. "Understanding" is used to refer to "knows the meaning of. . . ." "(Mis-)understanding" may mean this, or it may be used to refer to "appreciates, likes, has empathy with. . . ." To regard homonyms as synonyms is a common way of making commensurables out of incommensurables.

In addition to the barriers to "knowledge" that are here produced by definitions, the syllogism is, of course, as weak as its premises. The proportion of all conflict between persons and groups that is generated by "misunderstanding" is probably minuscule (Coser, 1956; Pelcovits, 1946; Simmel, 1955), and the contrary is always a lively possibility: Now that I understand you, I don't like you at all.

In summary, semantic explanation makes symbols clear. Making symbols clear is sometimes a first step toward making events clear. Language is learned, however, in such a way as to provide us with traps as well as tools, and he who becomes enchanted with words and their play runs the risk of becoming their addict.

Knowing, it will be seen, is a peculiar enterprise, intertwined with feeling, and judging and believing, and yet distinguishable from them. These are different "reasons for thinking." They are sometimes at loggerheads, and they may elect different styles of definition in their service.

The varied modes of definition are different ways of telling "what it is." Different views of "what it is" raise different questions, or none at all. As Gertrude Stein told us, the answers we get or give depend on the questions asked.

Put another way, definition determines the "kind of data" one puts into his explanatory tale. The "kind of data" one works with may affect the style of story he tells. The man who employs an operational definition of crime, for example, will end up knowing different things about it than does the student who starts his study from synonym or example.

It is no surprise, then, that theoreticians of different persuasion (or "of different temperament" — cf. Chapter Three, note 1) employ different concepts and prefer different modes of definition. Coan (1968), for example, reports a factor-analytic study of the dimensions of psychological theory. He had 232 "experts" in the history and systems of psychology rate 54 prominent theorists active between the 1880s and 1950s on 34 variables. Among other findings, Coan shows that explanations that prefer:

"conscious processes"
"unconscious processes"
"voluntarism"
"armchair speculation"

are *negatively* associated with a concern for:

"operational definition"
"determinism"
"immediate external determinants" of behavior
"learning"
"observable behavior"

Additionally, the explanatory style that emphasizes the "uniqueness of the individual" is *negatively* correlated with attention to the "social determinants" of "observable behavior."

We remain bound in our cage of symbols, and however we would proceed to know the world and explain it, the very mode of defining our counters-of-communication affects what we conclude. The definitions we use gather sentiments and observations under different rubrics; they stimulate disparate Pavlovian signals, and thus lend varied structure to our lives, and caution or zeal to our appetites.

Semantic explanation is one kind of knowledge-task, and a necessary step in a scientific enterprise that calls for interpersonal communication. Defining words and clarifying meanings, however, will not do everything one might want to accomplish in taking thought. Semantic clarification, in its variety, is a limited instrument of explanation, and, at some stage of knowing, a disappointing one. Not all that we think and feel about is knowledgeable, and much of it ought not to be so, at the peril of loss of its pleasure. Thus happiness defined and measured will appear as something other than happiness experienced.

NOTES

[1] An exception to the "exchange-of-symbols" definition of semantic explanation is to be found in some types of "operational definition." See pp. 14-24.

[2] This charge is not flippant. Social "scientists," being good men, are in a moral bind between their twin commitments: telling the truth and advocating love. The loving theme is that we are all brothers, God's children, part of the human family. If there are differences among us, they are, or should be, defined as unimportant.

But when truth-seekers observe *how people behave,* as opposed to how they think they should, it is apparent that man, like his mammalian relatives, discriminates. Men classify men and judge them.

This fact of life conflicts with the melioristic motives of many professional students. The impulse to moralize, to admonish the carriers of hatred, is inhibited by those who would be scientists. Moralizing is not their distinctive competence and such advocacy is felt to reduce both their actual "objectivity" and the public image of it. But educating, correcting error, *is* within the competence and the imagined role of the scientist. A way, then, is pointed to having our morals and our truths too. "Techniques of neutralization" can be applied against the other man's taxonomy and in favor of ours. The neutralization involves:

(a) Giving folk categories a pejorative label, "stereotype," that carries the cachet of science.

(b) Calling folk categories false (as well as immoral).

(c) Claiming that our classifications, by contrast, are true (and, if not moral, at least not immoral, as when we characterize people by socioeconomic status, or sex and age, or by "value orientation" and "personality type" like the "authoritarian" and "democratic" personalities, the "inner-" and "other-directed" men, and those who have "open" or "closed" minds with "radical" or "conservative" values).

(d) Holding that our morals — and we have them — are factual.

A "stereotype" is considered, as per Secord and Backman (1964:67), to have three characteristics: The categorization of persons, a consensus on attributed traits, and a discrepancy between attributed traits and actual traits. Krech *et al.* (1962:53) add to this definition the quality of rigidity.

This construct has never achieved a rigor that would permit its scientific use. There has been no specification of *how* categoric, *how* consensual, *how* rigid, and *how* inaccurate a folk image must be — as compared with what other taxonomy — before it deserves denigration as a "stereotype."

Fishman (1956) attempted to clarify the construct and to identify it, not necessarily with inaccuracy and rigidity, but with "inferior judgmental processes" and group allegiance. Nevertheless, the term continues to be used in the Secord-Backman-Krech *et al.* manner and, thus defined, stereotyping is condemned on three grounds: that it is illogical, immoral, and inaccurate. Much, but not all, of the charge of illogic and immorality is derived from the allegation of inaccuracy. We say "not all" because there are social psychologists who would continue to regard folk categories as immoral even if they were accurate.*

The alleged illogic of stereotyping is seen in such tendencies as these:

(*a*) What is "good" in our group becomes bad in theirs.

(*b*) The stereotyped categories are rigid while the entities they describe change.

(*c*) The categories are changeable (particularly in valence) with change in historical events (e.g., Pearl Harbor and the stereotype of the Japanese) where there is no evidence that the reference group has changed.

(*d*) Folk categorization ignores the range of individual difference in the other group.

(*e*) It generalizes from visible (and usually irrelevant or trivial) traits to less visible but more important characteristics.

(*f*) It is selective, partial, incomplete.

(*g*) Folk categorization *produces* the behaviors purportedly observed: Give a man a bad name, treat him that way, and that's the way he'll become.

The immorality of folk categories derives from the tendency of stereotypes:

(*a*) To deny the individual ("d" above).

(*b*) To foster group distinction and separation.

(*c*) To emphasize the wrong qualities. Stereotypes categorize by traits which are deemed irrelevant to the worth of a man as demonstrated by other qualities. This moral judgment follows, of course, from the judgment of illogic ("e" above).

Both of these charges — of illogic and immorality — are bolstered by the assumption that stereotypes are inaccurate.

A sadness of all this is that men of letters have addressed most, if not all, of the same charges against the sociologist's categories that the sociologist has advanced against folk classification.

Worse, having *defined* a stereotype as egregious, we can be led easily to believe it. Thus Harding *et al.*, writing in the *Handbook of Social Psychology* (Lindzey, ed., 1954:1039) stress . . . the low degree of correspondence between common stereotypes of various ethnic groups and the actual characteristics of these groups insofar as the latter are known through scientific research. We have discussed this problem in a previous section of this chapter.

When one turns to this "previous section," the scientific evidence reported there reduces to three studies of the accuracy of stereotypes, one of which [on occupational image (Rice, 1928)] shows some accuracy in the folk perception. The remaining two studies by Humphrey

---

*If there are innate differences between the races, that's all the more reason to say that there aren't any. (A social scientist, cited by Shuey, 1966)

(1945) and LaPiere (1936) are cited as proving that stereotypes "may emerge without any objective basis."

Alas, these studies do no such thing!

Humphrey's research attempted to "validate" the image of Mexican-American adolescents as "zoot-suiters," resident largely in the southwestern United States, against the perceptions of social workers and other "knowledgeable" residents of Detroit! No data are provided on the relative frequency of wearers of the "zoot-suit" among Mexican-Americans and other ethnic groups or of the distribution and existence of this one stereotyped image among Americans. Further, social workers' judgments constitute a tenuous criterion of reality.

LaPiere's paper, "Type Rationalizations of Group Antipathy," is more frequently cited as evidence of the inaccuracy of stereotypes. *Three* aspects of the in-group vision of a minority, the Armenians in Fresno, were tested against public records and found to be false. However, a reading of the doctoral dissertation (LaPiere, 1930) from which the published study was extracted shows that *only a portion* of the in-group's "stereotype" of the Armenian was, in fact, tested. Two of the published "type rationalizations" do *not* appear in the stereotypes listed in the dissertation. Some 25 additional pictures of the Armenian were elicited without validation against objective criteria, and, throughout the original work, there are indications of the accuracy of the stereotype (for example, pp. 172, 212, 260, 274, 389, 421, 439-451).

This lengthy note suggests at least these conclusions:

(*a*) Social psychologists, like all men, are vulnerable to the intrusion of hope upon thought.

(*b*) Much evidence of the existence of ethnic differences in conformity with some facets of stereotypes is ignored. (As examples of such: Akers, 1968; Clark, 1949; Erskine, 1967-68; Hertzberg, 1963; Himmelfarb, 1965, 1967; Post, 1962; Shuey, 1966; Sklare, 1968.)

(*c*) There is no scientific evidence concerning the accuracy of ethnic stereotyping. A first, methodologically sound endeavor in this direction is under way (Mackie, 1968).

[3]Differential preference among the tests of classification schema is suggested as hypothesis, rather than fact, and as an interesting project for research.

[4]One might think the need for reliability of definition obvious. Yet we are continually surprised at the amount of ambiguity we use and accommodate. As an instance, Hakel (1968:534) employed a magnitude-estimation procedure to find the meaning of "frequency words," and discovered, not astonishingly, that these adverbs are vague:

Variability is rampant. One man's "rarely" is another man's "hardly ever." "Often" and "rather often" have the same medians. "Very seldom" is very seldom less than "seldom."

We are exceedingly stable about being exceedingly imprecise.

[5]These disadvantages have, in turn, their own "causes," ably summarized by Benjamin (1955), particularly in his Chapter 5. A valuable symposium on operationism is to be found in the *Psychological Review*, 52 (September, 1945).

[6]For example, of the concept "social class," Glenn (1968:538) writes: There are now at least a dozen distinctly different meanings of the term. I have recommended elsewhere that the term be dropped from sociological discourse and that a synonym be substituted for it in each of its meanings. However, I obviously find it difficult to follow my own advice; there seems to be no suitable synonym for class in its traditional sense.

[7]"Projection" itself may mean more than one thing, as Holmes (1968) has shown.

[8]Gage and Cronbach demonstrate how to develop subtypes of operational measures in their proposal that "accuracy" in judging others refer to a positive correlation between ratios of scores: $\dfrac{WAS}{RS}$ and $\dfrac{WAD}{RD}$ where WAS refers to "warranted assumed similarity," RS to "real similarity," WAD to "warranted assumed dissimilarity," and RD to "real dissimilarity." A judge of others would be called "accurate," then, insofar as there was a positive relationship between his ability to predict correctly when he was similar to the target-other and his ability to predict correctly when he was dissimilar.

[9]A procedure for bridging the gap between the language of thought and the language of test is provided by Costner (1968:17-18). However, his technique is of limited application because, in his words, . . . the ties between very highly abstract concepts and the empirical world appear to take a form that is different from that assumed in this discussion. Specifically, highly abstract concepts are frequently designed to encompass a variety of different forms of a given phenomenon that are not necessarily intercorrelated with each other. There is no reason to assume a priori, for example, that all of the many forms of deviant behavior are intercorrelated. Similarly, frustrations are many and varied and the degree to which one suffers frustration in one guise is no clue to the degree of frustration of another kind. The admission of uncorrelated indicators for a given abstract variable renders the strategy discussed in this paper inapplicable.

[10]Fancher (1967) provides a neat test of the possibility that explanations may frustrate accurate perception. He shows, for his sample, that accuracy in judging others is *negatively correlated* with "validity in conceptualizing the other." Further, while such "conceptual validity" is positively associated with training in psychology, accuracy in perceiving others is negatively associated with the number of courses taken in psychology ($r = -.17$) and with course grades in abnormal psychology ($r = -.31$).

[11]This may be an unfair way of winning an argument—by definition. But it seems useful to distinguish "ideas," symbolizations, from that umbra of feeling and imagery that is also part of "mental life." Conventionally, "things known" are deemed symbolize-able, and the mental netherworld of feeling and imagery shades off from knowledge by degree of symbolic clarity.

[12]We grant that some aphasic individuals may "know what they mean" without "being able to say it." But we grant this *only when* the brain-injured person manipulates symbols other than the spoken word to articulate his meaning. When this ability is lost, our conventions of perceiving the other translate "knowing what he means" into feeling-states such as "drives," "wants," "needs." Thus, in describing idiots and infrahuman animals, we restrict the range of the others' expressions that we call "knowing."

CHAPTER THREE

EMPATHETIC EXPLANATIONS

"Explanation" has been treated as a sociopsychological phenomenon. That is, the explanatory process, however engaged, is held to be directed toward a human satisfaction that is socially conditioned.

Curious man asks "questions" and feels gratified when they are "answered." What counts as a question and a satisfactory answer is *social* (a function of who is answering whose question), *cultural* (a function of symbols learned in such a way that their evocation is deemed an "answerable question" or a suitable explanation), and *psychological* (in that our individual tempers affect curiosity and probably make one kind of explanation more satisfying to us than other kinds).[1]

In the public arenas of law, commerce, and domestic affairs, much explaining is accomplished by utterances that allow the interrogator to identify with processes conventionally held to make the explanandum (the events to be explained) "understandable."[2]

The processes that make human conduct understandable are usually amalgams of feelings, beliefs, and intentions that, from one's own life, seem to provide "good reasons" for the behavior. The processes referred to in empathy-building constitute, in Sorokin's words (1947:40), . . . the meaning or value superimposed upon the purely physical and biological properties of the respective actions.

The satisfying explicator varies the mix of emotion, idea, and purpose that he attributes to his actors within a framework of familiar thoughtways until his auditor experiences something like the "Ah-ha phenomenon": Oh, so that's why Alpha did it!

Such a response is an indication of empathy. The satisfied interrogator is saying that he can feel how the other must have felt (or believed or wanted) when he did X where, to the question-asker, "feeling that way" has some assumed association with doing X. *The heart of empathy is imagined possibility:* Under those circumstances I too might have behaved similarly.

Frequently, but not necessarily, the factors referred to by the empathy-building storyteller are assumed to have a causal connection with the matter to be explained. This assumption need not be a valid one, nor is it clear that it is always required for a satisfactory empathetic understanding of behavior.

Preliminary to a list of some contemporary Western techniques for explaining by empathy, it must be emphasized that "procedures for gaining understanding" are contingent upon the acquisition of those explainways conventional in the culture in which one is operating. These explanatory modes vary with the kinds of events to be "understood," with attitude toward them, and with a personal history that has taught one, perhaps idiosyncratically, which categories of question are satisfactorily or efficiently answered[3] by which classes of symbol organized in which style of answer.

Thus, for example, whether human behavior is explicable by reference to "will" or "purpose" is not so much a factual question as a culture-bound usage. In other words, the application of such concepts varies among cultures and, within a system of shared symbols such as ours, varies with conventions about what is a "proper explanation." We no longer explain the behavior of plants and trees by reference to spirits within them.[4] As events become more animate, we resort more frequently, yet inconsistently, to unobservable forces within the organism to account for its behavior.

The inconsistency is illustrated by Leifer's suggestion (1964) that the explanations that satisfy us about "normal" (that is, approved) behavior tend to be telic, whereas the explanations we prefer for abnormal conduct tend to be causal. When Millicent marries we "explain" her behavior by reference to her assumed purposes which, in an approved marriage, are congruent with the normative ends of this institution. When the psychologist interrogates the criminal, however, such "explanations" seem less satisfying:

Why do you rob banks?

'Cause that's where the money is.

A purposeful answer "explains" good behavior; it is not usually what we want to hear as the reason for bad conduct.

Tests of Leifer's point are as yet limited. The correlates that condition the relationship between attitude toward actor and preferred style of explanation adduced for his behavior have not been plotted. Evans' study (1968) is a beginning. However, it might be predicted that Western men make the tacit assumption that "free will" guarantees goodness and "causes" foster badness.[5] Conversely, even *within* a causal framework, good factors produce freedom of volition and bad influences limit it.

There is some evidence for the latter assumption. De Charms and colleagues (1965) report that when an external influence is approved, the person subject to it is perceived as more likely to be the origin of his own acts. Schiffman and Wynne (1963) find that the attribution of . . . causes of events either to other persons or onto the impersonal environment [is] a joint function of (a) whether the event itself was positive or negative, and (b) whether the other person was liked or disliked. If something pleasant happens to someone we like, or something unpleasant to someone we dislike, we tend to attribute causation to the person himself. If, on the contrary, something ugly happens to a loved one, or something fortunate occurs for a hated other, we tend to attribute causation to the environment.[6]

To attend to the varieties of explanatory style used in arousing empathy is not to prejudge them true or false. Rather than engage in the fruitless debates about whether men do or do not have "free will" or whether "reasons for acting" are the only acceptable explanations of human conduct (Louch, 1966), such explainways can be treated as assumptions used with varied success (and mostly untested results) in response to our social environments.

Empathy, then, may be variously aroused. And in the nonscientific forums that constitute the significant situations of interpretation of ourselves and others, empathy, however aroused, is a principal explainway. In clinic and court, in the novel and on television, the narrator "explains" to his audience by making the actions of his "subject" plausible, that is, produced by what we regard to be "sufficient reasons."

In contemporary Western cultures, the techniques of empathy-building include at least these five procedures:

(1) *Telling a history*

(2) *Depicting circumstances*

This is part of telling a history. Empathy is encouraged insofar as one has experienced similar situations in which he has felt as the storyteller describes his actor's feeling. Lacking such experience, the auditor may yet have his feelings appropriately aroused if he has learned to associate a set of circumstances causally with the actions to be explained. That is, whether the observer has, or has not, experienced similar urges in like situations, he may have learned to regard circumstance X as normally producing action Y. The assumed causal bond serves as "sufficient reason" for the action and, hence, is felt to yield an "understanding" of it.

(3) *Labeling "character"*

This can be done in several ways. One procedure is to appeal to generalized traits such as "intelligence" or "hostility." These may placate the interrogator despite their proclivity to tautology.

Another technique calls the behavior appropriate to a role and thus attempts empathy: Professors do that sort of thing.

And, more insidious, technical terms can be used to build "understanding" through connotation. "Psychoneurotic," "psychopathic," "character-defective" say more than they denote. In this surplus-saying lies their power to build empathy.

(4) *Postulating needs, instincts, and other drives*

In the current climate congenial to psychologizing, these drives attributed to the actor can be termed conscious or unconscious. When deemed unconscious, the motor of action is placed beyond test, but not beyond empathy-arousal.

(5) *Describing intentions and feelings*

Sociologists of the "social action" school call these attributes "meanings." Lawyers call them "motives." Such imputations may or may not coincide with the postulated energizers of action called "motive" by the psychologist. The differences in the use of the idea of "motive" correlate with larger differences in the models of man assumed. The concept "motive" is a metaphor and, as such, is sufficiently vague to be useful to explicators of varied style. Broadly, it refers to "that which incites to action."

A "determinist," who thinks in terms of "causes," sees motives as the antecedent, fateful conditions moving men. To such a philosopher, the idea of "destiny" is congenial.

Empathetic explicators resist this use of "motive" as that which *pushes* people into courses of action. They prefer, instead, the notion of "motive" as "final cause," that which *pulls* men in certain directions. Motives then refer to the ends of action, the goals sought. In lay language, a motive is "the reason he did it." "The reason why" may mean just that: a statement of the actor's purpose *made after the fact.* In this usage, motives become explanations when the intentions described are deemed "good enough" to account for the behavior to be explained.[7]

This empathetic account of behavior need not rest upon actual uniformities between a man's situation (including his "internal states" as well as his environment), his intentions (usually assumed to be a special kind of "internal state"), his after-the-fact "reasons," and his conduct. Motivational explanation may prove effective for certain classes of auditors whether or not such uniformities are known.

Motives constitute that portion of contemporary explainways usually reserved for human action, particularly its "higher" forms.[8] By definition, in the empathetic framework motives explain purposeful behavior.[9] They do not, except among psychoanalysts, explain "accidents,"[10] nor do they usually find employment in accounting for reflexive or habitual acts or purely expressive behavior.[11]

Motives may become part of a "scientific explanation" in ways described on pages 72, 97, and 136. For the present, it will suffice to remind ourselves that *the reasons men give for their actions need not be the causes of their behavior.*

It follows that the reasons men attribute to *others* in explanation of *their* behavior may be even further divorced from the necessary and sufficient antecedents of that action.

These distinctions in the application of motivational explanations are conventions. They have their own peculiar consequences, one of which is that the assignment of the "correct motive" will empathetically explain much of the behavior of human beings to many auditors. Such attribution doesn't work so well in the explanation of the acts of cats or the growth of trees. Sutherland (1959:159) sees it this way:

> It must be remembered that the fact that explanations of behavior are couched in everyday speech in words which are not used in the explanation of the behavior of animals or inanimate objects does not necessarily reflect a fundamental difference between men and the rest of creation: it merely reflects a difference in our way of thinking about them. It does not preclude the possibility of giving explanations of inanimate systems in terms of ends, if it were found convenient to do so. Thus the fact that words like "motive" are rarely used in explanation of animal behavior despite the obvious convenience of such explanations for certain actions of certain animals, may point not to any actual difference between ourselves and animals which makes it appropriate to give the type of explanation in the one case and not in the other, but to a reflection in language of theological views about the difference between men and animals.

Depending upon the audience, the narrator will combine these stories about circumstances, characters, needs, and intentions to produce the "feeling-in-with" that is popular explanation. The combination, in turn, may be poured into various thought-moulds. For example, "drives" and "intentions" (the "pushes" and "pulls" of ordinary thought) can be blended into a psychodynamic interpretation or read behavioristically as the result of reward and punishment.

Some attempted explanations via empathy, such as those frequently found in case histories recorded for forensic purposes, use a "shotgun technique" and include everything commonly held to be empathy-evoking: size of the subject's family, socioeconomic status, birth order, birth history, school record, sibling rivalry, peer accommodation, parental relations, physical defects, psychological test performance, dynamic interpretation, and psychiatric diagnosis. There is evidence that much of this "information" is noise,[12] but its notation busies official narrators.

The relation of information to empathy-building, of empathy-arousal to the quieting of curiosity, and of information, empathy and its sometime-consequent, "understanding," to predictive power is an open matter. It is here suggested that the connections among these variables — knowledge, empathy, sated curiosity, and forecast ability — are not so clear as current explainways assume. While empathy pacifies curiosity, it may not require knowledge (accurate information), and it may frustrate as well as assist prediction.

If these possibilities are true enough when one asks a psychological question ("Why did he do it?"), they become more tangled when the query is sociological ("Why does this society have a higher homicide rate than that one?").

Sociological questions of this nature receive many answers. Some portion of this multiplicity of reply derives from a continuing dispute among students of social behavior as to the necessity, or utility, of "reducing" societal explanations to answers given in terms of the behavior of individuals. This is a modern version of the nominalist-realist debate: Do groups have their own "laws" of behavior or is collective action to be explained by reference to principles describing the actions of the individuals who comprise the groups?

Attending to the motives of men and the meanings assigned to their situations, the empathetic explainaway is nominalistic, congenial to "methodological individualism," and subject, therefore, to reductionist errors in the explanation of collective behaviors. (Cf. pp. 69-71.)

The empathetic orientation in the explanation of group phenomena is exemplified in the writings of Max Weber, who formalized for sociology what has long been the empathy-building practice of saga-sayers. Historians who would make their plots come alive have told us stories that allow us to "understand" how their actors must have felt as they spun out their roles. This is "meaningful" history as opposed to the "mere" description of what happened.

Weber (1947:88) has argued that it is the distinctive objective of sociology to be a "science which attempts the interpretive understanding of social action." He goes on to claim that this understanding is necessary for the "causal explanation" of social behavior.

"Understanding," as Weber conceives it, is gained through the interpretation of the "states of mind" of actors. The "state of mind" that the Weberian sociologist seeks to comprehend is the "meaning" of the behavior to the actor. The "meaning" looked for by sociologists is the "actual meaning" of the act to its perpetrator. (This search distinguishes sociology from jurisprudence or ethics that tend to describe "pure" or hypothetical meanings.) And the "actual meaning" is found in the intentions of the actor.

In short, meaningful action (which is, for Weber, a definition of "social behavior" when it takes account of the behavior of others) is that for which motives can be explicated. Motives, in turn, are "known" by the actor himself or by his observer when "adequate reasons for the conduct in question" can be given.

Weber acknowledges that there may be "nonunderstandable" regularities associated with, or even underwriting, human behavior. These uniformities, such as physiological conditions, may be part of the causal chain but, for Weber (*Ibid.*: 99), a sociological explanation requires more than a statement of such probabilities: A correct causal interpretation of a concrete course of action is arrived at when the overt action and the motives have both been correctly apprehended and at the same time their relation has become meaningfully comprehensible.

Statistics of societal events, such as death rates, are not "sociological statistics" for Weber until they are given "meaning" through a linkage with the motives of men. A crime rate, therefore, is explained *only when* the motives of the criminals are understood and shown to be connected with variations in these rates.

Weberian sociology is, hence, nominalistic. Action in the sense of a subjectively understandable orientation of behavior exists only as the behavior of one or more *individual* human beings. (*Ibid.*: 101, emphasis in the original) And again, collective behaviors . . . must be treated as *solely* the resultants and modes of organization of the particular acts of individual persons since these alone can be treated as agents in a course of subjectively understandable action. (*Ibid.*, emphasis in the original)

We "understand" the actions of the other man either by perceiving his behavior as rational (as appropriate means toward the satisfaction of the actor's purposes) or by "sympathetic appreciation" (feeling as he must have). Both forms of understanding are often subsumed under Abel's definition (1948:212): We "understand" a given human action if we can apply to it a generalization based upon personal experience.

However, some empathetic explicators are more radical, more subjective and "humane," than even the Weberian idea allows. These students resist the generalizing function. They hold each man and each career to be unique and, hence, to be understandable only *ad hoc*. That is, understandable by stories peculiar to that man and that act. This approach to explanation is idiographic; it draws a picture of the unique person in his unique circumstances without reference to general "laws of action." It holds an explanation of human action to be moral explanation, and to be given when we see . . . that behavior as justified by the circumstances in which it occurs. . . . In appealing to reasons for acting, motives, purposes, intentions, desires and their cognates, which occur in both ordinary and technical discussions of human doings, we exhibit an action in the light of circumstances that are taken to entitle or warrant a person to act as he does. (Louch, 1966:4)

This view maintains, with Winch (1958:115), that "real understanding" is "grasping the *point* or *meaning* of what is being done or said." And for this, statistical regularities may be irrelevant. The argument holds that such regularities and even their enabling of prediction do not yield "real understanding," and Winch illustrates this by saying that . . . the difference is precisely analogous to that between being able to formulate statistical laws about the likely occurrences of words in a language and being able to understand what was being *said* by someone who spoke the language. (*Ibid.*)

We can "understand" Winch and others of his persuasion without agreeing with them, and our appreciation of this *verstehende* position does not prevent notice of the impropriety of Winch's antistatistical argument. There are at least two things wrong with Winch's "precise" analogy:

First, he is misled by his use of the word "meaning" into thinking that the "meaning$_1$" of a language is identical with the "meaning$_2$" of social events, and that, therefore, "understanding$_1$" an idiom is comparable to "understanding$_2$" human behavior.

These homonyms may, in some usage, approximate identity. Ordinarily, their referents diverge. "Understanding$_1$" the "meaning$_1$" of a language is a matter of conditioning. "Meaning$_1$" in this sense is not so much attributed as given by the learning contingencies. Now, we do have this kind of trained "understanding$_1$" of the "meaning$_1$" of other's acts. We can, for example, discriminate hostile from friendly advances. As Oliver Wendell Holmes, Jr., told us: Even a dog knows the difference between being stumbled over and being kicked.

We don't have to be able to "explain" how we can differentiate hate and love to be able to make the discrimination, but this ability, too, grades off into areas of dispute where meanings are more assigned than conditioned:

Alpha: That was a "crack."

Beta: No it wasn't. He didn't mean it that way.

Alpha: How do you know?

As one moves from the "understanding$_1$" of conditioned "meanings$_1$" to the explanation of complex social events, he becomes more involved in attributing and inventing "meanings$_2$." The "understanding$_2$" achieved by such assignment is imposed upon the events rather than trained into the interpreter. In his preface to Wittgenstein's *The Blue and Brown Books* (1958), Rush Rhees comments:

He (Wittgenstein) speaks of coming to understand what people mean by having someone explain the meanings of the words, for instance. As though "understanding" and "explaining" were somehow correlative. But in *The Brown Book* he emphasizes that learning a language game is something prior to that. And what is needed is not explanation but *training* — comparable with the training you would give an animal. This goes with the point he emphasizes in the *Investigations*, that being able to speak and understand what is said — knowing what it means — does not mean that you can *say* what it means; nor is that what you have learned. (P. vi, emphasis in the original)

He is raising the question . . . of what you know when you know what something means. (P. viii)

The debates about constructed interpretations and attributed "meanings$_2$" assume much and avoid a resolving test. They assume, as will be seen, a similarity between the man who would "understand" and the actor to be explained, and they equate this kind of implicit appreciation with "explanation." These quarrels also assume that, if sentences have "meaning," then acts must, too. But some sentences, written in familiar language and of correct grammatical form, are deemed nonsensical, and we have difficulty in stating the principles by which meaningful sentences can be distinguished from nonsense. If, with Wittgenstein, this is true of language, we should be chary of entering the lists where meaningful and meaningless acts meet.

Winch's poor analogy has a second failing: No one proposes that knowledge of the frequency distribution of words in a language is a procedure for comprehending the idiom. One counts "things" in the search for regularities when knowing the regularity or its lack provides an answer to *his* question. This does not indicate that one counts anything or everything for any purpose. Loving requires no tallying but, if one were to set up an insurance shop, he'd do well to count which kinds of people are risky bets.

Concerning language and its understanding, if one were interested in *how* language comes to be understood, his scientific answer would not derive from his being himself fluent, but from some process of hypothesizing tested against regulated observation. This has been done, of course. (For example, Staats and Staats, 1957.)

The crux of the argument concerns when one may be said to have (or feels himself to have) an "understanding." Winch *et al.* want to know (or want to feel) *why* the statistical regularities are there. They ask for "the meaning" of the regularity and their quest is made suspect by their characteristic intrusion of the adjective "real" before their "understanding."

(We read "real" to mean "the understanding *we* want, not the one *you* have.")

This kind of *verstehende* orientation cannot rest its curiosity where the behaviorist does. The behaviorist, a less belief-attentive chap, can accept the regularity as the meaning.

Explanations of this sort — which would provide "understanding" through a statement of the "sufficient reasons" for an act — state no rules, describe no regularities, are unconcerned with forecast, and can, therefore, provide only a timid guide to personal conduct and social policy.

These disadvantages do not deny Louch and Winch their point: *This style of empathetic explanation is, apparently, the preferred explainway regarding human action.*

To say this is to advance a hypothesis. No one has yet counted the frequency with which the explainways here described are used. If we cannot agree with the defenders of the empathetic mode that theirs is the *only* style of story deserving the label "explanation," we can, until such a count may contradict us, accord them the dubious honor of being popular. Most of us, most of the time, are comforted by explanations that allow us to comprehend behaviors as motivated by meanings.

The present intention is not to call this right or wrong. Rather, as with every way of knowing, each explainway carries its peculiar satisfactions and defects. There are intellectual purposes that "understanding" will answer; there are other purposes it will frustrate.

In the history of man's thinking about himself, such search-for-understanding, whether idiographic or, at times, nomothetic, seems to be associated with other thoughtways. This suggested association is intended to contrast the empathetic explainway with other modes, particularly the scientific, but it is recognized that the concordance is proposed rather than demonstrated. Tentatively, pending someone's definitive doctoral dissertation on the matter, it seems that those who favor explanation-by-*verstehen* argue for the irreconcilable differences between natural and social science, prefer cognitive to other determinants of human behavior, and are concerned with its moral evaluation.[13]

Verstehen is allied with protests in favor of a "human dignity" that would divorce the behavioral sciences from the other natural sciences since, it is believed, only man is self-conscious and only man has purposes — or, at least, is aware of them. This position gains strength from the difficulties of behavioral taxonomy. While it rejoices in these difficulties, it resents attempts to alleviate them since the classification of humans is regarded as demeaning.

THE SOCIOLOGIST AND THE MAN OF LETTERS[14]

Letters: Sociology is disgusting, if it is not downright immoral. You put everybody in a pigeonhole. Social class. Race. Role. You deny that we are individuals.

Sociologist: You write. You describe your hero with adjectives. He's tall. Bright.
Right. Are these not pigeonholes?

Letters: But I am using these words to describe my hero uniquely. To show the
reader what kind of man he is. And that means how he is as an individual.
One man!

Sociologist: But no one can understand any man except as he parallels some
other men. It wouldn't make sense to describe someone uniquely. Without
some behavioral matrix (pardon the expression) through which to view your
hero, no one could fathom him, not even his author.

Letters: Let's get a drink.

As part of its regard of man as unique and unpredictable, the empathy-
building orientation believes in the importance of belief. It stresses words
and attends to talk. It has faith in the power of ideas and the therapy of
symbol-manipulation. It is an outlook that dominates Western social psychology under the school-name "symbolic interactionism."

It explains actions by reference to motives which are often conceived as
arranged in a hierarchy of "values." It studies values as known, not so much
from what men do as from what they say.[15] In fact, it is part of the bias of
this point of view to consider "valuing" as coterminous with verbalizing.
(Does it need to be said that there is also justice in studying "valuing" by
observing what a man does?)

This orientation has contributed to the tremendous research interest in
"attitudes" and has assigned to cognition a prime role in the determination
of behavior.

Its point of view is variously expressed thus:

If men define a circumstance as real, it is for practical purposes real. (Thomas,
1923)

Most of the objects of social or human action are not "objective facts" in the
special narrow sense in which this term is used by the Sciences and contrasted
to opinions, and they cannot at all be defined in physical terms. So far as human
actions are concerned the things are what the acting people think they are.
(Hayek, 1955:26-27)

Men tend to confuse the *necessary* consequences of an act with the consequences that result from their beliefs about it and response to it. (Nettler, 1967*b*:1)

In order to explain why people do what they do we must know how they think. The chief source of information about how people think is what they say. (Lindesmith and Strauss, 1956:9)

Last, the *verstehende,* empathetic explainway is associated with, and is probably generated by, the proclivity to evaluate the behaviors being explained.

Much explaining is entangled with appraising. We find it difficult to describe human action, and more so to explain it, without judging it. This difficulty is demonstrated by the continuing debate concerning the logic of deducing prescriptions from descriptions. It is a difficulty rooted in our linguistic tools which give significance to the world largely by making judgments of it, as is shown in studies on the measurement of meaning (Osgood *et al.,* 1957). Such research repeatedly finds the *evaluative component* to be the principle dimension of interpretation of the social realm.

If we look at the world to judge it, then, say these *verstehende* philosophers, explanations that cleanse the "understanding" of its moral flavor are unsatisfactory. Such stories are not what we want to hear. Louch tells us (1966:4): Explanation of human action is moral explanation.

One can agree with Louch that most explaining of human behavior *is* moralistic. Evaluations are built into our language and, hence, into our thoughtways. To agree that men *do* explain by entwining description with prescription is not, however, to accord this mode utility for other purposes, such as prediction.

From a scientific point of view, the popular entanglement of judgments with explanations is a mischief, peculiar to the empathetic explainway with its advantages and limitations, and productive of illogic and perceptual inconsistency.

Still, there are philosophers who applaud the blending of evaluation with understanding. They hold that judging *must be* part of the explication of human behavior and that attempts to disentangle the two processes have ugly consequences. Thus Polanyi writes (1965:18): To assume that you can explain an action without regarding whether it is good or bad is to assume that moral motives play no part in it.

To extend this assumption to all social action is to deny the very existence of genuine moral motives in men.

To us, neither statement is true. Both are *non sequiturs.*

The intimate bond between "understanding" human conduct and assigning it praise or blame is further illustrated in a representative statement by Brodbeck (1968:84), who argues that "mere" statistical regularity is not enough. As an explanation, it doesn't satisfy. Brodbeck's explanation of this statistical sterility, please note, is not so much that correlations do not permit prediction (How else does one *begin* to forecast events?), but that statistics alone are devoid of moral assignment:

> Suppose that bankers usually vote Republican and we know that Brown, a banker, voted Republican. We cannot say that his being a banker was the cause of the way he voted. Causal laws permit the prior (sic!) prediction of behavior, and we could not have predicted how he voted from the merely statistical correlation. (Why not?) However, even if the law were universal and stated that such behavior invariably occurs, though we could predict it, we might still be reluctant to accept Brown's occupation as the cause of his behavior. Being a banker is not *in itself* a motive or reason for voting one way rather than another. (Emphasis in the original)

Note the ready association of causes with motives and reasons, in contrast with our earlier suggestion that reasons need not be causes. Brodbeck herself says elsewhere (p. 74) in the work cited: Sometimes motives are causes, sometimes not.

> It is a mistake to expect to universalize all such statistical correlations. . . . People are not all that conformist. We expect instead to find more basic laws about people's motives, needs, beliefs, and circumstances that will explain the statistical regularities. When we can do this, we will know not only why most bankers vote Republican, but also why some do not. When we do know the motives, beliefs, and expectations that cause behavior, then we find it intelligible. But there is nothing "irrational" about explaining a person's actions by means of his occupation, social status, habits, or, for that matter, his blood pressure. It *merely does not tell us what we in everyday life frequently want to know — namely, those causes by virtue of which we ascribe moral responsibility.* (Emphasis supplied)

> In general, there are two kinds of decision about causality that we may have to make. . . . We make a judgment, which does not depend upon our values, of *causal* significance. Second, . . . we make a judgment, which does depend upon our values, of *moral* significance. (Emphasis in the original)

Another philosopher (Walsh, 1959:302) puts the point directly: To say that history "makes sense" or is meaningful as a whole is, often at any rate, to say that we can feel morally satisfied when we contemplate it. To assert that history fails to make sense is conversely to proclaim that it offends our moral susceptibilities.

A CRITICISM OF EMPATHETIC EXPLANATION

Explaining through some form of empathy-building is undeniably common. Such ubiquity must mean, we think, that it "does something" for those questioners who use it. The most apparent result is a quieting of curiosity.

Some philosophers have advocated this explainway as "the best" or "the only" mode of thinking in explanation of human behavior. There is a rich tradition in the social studies in defense of this style of comprehension that runs from Vico through Comte to such moderns as Cooley, Weber, Znaniecki, Sorokin, and MacIver. (Cf. Abel, 1948.)

We will continue to use this popular explainway. Its weaknesses, therefore, deserve recognition. As formalized by its protagonists, empathetic explanations are subject to at least ten intertwined criticisms.

(1) *The techniques of empathy-arousal are unmethodical.*

Since attempts to generate empathy vary in effectiveness with the auditor's experience and his conditioned repertoire of explainways, what builds empathy for one observer may not for another.

Given this uncertainty, "developing an understanding of the case" remains art and, like art as opposed to craft, it is less taught than learned from model and practice. Some narrators have *Sprachgefühl* and can speak in empathetic tongues; others have difficulty with the dialect.

Insofar as "developing understanding" is an art, it can hardly be termed "a method," as the *verstehende* process often is. "Method" refers to an intersubjectively transmissible set of procedures. It refers to regularities in "doing things" so as to obtain reliable results. One can teach methods of vulcanizing rubber, strengthening biceps, or preparing Chicken à la Kiev, but the "methods" of "understanding," although alleged to constitute a "singular form of operation" (Abel, p. 211), have yet to be explicated:

While many social scientists have eloquently discoursed on the existence of a special method in the study of human behavior, none has taken the trouble to describe the nature of this method. They have given it various names; they have insisted on its use; they have pointed to it as a special kind of operation which has no counterpart in the physical sciences; and they have extolled its superiority as a process of giving insight unobtainable by any other methods. Yet the advocates of *Verstehen* have continually neglected to specify how this operation of "understanding" is performed — and what is singular about it. What, exactly, do we do when we say we practice *Verstehen?*

(2) *The procedures that are used, ad hoc, to develop empathy assume similarity between the actor-to-be-explained and his understanding judge.*

Schutz (1960) tells us: I am able to understand other people's acts only if I can imagine that I myself would perform analogous acts if I were in the same situation.

It is a truism that it is easier to "understand" people like ourselves.[16] What, then, if the clinician must "explain" the bizarre murderer to the morally distant judge? How evoke empathy except by appeal to conventional pity? Pity is here termed "conventional" because not any other man in any situation will stimulate it, and "understanding," however conceived, may be irrelevant to it. The judge's emission of compassion can represent a cultural encrustation upon his temperament. It may substitute for understanding, and any external observer will be hard put to distinguish conventional sympathy from empathy.

Nevertheless, there are observers of the other who tell us that they can "empathize" with Everyman and Anyman — the orgiastic murderer of children, the commandant of human abattoirs, the ascetic, the compulsive, the schizophrenic, or the zealous anarchist.

Homo sum: humani nihil a me alienum puto. Terence's definition of "a man" as one who calls nothing human foreign is fine motto. (1888) Whether such powers of identification with all things human characterizes anyone, the poet included, lacks independent test. But this side of such sensitivity, the evidence points to barriers to empathy with everyone, and the more so as the other man behaves, by our standards, extremely.[17]

In such instances, Trasler holds, we abandon motives as explanations in favor of circumstances: There are many cases in which it is not possible to account for a crime by pointing to motives with which the magistrates can feel sympathy. Some offenses, and some offenders, are unnatural. Then the exposition of the criminal's motives is either supplemented or replaced by another kind of explanation, which refers to his previous history. (1962:26-27)

The history-telling that substitutes for motives in the explanation of the immoral other man is often mixed with medical labels to produce the required satisfaction. In our post-Freudian climate, "sick" has become an empathy-building material.

If one joins Schutz in "trying to catch meanings" and operates with the undisciplined assumption that "the meaning for them, the actors (paranoid schizophrenics? retardates? sado-masochists?), corresponds to the meaning their act has for me," error can be forever covered with quarrel and incomprehensible meanings patched with psychiatric rubrics.

(3) *Empathy-building need not require truth-telling.*

Our Italian friends have a wonderful phrase. Translated, they say, "It may not be true, but it's a good story."

Similarly, the narrator who proceeds to elicit empathy for his subject need not tell a true tale. His story will always be partial, as is all telling and knowing but, more crucially, false hypotheses may work as well as true ones and, since the test of empathy is empathy, the observer who has "understanding" of the events before him, his curiosity sated, need never require proof of his insight.

Common sense, with all its *aperçus* and its errors, will satisfy as well or better than data-filled theory. This is so because independent tests of "having understanding" are lacking.

This possibility applies with greater strength as one moves from explaining an individual to comprehending history. As illustration, Weber's comprehensible thesis concerning the congruence of capitalism with Protestantism makes sense. Readers can "understand" how the union of Calvinist asceticism with the discomforts of predestination could be assuaged by "doing well." The lively questions remain, however:

Is the congruence causal?

How much distortion does an interpretation through "constructions" ("ideal types") involve?

Is that the way things happened? (Feuer, 1963; Green, 1959)[18]

(4) *Empathy employs vague indicators.*

It is part of the unmethodical procedure of empathy-building that it is difficult to know when one (particularly the other one) "has understanding."

Apart from those illuminations that are self-validating, reliable indicators of comprehension ("true comprehension") are missing. We rely on our own feelings and on the reports, verbal and gestural, from other auditors that they too have "understanding" as they assure us that they "know what the actor's life must have 'meant' to him."

But some men, who search for meanings outside ideologies, confess their failure in this search. The correspondent Sevareid writes (1967):

As journalists we are not keeping pace with the realities; we report them but we do not truly understand them, so we do not really explain.

I have read much and listened much but I do not understand what will really happen, to what end, when we have men on the moon; I thought I knew something about China but I am at a loss to perceive the inner meaning of the present convulsion in the world's biggest country. I have closely followed the civil rights story but if you asked me now to explain what lies in the deepest recesses of the heart of a Negro boy in an American ghetto, I could not tell you.

. . . It is not that we hide or alter the truth; it is often that we cannot penetrate the truth.

The trouble with the business of meaning-reading is that one man's comprehension will not be another's[19] and, lacking independent tests of interpretation, we debate. With debate, our thinking moves from evidence and inference to *argumentum ad hominem.* In the social studies *argumenta ad hominem* can be dignified as works in the sociology of knowledge which seek out the sources of the other fellow's "false understanding," as though knowing the origins of a proposition refuted it.

We are left with no adequate test of the "comprehension of the meaning of acts," although we are all engaged in the game of meaning-reading.

There is no accurate measure of the acquisition of empathy for one man by another (Gage and Cronbach, 1955), and what is true interpersonally holds as one interprets collectivities. We can be fooled by our own insights and by those of other judges, and where observers quarrel about their respective "understandings" of the other man or historic events, empathetic explainways provide no reliable procedure for resolving their dispute. Into this explanatory vacuum, ideology is drawn.

It would be an interesting exercise to take antagonistic "understandings" of contemporary issues and ask how the "method" of *Verstehen,* as opposed to other procedures for knowing, would resolve them. For instance:

A SAMPLE OF "UNDERSTANDINGS" OF CURRENT EVENTS

(I) *A Walk through the Mortuary Literature:*
Questions about Death and Dying

(Excerpted from Nettler, 1967*a*)

(*a*) Does the British government's campaign against tobacco-smoking "mean" a "rejection" of death (as Gorer urges)?

(*b*) If children seem not to think about death, are they "repressing" (as Wolfenstein contends)?

(*c*) Was the apparent "lack of affect" on the part of male adolescents to the assassination of President Kennedy "motivated [by] the arousal of vicarious guilt for a crime that bore the latent significance of parricide" (as Wolfenstein and Kliman argue)?

(*d*) If mourning practices change, does this signify an alteration in feeling (as Gorer interprets it)?

(*e*) If high-status persons express less grief than lower-status ones at the death of a Democratic president, can this be attributed, "in part," to guilt at having opposed the murdered leader's federal programs (as Barber reasons)?

(II) *Why Was Senator Robert F. Kennedy Killed?*

(*a*) The murder of Robert F. Kennedy is closely related to those of Martin Luther King, John F. Kennedy, Medgar Evers, the three civil-rights workers who died in Philadelphia, Miss., and the many anonymous victims of Southern racists. I believe that all of the murders were carried out to impede the process of social change now going on in America. (Gans, 1968:5)

(*b*) But it is every bit as possible that Sirhan Bishara Sirhan would have been moved to commit the act he is charged with if we had never intervened in Vietnam, if poverty and bigotry had been wiped out long ago, and if our popular entertainment dealt with nothing but love and gentleness and brotherhood. (Rovere, 1968:90)

(*c*) Sirhan grew up in Pasadena, a center of the John Birch Society, a center of radical right reactionaries, a despicable blot on this earth. The people of Pasadena are well-off. They hate the Jews, they hate the Negroes, the poor, the foreign. I find these to be really terrible people. Sirhan grew up in this atmosphere and I do not doubt that he heard many anti-Kennedy speeches. He simply accepted the way people in Pasadena think. He decided that Bobby Kennedy was evil and he killed him. (Vidal, cited by Buckley, 1969:124) (*d*) Another explanation for the wave of political killings is the presence of sick, demented men in our midst. . . . it is not at all certain that the assassins were sick. Oswald died before we could learn his motives; the killers of King and Robert Kennedy have not yet explained their ugly deeds. (Gans, 1968:5)

(*e*) We cannot blame the epidemic of murder at home on deranged and solitary individuals separate from the rest of us. For these individuals are plainly weak and suggestible men, stamped by our society with a birthright of hatred and a compulsion toward violence. (Schlesinger, 1968:19)

(*f*) Since the birth of this country, eight attempts have been made to assassinate presidents. Four were successful. With one exception, none of the murders, actual or attempted, was the result of foreign or domestic intrigue. Rather, each was the product of one man's disordered mind. The exception, the attempt by Collazo and Torresola in 1950 to shoot their way into Blair House and kill President Truman, was the result of a conspiracy by a few Puerto Ricans. . . .

Except for the two Puerto Rican gunmen, then, who probably were not insane . . . , the assassins, in my opinion, had schizophrenia, in most instances a paranoid type. (Hastings, 1965:27)

(*g*) The murder of Bobby Kennedy, postulates McLuhan, resulted from a breakdown between the new and old world of communication. In suggesting arms for Israel, Kennedy "spoke from a spacious and underpopulated world of highly fragmented, individualist culture — but he was also speaking straight into the ear of a highly tribalized corporate culture." (*Time*, 1968:40)

(III) *How Does One Read Riot? (The U.S.A. 1965-1968)*

(*a*) A riot is a social event which provides different opportunities to different participants. (Rainwater, 1967:23)

Riots . . . provide different kinds of ghetto dwellers with different opportunities to pursue highly varied goals. (*Ibid.*, p. 26)

(*b*) The full redefinition of certain property rights occurs next. The "carnival spirit" observed in the Newark and Detroit disturbances did not represent anarchy. It represented widespread social support for the new definition of property. (Dynes and Quarantelli, 1968:13)

(*c*) "The name of the game," a movement operative in San Francisco said recently, "is chaos." . . . [Brown] . . . may well sound too dangerous to be tolerated. "We are going to burn this town to the ground," he says. Apocalypse is the normal mood of ghetto talk, but on the outside it sounds like criminal anarchy. (Kopkind, 1967:4)

(d) At one level, there is no question that looting in civil disturbances is criminal behavior. But the laws that make it so are themselves based on dominant conceptions of property rights. Widespread looting, then, may perhaps be interpreted as a kind of mass protest against our dominant conceptions of property. . . . An attack against property rights is not necessarily "irrational," "criminal," or "pointless" if it leads to a clearer system of demands and responses, in which the needs and obligations of the contending parties are reasonably clear to themselves and to one another. . . . The looting that has occurred in recent racial outbreaks is a bid for the redistribution of property. It is a message that certain deprived sectors of the population want what they consider their fair share — and that they will resort to violence to get it. (Dynes and Quarantelli, 1968:14)

(e) The man who steals a six-pack of beer or breaks a store window does it not out of "criminal" motivation[20] (it would be hardly worth his while), but because he is expressing some important feelings about his world and trying to put these feelings "on the record." (Rainwater, 1967:26)

(f) I heard a friend of mine say, "Hey! They rioting up on 12th." That's all it took to get me out of the house. He said the police was letting them take it; they wasn't stopping it; so I said it was time for me to get some of these diamonds and watches and rings. It wasn't that I was mad at anybody or angry or trying to get back at the white man. If I saw something that I could get without getting hurt, I got it. This is nothing but pure lawlessness. People are trying to get what they can get. They have been denied these things and when the first brick was thrown, that's all it took. Let's get it while we can get it. They were trying to get all they could get. They got diamonds here, they got money here, they got clothes here and TV's and what not. . . . That's all. They're just getting something they haven't got. . . . This was a good way to get it. I really enjoyed myself." ("Arthur," as told to Parmenter, 1967:15, emphasis in the original)

Such opposition of understandings can be extended into any personal or social problem. The conflict of interpretations is a constant of the human condition and need be neither deplored nor praised. It gains contemporary relevance, however, insofar as professional knowers claim to have developed a distinctive competence applicable to the engineering of individual and societal reform. The claim to competence, usually based on academic accomplishment alone, is a bid for responsibility and power legitimized either by "truer understanding" or science.[21] About the sciences of behavior, more later; here it need only be noted that no evidence is available to support the expertise of scholarly empathy over the "understandings" of any men of like intelligence.

(5) *To empathize is, usually, to moralize.*

The tendency to fuse evaluations with descriptions is not decried by the "understanding" explicator as possibly contaminating the description but, rather, is defended as necessary for an adequate explanation (cf. pp. 45-47).

In opposition to this opinion, it can be argued that valuing the behavior distorts its perception (cf. note 13). Love and hate are blinding as well as illuminating. Those who would be scientific in their explanations seek to reduce the impact of moral judgment upon observation and inference. To exercise scientific explainways (or, more simply, to improve accuracy in judging the other) requires training in moral-free description. As with any exercise there may be some pain involved.[22]

The entanglement of moral judgment with "understanding" places a striking limitation upon empathetic explanation. The limitation follows from the earlier point about its being easier to "understand" people like ourselves. We can add to this fact another possibility: It is easier to "understand" people of whom we approve.

The ordinary use of the idea, "to understand," implies appreciation and it is no accident that people confound "knowing the other man" ("understanding$_1$" him) with "liking him" ("understanding$_2$" him). Nor is it surprising, then, that we find it difficult to "understand" behavior we dislike. The notion of "understanding" is buried in a web of connotation that refers "knowing" in this sense to preferring. This constitutes a restriction upon "empathetic knowledge."

(6) *Empathetic explainways suffer a cognitive bias.*

As has been seen, those who employ "understandings" in their explanations are meaning-readers—except, of course, when the other man's behavior becomes so bizarre as to be deemed "meaningless."

If there were method to the empathetic explainway, it would tell where to look to find the "meanings" of the situations to the actors playing in them. Method would also teach correct interpretation of these signs of significance. Neither locus of definition nor mode of reading is clear however.

Ordinarily, when one engages in the search for the meanings of acts, he looks for cognitions: beliefs, definitions, "attitudes."[23] For example, that popular variety of empathetic outlook known as "symbolic interactionism" tells us that human behavior is not merely "released" by stimuli, but that, or the contrary, man acts by . . . noting and interpreting features of the situations. . . . (Blumer, 1962:184) The point of view holds, repeating Lindesmith and Strauss, that to . . . explain why people do . . . requires knowing . . . how they think . . . and . . . knowing how they think . . . is to be gauged principally by . . . what they say.

This set of assumptions is popular. It has occupied the center of American sociopsychological attention since Thomas and Znaniecki (1918) put "attitudes" there.[24] Intuitively, there is a rightness about it. Each man knows from his own experience that his "attitude" makes a difference. Situations *do* vary with our definitions of them. When we play at competitive games, we know that we can be "up" or "down" for the contest, a matter of "attitude." When we engage in courtship or salesmanship, there, too, "attitude" affects us.

This outlook assumes, of course, that "attitude" is largely a matter of thought, and, in attest of the power of thinking, Western cultures have developed a wide spectrum of mind-mending facilities that range from meditational retreats through a gamut of counselors to group-therapeutic, "sensitivity-training" institutes. When the other man behaves unpleasantly, the vogue is to regard his "mind" as out of tune and to recommend an adjustment of the mental carburetors to put him back in acceptable running order.

In all this, the sign of "mind" is its product, "thought," which is usually considered as "that-which-is-verbalized." This is a narrow conception of "mental activity." It is an even narrower view of the sources of behavior.

There is a kind of general disease of thinking which always looks for (and finds) what would be called a mental state from which all our acts spring as from a reservoir. (Wittgenstein, 1958:143)

The "logic" implicit in the cognitive bias may be outlined like this:

Actions result from "interpretations of the situation." As determinants of acts, "objective situations" vary, then, with definitions.

Interpretations are mental processes and mental processes are known from utterances. This is what is meant by "how-people-think." (This point requires inclusion because it is conceivable that an actor's "interpretation," considered as his reliable bent to respond one way rather than another, need *not* be so cognitive as empathetic explicators would have it. Further, and repetitively, "how-people-think" need not be assumed as coterminous with "what-they-say.")

If you want to understand the other person, learn what the situation "means" to him. He can tell you.

If you want to change his (or your) behavior in a situation, change his (or your) interpretation of it.[25]

To criticize this group of assumptions is not to say, "All wrong and of no value." Rather, it is to say that the model of man as "frontal lobes with organism attached" is partial and productive of a systematic bias in explaining his conduct.

What needs to be said in criticism of a respectable explainway is difficult to say. For, once said, it may seem obvious; but, unsaid, the criticism is ignored and the valid assumptions of symbolic interactionism are stretched beyond their wise application.

At the outset, let it be clear that we consider it foolish to deny the power of belief and inconsistent in an educator. It is equally unbalanced, however, to attempt to explain behavior as if it arose from thought alone.

"How a man thinks, so is he." True. But only "true enough." For when one thinks about "how a man thinks," the phrase becomes vague, its measures imperfect, and the correlates with other acts less than the phrase has led one to expect.

It is a fruitful assumption to hold that man interprets his world and acts upon his meanings. But this is not the whole truth about the springs of human action and there are at least these difficulties in explaining behavior by attending to thoughts:

(*a*) *"How-one-thinks" is a vague phrase, and "what-one-says" its imperfect measure.* Henry Adams told us as much, long ago (1907), and succinctly: No one means all he says, and yet very few say all they mean, for words are slippery and thought is viscous.

Whatever else it might mean, "how-one-thinks" has been studied by social psychologists in terms of the putative dimensions of intending, believing, and evaluating—the conative, cognitive, and affective components of "attitude."

These three aspects of thinking bear each other a fluctuating relationship (Fishbein, 1967), do not exhaust "how-we-think" (Woodmansee and Cook, 1967), and omit from consideration that part of "mind" that is *feeling* (Langer, 1967). If one agrees with Langer and other philosophers that mental life ("thinking"?) is more than what appears in words, the symbolic repertoire is seen as inadequate to express those feelings that are part of "how-we-think," and "what-we-say" becomes its poor representative.[26]

Studies of perception and learning-without-awareness demonstrate that an equation of that which is "language-able" with that which is discriminated and learned (part of "how-one-thinks") is erroneous. Eriksen (1960), in his review of this research, tells us:

The subception effect as an effect is real enough . . . , and it . . . focuses attention upon the limitations of verbal responses in conveying the individual's perceptual experiences. (P. 290)

There is nothing profound in noting that language and words are highly abstract symbols and bear little or no physical resemblance to the objects, events, and relationships that they denote. A definition of awareness in terms of verbalization places a heavy burden upon the adequacy of language to reflect the richness of perceptual experiences and images. The equation of awareness with verbal report leads to a similar kind of confounding of response and concept that has occurred with perception and the responses from which perception is inferred. (P. 280)

There are most likely circumstances where a nonverbal response may be a better indicator than verbalization. (P. 291)

(b) *Studying thinking by "what-one-says" has its own difficulties.* If knowing "how-we-think" is introspectively difficult, it is more so as one tries to gauge the other man's mind. Everyone assumes that beliefs make a difference, but when we attempt to measure verbalizations and correlate them, one with the other and with the actions to which they refer, the results are disappointing.

This is not to hold that there is never an association between word and its logically linked deed. Some consumers, for example, do purchase what they say they intend to buy (Katona, 1951, 1957, 1960). Rather, the relationships lack that closeness and uniformity that would make attention to what people say the single, best way of knowing about men.

Some of the disappointment with studies of opinion as signs of "how-one-thinks" derives from a measurement problem. The varieties of difficulty in assessing beliefs have been treated extensively[27] and need not be reviewed here other than to note that, despite the application of sophisticated measuring techniques — scaling, factor analysis, multivariate analysis — the relationships found are no better than the responses gathered. It would be naïve to assume an isomorphism between "how-people-think" and their responses to interviews and questionnaires.

The naïveté is encouraged when we forget that asking is its own behavior. The very act of asking puts behavior in a different context. One can learn something about how Little Joe feels about his Daddy by watching them together and apart, but what one thus learns may be rather different from what he hears when he *asks* the child about his father. The swain who asks his inamorata "Do you love me?" is not likely to be happy with any answer he receives.

Yet, we persist in asking people questions:

Do you enjoy soaking in a hot tub?

Who, or what, do you think is responsible for the assassination of President Kennedy?

If you had to describe the total experience [of President Kennedy's assassination] as one which smelled bad or as one which left a bad taste — which would it be?

There are two ways to interpret the answers given to questions such as these taken from actual interview schedules. An empirical interpretation says the answer means whatever it correlates with. If responses to such questions differentiate among people for the investigator's purposes, then that is their meaning and their utility. But an empirical interpretation is not an "understanding" one and the empathetic explicator puts other meanings into the pattern of responses he obtains. For example, Tomkins tells us (1965:94) that *saying* that events smell bad or taste bad means something more than the empiricist can read:

In one choice (bad taste) another human being or any bad experience has been permitted to come close, to enter the body through the mouth. In the other choice (bad smell) the bad other person or experience has been kept at a distance. In terms of the underlying affects one is a response of shame, the other of disgust and contempt.

The practice of reading meanings from responses to interviews and questionnaires (beyond their empirical correlates) is sometimes supported by reference to "theory." But, it will be seen, theories of human behavior lack that specificity and generality that would allow for definitive decision among competing interpretations of "what-people-say."

The practice is also supported by the symbolic-interactionist assumption that other men must "note and interpret" their situations and think about their lives in some ways parallel to the way we think about lives. This assumption is projective; it supposes that others think about the matters in our minds, that our questions must have answers in their thoughts. It is a premise encouraged by the "responsible citizen" notion that, in a democracy, everyone ought to have an opinion about everything.[28] A result has been the proliferation of polls and questionnaires that put the "vacant question," or . . . one that elicits a response out of "nothing" — neither opinion nor information, neither feeling nor disposition to act. "Nothing" is perhaps too strong a term: since there is a response, one may infer a motive. But the answer's motivation may not be what the student assumes; it may be courtesy or the socially approved feeling that "one ought to have an opinion."[29] (Nettler, 1967a:343)

VACANT QUESTIONS — SOCIAL WORK AMONG THE SLUM CHILDREN

(Offenbacher, 1968:6)

Even specific and repeated questions often fail to elicit internally consistent responses.

CASE I

Social Worker: Why does your father want you to go to college?

Child: I don't know. I guess he wants me to be a real good mechanic; better than him, because he ain't that good.

Social Worker: But you don't have to go to college to become a mechanic.

Child: I know, you can do all sorts of things. That's what I want to be, a mechanic.

Social Worker: But do you think that in college they'll teach you how to be a mechanic?

Child: I'll study, anyway. That's what school is for, to study and learn. Right?

CASE II

Social Worker: In what ways do your teachers help you out?

Child: With grades.

Social Worker: How's that?

Child: Like I got 70's and 80's.

Social Worker: Don't you think you deserved that?

Child: Yeah.

Social Worker: So, how did they help you out?

Child: Well, I call it helping out.

CASE III

Social Worker: Why do you think social studies are important?

Child: Because they teach you things I never heard about.

Social Worker: Like what?

Child: Like Abraham Lincoln, and Washington and Napoleon.

Social Worker: And why is that important?

Child: I don't know. I guess just to learn. Everybody should learn everything about it.

One can't read these interrogations without feeling sorry for the children. One wonders what kind of answer would have satisfied the inquisitor, and what the inquirer had "in mind," and whether the questioner believed her respondents had ever "thought" about these matters.

It needs repeating that it is an assumption, not a fact, that people define every situation in the cognitive sense, in the sense of "having opinions about." It is a worse assumption to suppose that such opinions as people may hold about some facets of *their* lives are couched in the vocabulary of *our* questions.

There *are* Scarlett O'Haras, and their philosophy of postponing "thinking" may be an adaptive one, despite its antagonism to "middle-class," responsible mores. Some of us are Spaniards, as well as O'Haras, and our *dicho* tells us: Don't think. If you don't think, you don't remember. If you don't remember, you have no regrets.

A cute test of this argument is to ask of oneself that most difficult of all questions, so frequently posed in various forms to our "subjects": What do you want out of life?

(*c*) *Cognitive bias reduces motivation to verbalization.* Symbolic interactionism has *defined* "motives" as "understandable" when they are "language-able." True, the Gerth and Mills (1953) classic considers motivation on "organic" and "psychic" levels as well as on the "personal," but it is only on the latter level that motives are deemed to become socially significant and "understandable." Here motives are regarded as (p. 115) . . . the terms which persons typically use in their interpersonal relations. And again, . . . motives are acceptable justifications for present, future, or past programs of conduct. (*Ibid.*)

One may define the world as he chooses, but the unfortunate consequences of working with a concept of motivation constricted to vocabularies is that one omits much that generates conduct, and further runs the risk of confusing rationalization with motivation.

Justifications ("good reasons") may facilitate behavior without initiating it, and he who attends to the reasons may not attend to the motives, "the movers of action."

A result is a narrow causal picture and the possibility of ineffective response.

EXPLAINING EMBEZZLEMENT

D. R. Cressey (1964): The process of verbalization is the crux of the individual embezzlement problem. This means that the *words* that the potential embezzler uses in his conversation with himself actually are the most important elements in the process which gets him into trouble, or keeps him out of trouble. (P. 19, emphasis in the original)

I call the use of such a vocabulary a rationalization, which is different from the term "rationalization" in psychoanalysis. (P. 20)

The rationalization is his *motive*, a basic unit to be studied if one is to understand human behavior. (P. 22, emphasis in the original)

Prescription: A Twofold Defense:

(1) . . . company program designed to eliminate the number of nonsharable problems among employees. (P. 25)

(2) Educational programs emphasizing the nature of the verbalizations commonly used by trust violators. . . . [We must] . . . make it increasingly difficult for trusted employees to . . . think of themselves as "borrowers" rather than as "thieves" when they take the boss's money. (P. 26)

Another View (Nettler, 1969*b*): Suffice it to question that the rationalization *is* the motive, or the only motive. Justification becomes part of the energizer, but it need not be the source-motive. Most rationalizations of deliberated crimes come rather late in the process of decision. There are, of course, offenders who don't rationalize their crimes except as the official helper asks them, "Why did you do it?" (Fn. 17, emphasis in the original)

And Counter-Prescription: It cannot be argued that these measures [Cressey's] might not "do some good." But as point of emphasis, such prescriptions should *not* supersede alertness to vice, to the trusted officer's living beyond his means, and, most important, to rigorous audit.

"Educational" attacks on the rationalization process run into the same possibility [of evasion]: man is ingenious. Everyman justifies himself . . . with or without unsharable problems, rationalization is part of ego-defense and hardly to be abandoned before monthly talks about "borrowing is stealing." (P. 15)

(d) *"What-people-do" is a vague phrase.* Those who propose thoughts as causes of actions do not mean *any* action. A sneeze? Stuttering? Being anxious? Marrying Millicent rather than Virginia? Behaving "antisocially"?

To mention such a gradient of behaviors from the reflexive to the chain-of-acts is to suggest that each explicator chooses some cutting-point below which he deems behavior "thoughtless." This cutting-point will vary with ideology. The Freudian, for example, will accept thought-as-cause at "lower levels" of behavior than some other interpreters:

Wife: But why does Oscar cough like that?

Analyst: His coughing is psychogenic. It occurs whenever he is in a tension state, particularly when his impulses are unacceptable to his super-ego. For example, Oscar hates his mother-in-law. She talks all the time, mostly, what is to him, nonsense. He dares not express his own counter-opinions for fear of losing control. But a cough, at the right moment, interrupts the hated woman and allows Oscar to ventilate his hostility without fear of reprisal.

To the problem of what counts as an "act," the empathetic explicator replies that he is not interested so much in the meaning of reflexes as in the significance of purposeful behaviors. But "purposeful" is itself in need of definition and, as with the Freudian example, *where* one reads purpose, and *how much* purpose he sees, is a matter of assumption.

Those who adopt scientific explainways prefer to check assumptions against the predicted consequences of acting upon them. This is not a popular procedure, however. Meanwhile, the twin ambiguities of "how-one-thinks" and "what-people-do" encourage unproved assertions about their priority.

(e) *The causal priority of belief is assumed rather than demonstrated.* Freud and Pareto were neither the first nor the last observers to show that some portion of belief is rationalization. As with certain legal judgments, the process may be "decisions first, reasons afterward."

A cognitive bias leads interpreters to give priority to thoughts as determinants of acts where a more accurate picture might fuse thinking-acting or, at times, place thoughts *after* acts, much as James and Lange regarded emotions as effects as well as causes of behavior.

As an illustration, is phobic behavior—a fear of snakes, let's say—*produced* by ideas about snakes? Or is the phobia otherwise generated with the ideas as consequents?

Anyone who today believes that such emotionalized conduct is caused by thoughts is confusing the frightened man's reasons, after the act, with the neural motors of the fear.

A logical consequence of this belief — that sick thinking produces sick acting — has been that phobias and other unwanted behaviors have been "treated" by attention to beliefs.

The talking-therapies have a remarkable record of failure,[30] accompanied by a remarkable persistence of faith.[31]

The faith in thought-reform is defended by denying the fairness of testing hypotheses by acting upon them. If the consequences of such action falsify assumptions, the defender of a faith can argue that any or all of the following happened:

Those actions (those therapies, for example) did not follow from *his* assumptions.[32]

The testing actions were improperly administered.

Extraneous variables produced the unpleasant results.

The original objectives were not the only ends of action, and if the original goals were not achieved, well, other benefits (untested) may have been derived.[33]

There is yet another style of defense of causal hypotheses disconfirmed by action upon their premises. This is not a popular mode of argument since it runs counter to the cliché that knowledge is power. But, to the contrary, it can be argued that knowledge of causes need not yield cures.

In the case of thoughts assumed to produce actions, the failure of allopathic remedies of behaviors — healthy ideas healing sick conduct caused by unsound notions — need not be accepted as disproof of the causal priority of ideas. Perhaps, once caused, seldom cured.

All these defenses of a cognitive bias *may* be true. They will be accepted or rejected in accord with a host of concatenated ideas about heredity and environment, man-as-mechanism versus man-as-moral-agent, and the kinds of behavior to which "purpose" is to be imputed.

The present point is this: If one will allow that *some* acts are not initiated by thoughts, although they may be justified and maintained by them, then the range of behaviors of which this is true is indeterminate. If one will permit "phobias first, thoughts second," then this may be as true of a wider spread of acts and sentiments—let's say, of a family of behaviors and be-liefs called "neurotic." If this expanded spectrum is begun and maintained less by "definitions of the situation" than by training given a chemoneural system, then the possibility is open that many other behaviors, defined by the symbolic interactionist as resulting from "how-man-thinks," may be less thoughtful and more conditional.

In short, the "cognitive bias" assumes a dichotomy that may be less than real. It has placed learning in the frontal lobes and denied it to the viscera and it has argued for the superiority of the first learning-locus over the second. Miller (1969:434) notes:

> Since ancient times, reason and the voluntary responses of the skeletal muscles have been considered to be superior, while emotions and the presumably involuntary glandular and visceral responses have been considered to be inferior. This invidious dichotomy appears in the philosophy of Plato, with his superior rational soul in the head above and inferior souls in the body below.

Miller shows learning to be less segmented than Plato assumed. It is more all of a piece. "Reward" changes autonomic processes as well as central nervous system function.

If symbolic interactionism is to work with its preferred dichotomy, and if it is to move beyond the formalization of folk knowledge ("beliefs make a difference") to an approximation of scientific knowledge, it will be neces-sary to specify the regularities between antecedent conditions, definitions of the situation, and consequent behaviors. Thus far, attempts to relate cir-cumstances to beliefs to acts have produced low-order generalities. There are as yet no "laws" stating the invariant, or even highly probable, relation-ships between perceptions and actions. Lacking such rule-fulness, the empa-thetic explanation via symbolic interaction is always *ad hoc*. As an *ad hoc* invention, plausibly conceived to "fit the facts," it works best *after* the events it explains and it runs thereby a high risk of tautology.

Other views would hold the beliefs abstracted as explanations of acts to be themselves part of the acting-complex to be explained:

A QUARREL

Questioner: Why does Danny the Red try to destroy the social order?
Explicator: Because he believes it to be unjust.
Questioner: Why does he believe it to be unjust?
Explicator: Because it is.

Questioner: "Is"! That's a hard verb. "Justice" and "injustice" aren't. They are words that refer to moral-feeling-states assigned — like shouts, groans, curses — to social relations which themselves are always dimly perceived.

Explicator: You sound like old Freddie Ayer.* You're quibbling.

Questioner: No, I'm not. You've told me that Danny is destructive because of "conditions out there" about which Danny believes something. You are correct. Danny believes; Danny destroys. But, where *you* would *separate* the belief and the action, to me they are part of the same parcel. For me, what I want explained is "why" (confound that word!) Danny believes and acts *that* way. His thoughts are not enough. They do not seem to be the *variable.* (Maybe thinking with "variables" is what fouls us up.) That is, other men "knowing" the same things believe differently, which means they feel differently, and they apply different interpretations to the same "reality." What is not clear from your explanation is what comes first (if any of these), which varies most, and independently: feeling, thinking, reality, or "the facts."

Explicator: I don't understand you.

Questioner: Well, if I wished to change Danny, and assuming the power to manipulate these matters mentioned in explanation of his behavior, should I work on his attitudes (beliefs), his acts, his facts, or the reality he attacks?

Explicator: That's a hypothetical question. You don't have the power.

Questioner: Fortunately?

Explicator: Possibly. But, if you did, I suppose you'd do what you could.

Questioner: As do we all. And feeble doing failing, men, from all times, yield to an ancient resort, anthropoemia.**

The disappointment that results from working from a cognitive bias is aggravated and illustrated when one examines the disparities between what men say (one measure of their "thought") and what men do.

  (f) Words and deeds continue to say different things. Studying "how-people-think" by "what-they-say" has not produced clear and close relationships with "what-people-do."

  If, as proposed by the empathetic explicator, actions are to be understood from the thoughts of the actor, and thoughts are known from utterances, the explanation is left to leap a chasm between words and deeds. The width of the chasm varies and the understanding interpreter bridges the gap with improvisations.

*A reference to Ayer, 1936.
**A Greco-ism: "to throw the man out."

The inventory of slippage between what men do and what they say is long. It has been ably summarized by Deutscher (1966), and has often been memorialized:

> The citizens of Mississippi will vote "dry" as long as they can stagger to the polls. (Will Rogers)

> The lie is a condition of social life. (Nietzsche)

We do not merely lie to others; we also lie to ourselves. Awareness of this is part of the contribution given us by Shakespeare, Freud, and Eugene O'Neill, in particular. Their lessons have been proved experimentally: that self-deception is a constant possibility and that it is greater where our desires conflict with our trained morals (Hurlock, 1956:406, 411-412; Hartshorne and May, 1928: *passim*). More, we can be conditioned to believe our own false reports:

> Thus, telling a lie under conditions normally associated with telling the truth produces dramatic alterations in the perception and recollection of facts—a simple light can color one's thinking!

> Our theory that each person would believe more false confessions made in the presence of the "truth light" than in the presence of the "lie light" was certainly correct. (Bem, 1967:23)

It is no news that those who earn their livings in the reading of other's "minds"—prophets, salesmen, con-men, detectives, and counselors—do not work with words alone. Eriksen (1960:290) notes:

> There is reason to suspect that a considerable amount of the evidence that the clinician finds for unconscious processes is in the nature of discrepancy between concurrent responses. The clinician may note the S's autonomic responses and evidence of emotion do not correspond, i.e., do not correlate very well, with his verbal statements. This lack of correlation is a basis for the clinician's inference of unconscious processes or defensive mechanisms at work.

THE LOVING MOTHER AND THE DOUBTING PSYCHOLOGIST

Mother: I love my child and I want him back, but you don't seem to believe me.

Psychologist: I hear you. I even think you think you believe what you say. But this does not mean to me that you feel this, and only this, and really this.

I *listen* to what you say; I also *believe* what you do.

Self-deception is not merely a matter of individual psychology. There is abundant evidence of collective hypocrisy where "official moralities" are divorced from personal ethics for good reasons (Warriner, 1958). The structure of assumption, abetted by functional theorists, that sees institutions as interdependent, and beliefs and institutions as forming an interlacing network, leads too easily to the conclusion that the interrelationship is causal and that there is some neat geometry among beliefs, institutions, and everyday practices. Morgenbesser (1958:288) summarizes thus:

> Nor is there any basis for the thesis that once we know the beliefs of a group, we will be able to completely understand or to predict its behavior. There are no mechanical rules for the translation of belief into action, and not all primitive peoples act according to their beliefs. Malinowski himself noted many discrepancies between the beliefs or ideals of the people he investigated, and their actions. This discrepancy is not accounted for by any of the functionalistic theories of the types we have reviewed.

In the light of the repetitively demonstrated tension between saying and doing, there need be little surprise that fifty years and reams of research after Thomas and Znaniecki made "attitudes" central to actions, we can generalize thus: Beliefs make a difference in actions. No one knows how much. This means that no one knows:

which beliefs
held with what intensity
in what relationship to other beliefs in the "personality system"
under what quality and degree of peer support or indifference
with what history of acting-upon-belief[34]

will become operative as determinants of:

which kinds of action for
which "kinds of people"
under what circumstances.

It would seem difficult, then, to maintain without qualification the position of the empathetic explicator that actions result from meanings and meanings are to be known from sayings. There is too much evidence reducing the power of thought as a determinant of behavior. There is also too much evidence against the efficacy of manipulating words that would alter interpretations that would, in turn, change behaviors in situations.

These reductions in the independent power of thinking are met by some students who tell us, rightly, that . . . under varying conditions we ought to expect positive, zero, and negative correlations between words and deeds. (Deutscher, 1967:2) This is so, continues Deutscher, because . . . the *orientation* of an actor toward any social object is constantly undergoing such reconstruction. Therefore, we can expect not only to find "attitudes" shifting in the process and behaviors shifting in the process, but the relationship beween the two becomes tenuous. *(Ibid.:* 3, emphasis supplied)

"Orientation" serves here as a *deus ex machina* to save *symbolic* interaction from the failure of measures of words as measures of meanings to correlate highly with what men do. To the interpreter less converted to a cognitive view of man, "orientation" might be a useful concept, to be read as the actor's "reliable bias" (Nettler, 1968a). This reading of actions as continuities of past postures tends to attenuate words and thoughts, however, and the *symbolism* of the interaction is diminished.

In fact, with "orientation" substituted for belief, one must ask the empathetic explicator yet again, "What does one attend to in order to acquire 'understanding' of the 'meanings' with which men define their situations?" Certainly, we have learned by now, not alone to what men tell us with words.

With such slippery connections between doing, thinking, and telling, explanations that attend predominantly to what people say will sometimes be right and sometimes wrong (where there is any test of this), and always partial. This may be a description of every attempt to think about one's life and his world, in which case intellectual humility seems recommended in preference to any one-and-only explainway.

The parting advice on this point is not that we should never believe in what people say, but that a "cognitive bias" is a bias that attends excessively to talk and insufficiently to other behavior.

Having renewed acquaintance with the loose connection between words and deeds, students look to some of the sources of this slippage.[35] Many of these roots have been admirably described by Deutscher (1966). To his inventory may be added the *underwriting error* in accepting what people say as determinants of their actions. This is that men take thought for a variety of tangled purposes. We do not think only to intend, to believe, or to evaluate, as the student of "attitudes" has assumed. We also exercise symbols to stimulate feelings and to express them. The joy of playing with words goes beyond individual gratification and may also be a means of affiliation with others, like sounding the national anthem. Words can make us "feel good" (or ill) whether or not we know their meaning.[36] The jealous professor who commented on the incomprehensible lecture by the Great Name, "He should have played it on a violin," was resenting the substitution of one purpose of symbol-dexterity for another.

If there are, then, these limitations to knowledge of others from attendance to their talk; if, as Turner has recently remarked (1968), . . . it has long been known that the best way to predict behavior is to look at earlier samples of similar behavior and simply predict continuance; what is gained from the imperfect study of "how-people-think"? The answer, of course, is "understanding" which, in this case again, bears a tenuous relationship to either knowledge of causation or the control of events, but carries a more satisfying connection with evaluating men and justifying their deeds, *after the act.*

The "good reasons" given for the actions will satisfy curiosity. They may, or may not, describe the sources of behavior.

(7) *Empathetic explanations suffer a nominalistic bias.*

Since this explainway appeals to stories about the human individual, it cannot afford the possibility that what is true of individuals need not be true of societies. The prejudice lies in the mandate that collective activities be understood through reference to individual wants, individual thoughts, individual acts. This bias is recognized as "methodological individualism" (Lukes, 1968). Its call to would-be scientists of the social is "to bring men back in" (Homans, 1964), and its orientation is well represented by this statement: Sociology is a corollary of psychology at least in the sense that social phenomena require general psychological propositions for their explanation. (Homans, 1967:60)

The polar perspective is Durkheim's extremity, that . . . every time that a social phenomenon is directly explained by a psychological phenomenon, we may be sure that the explanation is false. (1963:103)

We ancient Greeks would avoid these antipodes. The question for us is pragmatic. Does reducing the description of the behavior of aggregates to the behavior of their individuals add to some purpose of explanation, like prediction, or does it detract? Are the regularities among collective behaviors "better known" on their own level than by reduction to the level of their particles?

To the latter, the answer is "Often, yes."

Such affirmation does not deny some of the challenges of the methodological individualists:

(a) That there is a risk to "realism" of hypostatizing the metaphors with which collectivities are described. Talk of "group minds" and "folk souls" and "the spirit of the age" permits too much.

(b) That one aspires to a concordance between explanations on the individual level and those on the societal. We should like to be able, intellectually, "to walk up and down the abstraction ladder" without stumbling over our inconsistency.

But, again, satisfaction or dissatisfaction with the individualist position will be a function of what one is attempting to do with his explanation. One may be content, for example, with a statement of the *societal* correlates of warring as an explanation of war without reducing the explanans to statements about what individuals want. The predictive test of explanatory utility, applied to warring, seems to favor the realist outlook (Sorokin, 1937).

Similarly, if one accepts Popper's assignment (1962:346) that . . . the main task of the theoretical social sciences . . . is to trace the unintended social repercussions of intentional human actions, he resists understanding with empathy.

Economists have abandoned this debate that still intrigues the more empathetic sociologist. "Macroeconomics" has been developed as . . . a separate discipline with its own rules because aggregate economic behavior does not correspond to the summation of individual activities. (Dernburg and McDougall, 1968:2, emphasis supplied)

Eugenicists also have long recognized that there are "levels" of explanation — that, for example, benefits to individuals do not necessarily summate to the benefit of the collectivity, and that the Benthamite goal of "the greatest good for the greatest number" cannot be realized (Hardin, 1968:1243).

Not only are the truths about individuals not necessarily additive to truths about collectivities, but the moral judgment of individual and group behavior will also differ (Niebuhr, 1932). Worse, the moral stance that calls certain freedoms "good" for the individual may have to call "evil" the collective consequences of its exercise. This moral dilemma is encountered, for example, in "the tragedy of the commons," as Hardin (p. 1246) has termed it. The tragedy, "the remorseless working of things," is that the free employment of an "individual right" eliminates its proponents, although not necessarily its users. What one might declare as a moral prerogative of the individual becomes a collective menace. Thus, the freedom to breed, "guaranteed" by the United Nations in its 1967 "Universal Declaration of Human Rights," is seen as dysgenic.

In sum, it is helpful, particularly for predictive purposes, to be able to separate "levels of analysis" and to seek truths about groups apart from knowledge of their individuals. In explaining behavior, as in judging it, one may try to build ladders between these levels, but climbing them may make one dizzy. The empathetic explainway avoids the heights of collective perspective and misses some of the view.

(8) *As explanations of behavior, the empathy-arousing processes are vulnerable to tautology.*

Because empathy satisfies itself, explanations in this mode are peculiarly vulnerable to redundancy. The path into *circulus in probando* begins with the use of explanatory concepts that are but variant definitions of the behavior to be explained.

CASE I

Probation: Why, doctor, does our client continue to steal?
Psychiatry: He is suffering from antisocial reaction.[37]
Probation: What are the marks of "antisocial reaction"?
Psychiatry: Persistent thievery is one symptom.

CASE II

Defense: Whether one calls him insane or psychotic, he's a sick man. That's obvious.
Psychiatry: I should think that's largely a matter of terminology.
Defense: Do you mean to suggest that a man could do what that boy has done and not be sick?[38]

These battles of words mistake definitions for propositions. We are vulnerable to this confusion because we have learned language through an associational process that is highly conditional. Such acquisition makes language an imperfect tool of logic, but an effective instrument of word-music: poetry, drama, exhortation.

The linguistic legerdemain through which we confound definitions with propositions can satisfy us with an "understanding" that is vacant. The vacuity of such comprehension lies in its failure to predicate. This is another way of saying that it satisfies curiosity with nonempirical utterances, irrefutable because nonpropositional, plausible, but unpredictive.

What man has done, man can do. (W. C. Fields)

You can observe an awful lot just by watching. (Yogi Berra)

You won't get bald if you don't lose your hair. (An American mother)

(9) *Empathy-building explanations encourage nonpropositional understandings.*

The tautological style of explanation, to which the defects of language make us vulnerable, is further stimulated by attempts to understand behavior through the assignment of motives.

It is not that motivational explanation is *necessarily* faulty. Nor is it being contended that men do not, at any time, have objectives that guide their actions. Nor need one hold that such purposes can never be known by the actor or his student prior to the emission of the behavior to be explained.

Rather, the issue is that when we attempt to explain behavior by building empathy through a description of "what the man wanted" or "the reasons for his actions" we run the risk of satisfying ourselves by begging the question—that is, by proving the motives from the acts. "Inner states" are inferred from behaviors; the behaviors are then explained by reference to the "inner states."[39] This need not be circular *if* the explanandum is not the same behavior as is referred to in the explanans. This style of intellectual enterprise carries the hazard of redundancy.

Pierce (1956:137) puts it well: Any proposition about the relationship of the behavior of an "actor" relative to his presumed "ends" or "goals" is inherently nonempirical if the type behavior is logically implicit in those "ends" or "goals," e.g., using "the death wish" as a causal explanation of suicide.

The possibility Pierce describes is illustrated by that form of empathy-induction that talks about functions served: Suicide is a means for overcoming perplexing problems and anxieties, and it reduces a variety of tensions, but in doing so it also kills the person. (Honigmann, 1954:27)

Explanations that would understand through empathetic appreciation are built upon after-the-fact inventions. The successful practitioners of such explainways are artists in the construction of *post factum* plausibilities. Insofar as their means-ends analyses are nonempirical, they become irrefutable.[40] They may, for this reason, prove quite satisfying to some interrogators, but such satisfaction ought not be confused with the kind of knowledge from which one may draw forecasts.

(10) *"Having 'understanding'" may be unrelated to predictive ability.*

A powerful test of knowledge, and a principal reason for taking thought, is prediction, where *"prediction" is a forecast made on the basis of public procedures for the symbolic manipulation of representations of past and present observations.*[41]

This is not to say that "knowing" and "explaining" are engaged only for predicting. There are other satisfactions, and satisfying explanations need make no predictions.

But all men, at some time, raise the question "What will happen if . . . ?", and a common justification of explanation is that it leads to foreknowledge. Expectations are implicit in understandings. To wit:

If we know why we do things, we become free to do them, or not.[42]

If we are to get along with each other, we must understand each other.

Lacking legitimate tools of trade, he resorted to armed robbery. Giving him a vocation will assist him to be lawful.

The first two quotations may, of course, be only definitions and, as such, circular. If they are not used as definitions, they are prophetic. To such understanding, prediction says: "Put your forecast where your empathy is."

Empathy-building by its nature militates against counting one's predictive score. "Sympathetic understanding" is one kind of prejudice, and a prejudice is always excused. The inventory of common excuse is large and usually true:

The data are not all in. (They never are!)

The conditions of individual behavior that might make it predictable are not constant.

Maybe our program did not achieve its objectives, but things might have been worse if we hadn't tried.

Truth-possible statements such as these allow us to persist in "understanding" ourselves and others without the ego-damage of an error score. Thus, although explanations develop promises, most insightful explanations are blank checks. Few people cash them against the bank of expectation.

Since the indicators of "understanding" are vague, tests of its predictive power are necessarily difficult to construct. In the prediction of collective behavior, there is no evidence to support the forecast efficacy of a *verstehende* sociology. Scholars who work on this task use other methods (Brown and Helmer, 1964; Gordon and Helmer, 1964; Kahn and Wiener, 1967) which may be deficient in their own right (Nisbet, 1968; Shonfield, 1969), but which have not yet been compared with "historical understanding" for forecast power.

While awaiting test of competing ways of predicting the behaviors of aggregates, it is hypothesized that the nominalistic bias inherent in the empathetic explainway, the bias which assumes that understanding individuals leads to knowledge of groups, deters the student from counting those regularities of collective action that are not derivable from the "understanding" of human individuals. Our wager is that such neglect in keeping the collective score reduces comparative predictive ability.

As concerns the prediction of individual conduct, the evidence is, to say the least, discouraging to the practitioners of "human understanding," and major efforts to improve the accuracy of verified prediction tend toward other procedures.[43]

The questionable relationship between "understanding" the other person and becoming an accurate forecaster of his behavior seems generated by at least these correlates of the empathetic orientation:

Much that may be cause is omitted from the understanding. (For example, Weber's "nonunderstandable uniformities *underlying* . . . meaningful action." Emphasis supplied.)

Much that may be effect (part of the events to be explained) is omitted from the interpretation. (For example, behavior that appears to be nonpurposive.)

The linkage ("meaning") of the events may be wrongly assigned.

"Understanding" is entangled with moralizing so that predictions without "comprehension" become, à la Brodbeck, unsatisfactory. "Understanding" demands "something more" than forecast, and this "something more" (the evaluation) may make the "understanding" less predictive.

When "understanding" promotes this blindness to what is happening, it does so for all the reasons listed above — that "sympathetic comprehension" is selective, moralistic, and hence liable to truth-denial. As Ivan Karamazov tells his brother, Alyosha:

I understand nothing. I don't want to understand anything now. I want to stick to the fact. I made up my mind long ago not to understand. If I try to understand anything, I shall be false to the fact and I have determined to stick to the fact. (Dostoyevsky, 1950:289)

In sum, empathy-building is a popular explainway. Its recognized product, "understanding," is seldom given independent test, so that neither its "method" of induction nor sign of its presence is sure. We don't know, reliably, how to get "it," which means that every man's "understanding" may be his own. Once we "have understanding," there seems little we can do with it except to rest our curiosity upon it. Empathy seems of little value to prediction, and may even hinder it.

Nevertheless, this may be the best we can do, most of the time. As will be seen, the knowledge of behavior that might be scientific is difficult to extract. Given the daily need to act upon our explanations, we will continue to empathize. Our terminal advice here is not to abandon "understanding" social behaviors — an impossible waiver — but, rather, not to confuse art with science, and appreciation with knowledge. Thus unconfused, we may resist the temptation to claim the expertise of a scientist when we don the robes of the official explicator of behaviors or social engineer.

NOTES

[1] The possibility of temperamental differences underwriting preference for explanations is suggested by William James' hypothesis about "tender-" and "tough-minded" people (1907:12).

Bromley's study (1968:158) of the kinds of account given in explanation of individual adjustment leads him to suggest that . . . an "adequate" argument accounting for the behavior of a person in a given situation is one which contains enough evidence, marshalled by a sufficiently cogent argument, to convince someone that he now understands what he did not previously understand. So, naturally, the kind of explanation which will satisfy one person will not satisfy another.

Although definitive tests are lacking, it is conceivable that preferred explanatory modes may be projective: Different kinds of people prefer different kinds of explanation in answer to different kinds of questions. For example, Körner (1959:138) suggests that propositions about final causes are satisfactory explanations for some persons but not for others. All the variance in response to Körner's questions cannot be explained by cultural differences.

Studies that bear on the possibility that temperament interacts with culture to create differential predilection for explainways are to be found in the work of H. Witkin et al. on "cognitive style" (1962). There are also implications in the factor-analytic research of Coan (1958) on the "dimensions of psychological theory."

Longitudinal study of Witkin's measures of cognitive orientation show it to be a stable feature of personality. Schimek (1968), for example, reports reliable performance among male subjects tested at ages 14, 17, and 24. Of interest here is the suggestion in Schimek's work that a preference for a scientific explainway over a "looser," empathetic one is in some part a function of cognitive style. Note his definition (p. 576) of "intellectualization," a trait found to persist: Intellectualization [is] one of the main techniques through which the broad defensive aim of isolation of affect can be achieved. Intellectualization is manifested by a general style of thinking and verbalization characterized by an extreme emphasis on objective judgment, technical knowledge, a need to view everything as an intellectual task, and a preference for dealing with words and abstractions. The maintenance of such a detached, impersonal, precise, and dissecting approach allows avoidance of the immediate raw impact of the more affective and subjective aspects of one's experience.

[2]Trasler (1962:26) tells us: To the ordinary man the notions of *understanding* behavior and *explaining* it are identical; X is said to have explained Y's behavior to Z when he has described the situation as it appeared to Y vividly enough to enable Z to feel, intuitively, impulses which might have caused him to act as Y did. The attraction of this procedure is that it "makes sense" of an action which is *prima facie* puzzling. (Emphasis in the original)

[3]What "satisfies" may not necessarily be what is "efficient."

[4]But, other times, other places, other beliefs in the animation of plants (Nida and Smalley, 1959).

[5]This assumption does not belie the fact that in some men's minds sin is underwritten by "free will." Consistent belief in free will is probably more difficult than the consistent assumption of determinism. Thus Russell writes (1955:79): Free will is always unhesitatingly rejected except when people are thinking about the free will problem. And Carney (1967:238) speaks of . . . free will [a notion] which is inconsistently applied to the usual, but not to unusual behavior.

[6]The discussion above of Leifer's and others' hypotheses is extracted, with publisher's permission, from the author's paper, "Using Our Heads" (1968b).

[7]Douglas (1967:273), a proponent of the "meaningful" interpretation of sociological phenomena, expresses this point thus:

By meaningfulness is meant that the individual members of this culture consider the phenomena to be "meaningful." Something is considered to be "meaningful" in our culture when it can be interpreted or explained in some way considered by the members to be adequate. What constitutes an "adequate" interpretation is by no means clear and is not our fundamental concern here: we are concerned only with the "things" considered to be relevant to an "adequate" interpretation of suicidal phenomena. The "things" considered to be relevant in this respect are . . . certain "motives," certain "situations," "intention," and, perhaps, some other specific "things." But it is only *certain* motives in certain situations that are relevant for giving an "adequate" interpretation of the suicidal phenomena. . . . Most important in this respect, as the most frequent dimension of meaning relevant to the imputation of the category of "suicidal," is "intention." (Emphasis in the original)

[8]We still find it convenient to explain infrahuman behavior by reference to motives (The dog is looking for his bone), but as we become more biologically sophisticated we learn to discount such an explainway as a metaphor.

We no longer—most of us—apply purposes to the working of inanimate objects.

[9]The fact that purposeful behavior is often explained by reference to a "motive" (purpose) makes this explainway vulnerable to tautology:

Bereaved: Why did he commit suicide?

Explicator: He had a death wish.

Cf. pp. 71-72.

[10]It is a commentary on the interaction of language and explainways that psychoanalysts who use "motives" to explain "accidents" don't think our "accidents" are accidental.

[11]The motivational explainway is so expansive that one finds educated men who don't believe that human beings can be conditioned (I know an American physician who denies this possi-

bility), or that any human behavior may be called "purely expressive" (one encounters religious students who believe that "*all* behavior is directed toward a purpose").

[12] The relationships among the predictive utility of varying quantities and qualities of information and the comfort of curiosity remain an intriguing field of research. For example, Lady Wootton tells us (1965):

> Information . . . makes the courts feel cosy. . . . But cosiness is not the same thing as rationality; and for a decision to be rational, the information upon which it is based must be relevant. Up till now, however, the criteria by which relevant information can be distinguished from irrelevant are by no means firmly established. Probation officers' reports are full of personal details about a man's relation with his wife and children, his work habits, the measure of his liking for alcohol and a hundred and one other personal details all of which make fascinating reading. But an American experiment described by Leslie Wilkins showed that even those who write these reports, let alone those who have to act upon them, do not at present have a common mind as to the respective value of the various items of information which they contain.

The reference to Wilkins and Chandler's research (1965) concerns a study of the decision process among 17 probation officers in an East Coast American city. Their findings include these:

(1) As they are fed additional information, some decision-makers continue to vacillate between a "yes" and a "no" decision right up to the time of exhaustion of the total of available information.

(2) In general, the probability of a change in decision *decreases* as information increases. Stability of decision is usually reached at a very early stage.

(3) There is a general lack of concordance with respect to information which may be regarded as of most utility.

(4) Decision-makers seemed able to reverse a decision without loss of confidence.

(5) There is a tendency for a more *lenient* decision to be made with more information, regardless of the content of this information.

(6) One thing would appear to be clear from research of this kind; the assumption that better decisions (in any sense) are more likely to be made as a direct result of the supply of more information is not justified.

(7) It is clear that the amount of information which can be processed effectively by the human mind is quite small.

The way in which "information" may become "noise" is further illustrated by Bartlett and Green (1966) who compared the abilities of six psychologists to predict grade-point averages from either 4 or 22 predictors. Using *valid* predictors, it was found that the average validity per psychologist was .65 with 4 predictors, but .56 with 22 predictors. The authors suggest that the situation may be even worse in those quite common circumstances in which one adds "information" that gives an incorrect prediction.

Similarly, Meehl and Rosen (1955) have shown that, if a test has only moderate validity, it is possible for a clinician to make more *wrong* identifications with its "help" than he would likely make without it. In this vein, Savitz and Tomasson (1959) report a study in which the accuracy of identification of an ethnic minority was *reduced* as more cues were provided.

Not surprisingly, Sines (1959) finds that the relationship between amount of information and accuracy of judgment is complex rather than linear, and varies with the particular type of data made available to the clinician.

[13] One critic, noting our correlation of empathetic explanation with moral evaluation, asks "So what?"

The "so what?" proposed throughout this work seems demonstrable: That men often think they are describing while they are evaluating, that they confound defining with praising or blaming, and that knowing, in the scientific sense, is hindered, not helped, by its entanglement with judging.

Arguments and evidence are given in note 2 of Chapter Two, notes 5 and 12 of Chapter Four, on p. 166 of Chapter Five, in note 1 of Chapter Six, and on p. 54 of this chapter.

[14] A reminder (cf. note 4 of Chapter One): As with all illustrations in this volume, the stories, verbatim or paraphrased, are true.

[15] Recent expression has been given this point of view by Rokeach (1968-1969:550), who defines values as beliefs: To say that a person "has a value" is to say that he has an enduring belief that a particular mode of conduct or that a particular end-state of existence is personally and socially preferable.

Although Rokeach would distinguish "values" from "attitudes," in his conception both are to be known from the respondent's verbalized "beliefs." Thus, he says, . . . I will define an attitude as an enduring organization of several beliefs, focused on a specific object . . . or situation, predisposing one to respond in some preferential manner. (Ibid.)

[16] Similarity is a principal condition of accuracy in judging the other. Whenever . . . information is utilized in a simple fashion, or whenever it is presented in less than optimal manner, similarity between oneself and the other emerges as the single, highest correlate of predictive success. If we further assume that these conditions are frequently encountered, it is possible to conclude that the similarity between perceiver and perceived is a factor of primary importance in describing predictive accuracy. Predictive success, in the absence of actual similarity, is an exceptional occurrence. (M. Wilkins, 1965:22)

We not only predict the behavior of persons similar to ourselves with greater accuracy, we also like such people better (Bonney, 1946; Broderick, 1956; Byrne and Griffitt, 1966; Byrne et al., 1966; Byrne et al., 1969; Precker, 1952; Richardson, 1940; Winslow, 1937). Conversely, people whom we like are perceived as similar to us (Fiedler et al., 1952).

In these facts may lie a source of the violation of the semanticist's canon of singularity such that "understanding$_1$" (knowing the other) is confused with "understanding$_2$" (liking him).

[17] There are some provisional tests which indicate that the tendency to punish others (by definition, one sign of lack of sympathy, if not of empathy) may vary with the "moral distance" between the judge and the actor. This is suggested where "moral distance" is defined as the "perceived possibility by the judge that he, too, might, or might not, behave as has the actor he is judging" (Nettler, 1969a). The greater the perceived distance between judge's "possibility" and actor's behavior the more harshly will the judge regard the offender (Nettler, ibid; Reichstein, 1965).

[18] "Is that the way it happened?" Apropos, Feuer writes (1963:5-6): While Weber, on the other hand, held that the Protestant ethic was a precondition for the rise of European capitalism and science, Marx said it was, rather, the concurrent consequence of this rise. Yet Marxists and Weberians alike shared the view that the Protestant ascetic ethic somehow made it likely that its adherents would become more effective seekers after scientific truth.

Has this concentration on the Protestant ethic, however, radically misperceived the origins of modern science? Misgivings have persisted. Pitirim Sorokin . . . noted the scientific contribution of Catholic Italians during the first half of the seventeenth century was higher than that of any other country. This fact alone, he held, would refute the notion that there was a direct causal relationship between the Protestant ethic and the emergence of modern science. Even those who acknowledge that Protestant England had led European science at the end of the seventeenth century were uncertain as to what exactly the alleged connection between Puritanism and science had been. "The influence of Protestantism on natural science," wrote Richard S. Westfall, "is nebulous and difficult to determine." S. Killey accepted the documentation by Robert Merton and Dorothy Stimson, which purported to prove that Puritan beliefs had been a driving force in the origins of modern science, but both he and James W. Carroll wondered whether "Protestant" and "Puritan" were being used so loosely as to conceal under their rubric rationalistic, empirical, skeptical, and even atheistic tendencies. Was it possible that two disparate contemporary phenomena were being assigned a relatedness that had never obtained in actuality?

[19]This is the more polite phrasing of "the trouble with meaning-reading." There is a rougher version. It would pose an unpopular answer to Sevareid, phrased as a question: On what grounds do you assume that there *are* "ends to moon-walks," "inner meanings," and "truths to be penetrated"? Perhaps your quest is improper and there are no "true explanations" other than those men invent for faithful acceptance.

One is reminded of the sarcastic definitions of "metaphysics" and "religion": Metaphysics is a blind man in a black room searching for a black cat. Religion is a blind man in a black room searching for a black cat, only the cat isn't there.

[20]The placing of quotation marks around the pejorative label "criminal" is itself an interpretation. It assumes some unstated, *essential* "criminal motivation." It proposes a category of such motives, to be called "criminal" or not, dependent upon the moral judgment assigned a breach of the criminal law by the motive reader. In the Dynes-Quarantelli conception, for example, crimes become "less criminal" if the lawbreakers do not accept the legitimacy of the laws broken.

The effect of such redefinition is to dilute the concept of crime. This may not be a great loss since the word already carries a heavy load of reference. However, such attenuation of meaning renders the term more useful for ideological purposes than for description. *The moral infection of a once-legal concept permits an ethical assessment under the guise of behavioral interpretation.* And, since there is no independent test of accurate motive-reading, acceptance or rejection of the sympathetic explanation becomes a matter of "sides taken."

As will be seen later, ideologies are powerful explainways regardless of their truthfulness. With "understandings," ideologies allow moral evaluations to be made in the process of explanation. It is our continuing theme that such mixture of evaluation with description is satisfying to most question-raisers. At the same time, it is an obstacle to that description of behavior that might permit causal analysis and some degree of accurate forecast.

[21]A recent expression of this bid is given by Hoult (1968): . . . social and psychological scientists are, by far, the theoretically best qualified people in the land to sketch the dimensions of, and to lead others toward, the "good society." . . . We are the specialists in the principles of human behavior; we, better than anyone else, can properly assess previous faltering attempts to improve the general welfare; we, above all, . . . know how to create and apply the measuring

techniques and devices which can pinpoint the real sources of social discord and dissatisfaction and thus reduce to a minimum the supposed need for "educated guesswork" on the part of leaders of vital human affairs.

We're big boys now! And, like other "real scientists" such as physicists and biologists, we're qualified to make judgments about what apparently will and won't contribute . . . to the betterment of man. (Pp. 4-5, emphasis in the original)

Apropos, some Canadian professors who call themselves "The University League for Social Reform" tell us, in a flier advertising their book (Lloyd and McLeod, 1969), that . . . they like to think of themselves as the first wave of the drive for Ivory Power. This surgent movement was foretold in Bell's papers (1966*b*) on the changing role of the intellectual. Its consequences remain moot.

[22] The pain is not merely that nonevaluative observation of people is abnormal. There is a risk involved that the practice of amoral description reduce one from ethical relativism to nihilism.

[23] "Attitude" is placed in quotation marks here because, while it may indicate to the behaviorist the way a man "lists" (his "reliable bias," Nettler, 1968*a*), it is the "cognitive component," the thinking part of an "attitude," that symbolic interactionists have emphasized in their research.

[24] Social psychology, they wrote, is precisely the science of attitudes. (I:27)

[25] This premise in the logic of symbolic interactionism is used or ignored by its devotees as other parts of their belief systems find it advantageous. It is a preference for intervention, rather than a confirmed causal chain, that seems to determine whether, for any particular issue, the student of society emphasizes the impact of "reality" upon behavior or the impact of its definition.

Without research that would prove this, it is suggested that symbolic interactionists more frequently resort to the determinism of ideas as reformative when the behavior to be explained and remedied is seen either as a matter of personal policy, or as a conflict in public policy between underdogs and their exploiters. (The terms used here indicate which side is favored.) In the former instance, individual psycho-purging is recommended. In the latter, the definitions of the underdogs are held to be more valid than those of topdogs so that, for example, crimes defined by the masters are not crimes for the downtrodden. It is recommended, then, that topdog definitions (laws) be changed.

There is a third use of this definitional assumption. It is a use in disfavor today, but congenial to some dispassionate observers and topdogs. It holds that public policies addressed only to material conditions to the denial of the interpretations customary among those "helped" will fail. It is a doctrine advanced by the founders of this school, Thomas and Znaniecki (1918, I:12-14):

There are two other fallacies involved to a certain extent in social practice. . . . These assumptions are: (1) that men react in the same way to the same influences regardless of their individual or social past, and that therefore it is possible to provoke identical behavior in various individuals by identical means; (2) that men develop spontaneously, without external influence, tendencies which enable them to profit in a full and uniform way from given conditions, and that therefore it is sufficient to create favorable or remove unfavorable conditions in order to give birth to or suppress given tendencies.

The assumption of the spontaneous development of tendencies if the material conditions are given is found in the exaggerated importance ascribed by social reformers to changes of material environment and in the easy conclusions drawn from material conditions on the mentality and character of individuals and groups. For example, it is assumed that good housing conditions will create a good family life, that the abolition of saloons will stop drinking, that the organization of a well-endowed institution is all that is necessary to make the public realize its value in practice. To be sure, material conditions do help or hinder to a large extent the development of corresponding lines of behavior, but only if the tendency is already there, for the way in which they will be used depends on the people who use them. The normal way of social action would be to develop the tendency and to create the condition simultaneously, and, if this is impossible, attention should be paid rather to the development of tendencies than to the change of the conditions, because a strong social tendency will always find its expression by modifying the conditions, while the contrary is not true.

. . . innumerable examples could be cited from all departments of social life. But it is easy to understand that in the absence of a science of behavior social reformers pay more attention to the material conditions of the people than to the psychology of the people who live in these conditions; for the conditions are concrete, and tangible, and we know how to grasp them and to conceive and realize almost perfect plans of material improvements, while in the absence of a science the reformer has no objective principles on which he can rely, and unconsciously tends to ascribe a preponderating importance to the material side of social life.

Thomas and Znaniecki's classic statement of the importance of definitions of the situation has been given recent support by Myrdal's ten-year study (1968) of Asian economic development. A reviewer notes (Bliven, 1969:116): The mistake of Communist economists was their reliance on Marx's belief that a change in methods of production would impel a change in everything else.

. . . South Asian planning must try to change the individual South Asian. Economic progress will not automatically modernize the people. Unmodernized people prevent economic progress. Therefore the plan must alter social as well as economic behavior, and change attitude and institutions that in the West are not ordinarily thought of as economic.

[26] Wilson and Patterson (1968) argue that: Analysis of the probable central processes occurring when persons respond to traditional statement-form items suggests that two sequential stages are undergone:

(1) An immediate, emotional response to the central, controversial issue involved in the statement.

(2) Suspension of judgment while qualificatory and justificatory details of the statement are examined. . . .

In short, his eventual response becomes more a function of cognitive processes than affective.

Ideally, if assessment of attitudes is to facilitate prediction of actual behavior, it is the first (affective) stage which we should seek to measure. (P. 265)

[27] For a critical evaluation of "scientific" studies of how men think politically, for example, see Berns (1962). A review of the attitude-assessment literature will be found in Fishbein (1967).

[28] Riesman and Glazer (1948-49) comment: An opinion is considered a free gift in a culture where privacy is at a minimum, and people will feel that the interviewer is entitled to an opinion irrespective of whether they also try to guess which of several possible opinions he may want of them.

[29] Relevant to this possibility, see Hofstaetter (1950).

Other students of the social scene have recently expressed concern with professional over-consumption of opinions (Webb *et al.*, 1966:1): Today, some 90 percent of social science research is based upon interviews and questionnaires. We lament this overdependence upon a single, fallible method. Interviews and questionnaires intrude as a foreign element into the social setting they would describe, they create as well as measure attitudes, they elicit atypical roles and responses, they are limited to those who are accessible and will cooperate, and the responses obtained are produced in part by dimensions of individual differences irrelevant to the topic at hand.

[30] An able summary of psychotherapy research and quarrels of interpretation is to be found in Eysenck (1966). Findings similar to Eysenck's, but with regard to the ineffectiveness of psychotherapy with children, are reported by Levitt (1957).

[31] The tenacity of faith in the face of disconfirming evidence has long been noted and, depending on one's stance toward the particular faith, praised as indicative of courage and dignity or derided as folly and dogmatism. A record of such tenacity when confronted by failed prophecy is given by Festinger *et al.* (1956).

Similar thoughtways are experienced in response to failures of thought-reform. (See note 32 below.)

[32] Other counselors . . . felt that research was superfluous, since all the necessary rules of conduct in therapy were already known. When they were informed of the outcome of the study, they reacted in a characteristic fashion: those who were analytically trained and oriented asserted that the results would have been positive, had analytic principles been applied by all staff members, consistently, throughout the course of the treatment period. Conversely, those counselors who were followers of Carl Rogers' non-directive approach averred that a systematic use of non-directive methods would have produced more definite success. (Teuber and Powers, 1953:145)

[33] Teuber and Powers (*ibid.*) describe this defense against recognition of the failure of a delinquency prevention project: To some of the counselors, the whole control group idea, and our insistence on an objective description of the counseling process, seemed slightly blasphemous, as if we were attempting a statistical test of the efficacy of prayer. Theirs was an "ethics of sentiments" rather than an "ethics of consequences." They insisted that the relationships established had their value in themselves, irrespective of their possible effect on the boys' behavior, and they were not perturbed when the seemingly negative results of the delinquency prevention program became known.

[34] The history of "acting-upon-belief" will be viewed by the behaviorist as the organism's record of reinforcement.

With or without this perspective, "acting-upon-belief" may also be regarded as a personality variable. That is, we should expect to find a wide and consistent variance in the approximations of beliefs to actions among life histories — from the pole at which action and belief are closely wedded (as in the "man of character") to the antipode where practice and preachment are divorced (as in the "hypocrite").

Although the Hartshorne and May (1928) studies pointed in this direction, this remains a neglected aspect of personality research.

[35] Thus Campbell (1963:157-162) proposes that words and deeds have different "situational thresholds." And Schwartz (1968) suggests another cognitive variable intervening between a

set of words formally collected from a respondent and his nonverbal acts later observed; namely, that a congruence between word and deed is to be expected only as norms (definitions) of personal responsibility and perceived consequences of one's acts are activated.

From this research, Schwartz reports that . . . Within groups presumed to experience little activation of norms, no correspondence between norms and behavior was observed. Increasingly positive correlations were found within groups more likely to experience activation of norms. (For a summary index, $r = .02$ in the lowest group, and $r = .58$ in the highest.) (P. 232)

[36] Loudon Wainwright (1968) describes the evocative use of nondenotative symbols on the part of a political campaigner thus: "As George Bernard Shaw said," he continued, and there is a rustle in the crowd. This is his windup line and the reporters all begin to run back to the train. "You see things; and you say, Why? But I dream things that never were; and I say, Why not?" Unsure of its meaning but certain that the line calls for response, the crowd cheers him, and the bright stranger . . . fades away into the growing dusk.

[37] "Antisocial reaction" is a nosological entity (a disease?) in the *Diagnostic Manual* of the American Psychiatric Association (1965).

[38] The verbatim response of an attorney defending a 17-year-old boy who had butcher-murdered a young woman previously unknown to him.

[39] For an instance of this kind of reasoning in criminology, see Tucker's review (1967) of Cohen's *Deviance and Control*. Tucker argues that Cohen confuses observable behavior with unobservable motivation and that the term "motivation" is itself variously used: at one time to refer to action; at another, to refer to (unobservable) predispositions to action.

[40] Ex post facto "explanations" of behavior are, of course, always possible. There is no such thing as an observable act of behavior that cannot, by some mental gyration, be shown to be consistent with, and hence "validate," any "end" or "goal" one wishes to conjure up. In short, the approach has no criteria of relevance for its "facts" other than conformity to its own propositions.

With no acceptable criteria of relevance for its "facts," the Weberian type of action analysis cannot be confirmed empirically in any scientifically acceptable sense of the term. . . . it relates "meaningful" behavior to concepts which logically imply it; i.e., "ends," "goals," or "norms." (Pierce, 1956:137)

[41] Some students distinguish "prophecies" from "predictions" on the grounds that the former forecast from privy "knowledge" (intuition) whereas "predictions" are public drawings.

Meehan (1968) goes further and calls predictions "forecasts" when they don't lead to control of the future and "explanations" when, in principle, they do. For present purposes, Meehan's distinctions may be ignored.

[42] This statement is a working assumption of psychoanalysis and a reflection, again, of a common cognitive bias. As with many defenses of the power of insight, it defies test. Independent criteria of the key terms, "knowing why," and "being free," are usually lacking. When psychologists observe neurotic behavior persisting in the face of the patient's presumed "knowing why," the analytic explicator can retreat to the defense that the knowledgeable neurotic's "insight is intellectual, but not emotional."

To this clinician, the sentence equating knowledge with freedom is either "merely" a definition or, if a proposition, mostly false. "Knowing what you are" will not free you of it. We agree with a psychologist's review of Nabokov's *Lolita* (Brown, 1959):

Humbert's troubles are not caused by an unwillingness to be aware of disagreeable truths. His self-perception is accurate and complete. But his state of psychic grace does not have the consequences we have been taught to take for granted. Fully aware though Humbert is, he does not understand why he should be what he is; nor can he accept what he is; and he cannot change. No flood of therapeutic insight will help Humbert. In fact, there is no help for him except the gratification of making art from his plight. In these respects the novel challenges the axioms of the Age of Psychology.

[43] Summaries of assessment procedures are given in Jackson and Messick (1967), Megargee (1966), and Whitla (1968).

Pertinent here is the contest between clinical and statistical prediction. To date, the score favors the statistical over the clinical arts (Danet, 1965; Goldberg, 1965; Grebstein, 1963; Hiler and Nesvig, 1965; Kleinmuntz, 1967; Lindzey, 1965; Meehl, 1954 and 1965; Sawyer, 1966; Sines, 1959; Smith and Lanyon, 1968; Stricker, 1967).

One ought not expect a wide range of predictive accuracy from empathy-building processes, if only because of the observed relationship between similarity and accuracy in person-perception. (See note 16.) Thus Gage and Cronbach (1955) report that accuracy in perceiving the other does not seem to have high generality "across" persons and situations and that, where accuracy is found, it need not rest upon "genuine understanding" of the other.

Fancher (1966; 1967) finds that accurate, as opposed to inaccurate, judges of the other tend, among other differences, to assess the "psychological environment" of the person being evaluated. In some vocabularies, such assessment defines empathy. However, in opposition to common connotations of "understanding," the accurate judges in this research, while able to comprehend the actor's "subjective frame of reference," used "objective and nonevaluative" judgmental concepts. Since empathy often connotes sympathy, this additional finding qualifies the meaning of those global evaluations of the other man's psychological environment engaged in by the more accurate judges.

In this light, a Machiavellian or a psychopath may be an accurate judge, taking into consideration the actor's "subjective frame of reference" without "feeling in with it." All good con-men do so (Kesey, 1964; Maurer, 1940).

Further, as previously seen (note 10 of Chapter Two), Fancher shows that judging the other accurately is *negatively* correlated with "validity in conceptualizing" him.

CHAPTER FOUR

SCIENTIFIC EXPLANATIONS

"Explanations" are stories men tell to which they accord this title and satisfaction. The stories vary in content as a function of our heritage of symbol-attachments and what men wish to do with their explanatory tales.

The symbolic culture channels questions and, hence, affects what will be deemed a satisfactory answer. The "real world," and how we have learned to respond to it, also determine which tale, which time, will count as explanatory.

There is a reciprocity between the explanations we employ and the results we effect. Explanations do make a difference. The difference, however, is not always that which the storyteller intends. And what he intends is not always comforted by the "truth" so that "useful" explanations need not be "realistic" ones.

In semantic explanations the story-style is that of making connections among symbols. Words are clarified by showing the rules of their exchange.

Definitions are developed and accorded priority. They dissect the world. They pay attention, selectively, and in this manner guide questions and answers.

In empathetic explanations the art is that of making events seem plausible to the auditor and explicator through such symbol emissions as may constitute "good reasons" for acts. Believing the reason "good" is a function of emotion as well as cognition, feeling as well as fact. The major test of a "good reason" is that it allays curiosity. This test, in turn, rests upon a common fund of experience, similarly interpreted, between the explicator, his auditor, and the "subjects" being "accounted for." This foundation is limiting and biasing, but, from some cosmic stance, all knowledge is partial and thus-biased.

For most men, most of the time, the feeling of identification with the actor being understood guarantees the explanation of his behavior. This explainway is a folkway. It is expressed in literature and law and obtrudes into that more self-conscious mode of explanation called "scientific."

Empathy-building is the popular mode of explanation, but "science" is the prestigious thoughtway. The honor accorded scientific explanation is not a function of its being understood by those who defer to it, but of its intellectual distance and reputed results. "Science," at least "physical science," works, whether its benefactors and victims like it or not or know what it is.[1]

The word "science" derives from the Latin root meaning "to know," and for many moderns "knowing" and "sciencing" are coterminous. All knowledge that men have is scientific knowledge, says Hook (1957:219).

The distinctive feature of this kind of believing called knowing is *generalization from facts according to rules.*

The essence of knowledge is *generalization*, Reichenbach claims (1957:5), and generalization is (therefore) the origin of science. Dictionary definitions concur. The entry for "science" in *Webster's New International Dictionary,* Second Edition, begins:*

1. Knowledge; knowledge of principles or facts.
2. Specif., accumulated and accepted knowledge which has been systematized and formulated with reference to the discovery of general truths or the operation of general laws. . . .

*By permission. From *Webster's New International Dictionary,* Second Edition, © 1959 by G. & C. Merriam Co., Publishers of the Merriam-Webster Dictionaries.

Having said all this, one is left with problems that reside in the ambiguities of these glorious words: "knowledge," "fact," "truth," and "general laws."

How one knows "truths," how one develops generalizations from them, and how one puts these general propositions together to form scientific explanations is a continuing enterprise full of change and conflict. Thus those explanations considered scientific are not all of a piece. There are fashions and a variety of models available within the explanatory style. *What distinguishes the scientific explainway is an objective which, in turn, is supported by an attitude which, in turn, begets some preferences in thinking and peculiar tests of knowing.*

Objectives, attitudes, preferences — like all desiderata — may be held by degree and so attained. Thus some scientific explanations are "more so" than others, and explainways that fall short of the scientific qualities may not lack them completely.

The objective of a scientific explanation is to cite an empirical rule of which the explanandum is an instance.

The search for empirical rules is supported by an attitude. The scientific attitude is truth-seeking, where a true statement is regarded as a declarative sentence that predicates observables subject to public scrutiny. True statements, alternatively called "facts," are, for the scientist, propositions about phenomena verifiable by reference to publicly replicable and communicable experience. "Facts" have their own problems,[2] as will be seen, but, for the nonce, a distinguishing characteristic of the scientific explainway is its self-conscious use of facts as the building blocks, the elements, of its story.

By contrast, empathetic and ideological stories talk to the heart. What elicit sympathy and action are not so often facts, but feelings and moral judgments.

The fact-finding preference of a scientific explanation is associated with other desiderata:

(1) That the rules that explain be nontautological.
(2) That clarity be preferred to obscurity.
(3) That simplicity be preferred to complexity.
(4) That accuracy be preferred to familiar error.
(5) That objectivity be preferred to subjectivity.
(6) That experience be expanded.
(7) That the explicator be aware of, and comfortable with, abstraction.
(8) That this awareness be associated with a sensitivity to the impact of language and construct upon observation.

(9) That the empirical regularities have a *particular* utility. This is their contribution to an increase in the accuracy of our anticipations.

In summary, *to explain an object/event scientifically is to cite a nontautological empirical regularity of which the explanandum is an instance.*

The scientific attitude to be described follows from the definition of an "empirical rule." The desiderata attached are considered aids to the construction of these regularities.

A PECULIAR PREFERENCE: CONCERN FOR TRUTH

The scientific attitude is experience-committed. It seeks truths as these have been defined: as statements about empirical phenomena subject to public verification. Statements about events that transcend communicable experience cannot be included in the scientific endeavor. This does not mean that such events may not exist. It does mean that, if one wishes to be "scientific" about the objects of his belief, he must at some point bring his beliefs to a test in experience.

It means, further, that the fabric of a scientific story is woven out of facts. The story puts facts together and tells of a variety of empirical regularities, as will be seen. But factual tales leave out much that men like to hear, and much that they find in other types of fiction: moral evaluations, exhortations, a purge of feelings, and a promise of victory.

It is no surprise, then, that a preference for true tales of an empirical bent is time-limited and culture-bound. Many men will not have them and some men call them "ideologies" because these scientific stories, truth-rooted, favor some interests over others. In this spirit, Friedenberg (1960) argues that there are two approaches to "truth": the objective and the subjective. The "objectivist, empirical" conception of truth (scientific truth, that is), Friedenberg holds to be "middle-class," whereas personal and "essentially incommunicative" truth is, he feels, more congenial to lower- and upper-class individuals.

Such "private truths," like "moral truths," are nonfactual, in the sense defined, and, hence, *not* "truths" as the scientist uses the term.

It would be interesting, but digressive, to trace the cultural correlates of science-mindedness (Barber, 1952). It can be assumed that, like any other product of civilization, it is fragile. It is a preference that has evolved. It is changing, and it may give way as the peculiar conditions friendly to it fluctuate. These conditions are widely acknowledged to rest upon some luxury, some freedom from immediate necessity, and some "openness" in one's social connections. The particular personal conditions include disinterest, detachment, and, hence, some loneliness.[3] Cohen and Nagel (1934:402-403) put it this way:

> The safety of science depends on there being men who care more for the justice of their methods than for any results obtained by their use.
>
> Hence, while sectarian and partisan faiths are based on personal choice or temperament and divide men, scientific procedure unites men in something nobly devoid of all pettiness. Because it requires detachment, disinterestedness, it is the finest flower and test of a liberal civilization.

Whether one approves of this "flower of civilization," as do Cohen and Nagel, or regards the blossom as pernicious, as do many humanists, the statement of the conditions favorable to its growth seems accurate. Apropos, Arendt (1967) comments:

> To look upon politics from the perspective of truth . . . means to take one's stand outside the political realm. This standpoint is the standpoint of the truth-teller, who forfeits his position — and, with it, the validity of what he has to say — if he tries to interfere directly in human affairs and to speak the language of persuasion or of violence. (P. 83)
>
> This is the root of all so-called objectivity — this curious passion, unknown outside Western civilizations, for intellectual integrity at any price. Without it no science would ever have come into being. (P. 88)
>
> The standpoint outside the political realm — outside the community to which we belong and the company of our peers — is clearly characterized as one of the various modes of being alone. Outstanding among the existential modes of truth-telling are the solitude of the philosopher, the isolation of the scientist and the artist, the impartiality of the historian and the judge, and the independence of the fact-finder . . . . These modes of being alone differ in many respects, but they have in common that as long as any one of them lasts, no political commitment, no adherence to a cause, is possible. (P. 84)

Arendt's description of the lonely truthseeker is substantiated by the detailed psychological study of American physical scientists conducted by Roe (1963). She found:

Younger scientists (those in training during the 1950's) to exhibit the same psychological characteristics as older scientists.

These distinguishing characteristics to have been exhibited *early in life.*

The distinctive traits of creative physicists and biologists to include.

(a) High intellectual ability, particularly spatial and mathematical.

(b) Persistence and joy in work.

(c) *Extreme independence:* showing itself in childhood as a preference for a few close friends rather than an extensive or organized social group, preferences for working alone and, in adulthood, a marked independence of intense relations with others and a preference for freedom from all supervision.

(d) *Apartness:* low interest in social activities, with neither preference for an active social life nor guilt concerning such tendencies toward social withdrawal.

Roe's characterization is supported by some of the findings of studies by McClelland (1962) and Eiduson (1962). With Roe, McClelland also reports that physical scientists seek to avoid interpersonal relations, particularly when these are associated with emotionalized expression, and that they are absòrbed, almost "obsessively," in their work. Eiduson adds that the scientist's activity is felt by him to be personally expressive and *motivated chiefly by curiosity.*

This description of the practitioner of scientific method brings us full circle from the ideal of the "understanding observer" who knows about social life by his being "part of it." It is one of the difficulties of a social science that its developers are so close to their data. We are trained in, committed to, common sense about ourselves, and this common sense may, at times, be at loggerheads with scientific sense. Further, we wish to evaluate as well as to know, and to "do something" about the social realms we study as well as "merely" observe them. There are other difficulties, to be proposed later, but the intrusion of preference upon observation makes social facts and sociological propositions, of a scientific character, a tough ore to mine. This may be a meaning of Wiener's comment (1961:189-190): All the great successes in precise science have been made in fields where there is a certain high degree of isolation of the phenomenon from the observer. It is in the social sciences that the coupling between the observed phenomenon and the observer is hardest to minimize.

The scientific attitude, when applied to the study of man, runs against the grain of the humanistic attitude. Where the latter is moral *and therefore* unavailable to all true statements, the scientific attitude concerns itself with all true statements about man whether of "moral value" or not.

This confrontation of attitudes is observable in the familiar debates between truth and utility, the debates that inform us, not merely that some truths are uncomfortable, but, worse, dangerous.[4] The humanist, aware that his morals are offended by some facts, regards the disinterested search for truth as immoral, and not merely amoral, as the scientific attitude denominates itself. For the moralist, to be amoral is immoral. Thus Kristol (1961: 152-153):

> The "positivist" answer . . . like the nationalist answer . . . is of more symbolic than practical significance, since it involves only the corruption of professors. It belongs to the twentieth century and most particularly to America; though it was first stated by Francis Bacon ("We are much beholden to Machiavelli and others that wrote what men do, and not what they ought to do"). . . . According to his view, Machiavelli was a predecessor to Professor Harold Lasswell in trying to formulate an "objective" set of political generalizations derived from, and to be tested by, experience. His seeming amorality is nothing but the passionless curiosity of the scientific imagination. It proposes to establish demonstrative "truths" about men in politics that will be available to whatever set of "values" wishes to employ them.
>
> Were this line of thought as fruitful as its proponents think it might be, it would itself pose a major political problem. No government could allow such potent truths to enter freely into political life — any more than it can permit the knowledge of how to make atom bombs to circulate freely.
>
> It is interesting, nevertheless, that the assertion should be made — that an influential and reputable group of scholars should insist that it is *right* for political knowledge to be divorced from *moral* knowledge. (Emphasis in the original)

It is not necessary to engage Kristol in a debate about *morals:* whether or not . . . it is *right* for political knowledge to be divorced from *moral* knowledge. The present point is advanced, not as an ethical prescription, but as a proposition: namely, if one wishes to study human behavior scientifically, this wish will be facilitated by disinterest in the outcome of one's observations.[5] Conversely, and *a fortiori:* the more intensely and repeatedly one observes man from a moral site, the more partial and distorted his view.[6]

The argument thus far may be summarized as saying that:

(1) Scientific explanations, in their varied forms, share an attitude.

(2) This attitude gives priority to the search for "truth" where "truth" refers to statements verifiable by reference to publicly replicable and communicable experience.

(3) The scientific attitude is recognized to be fragile, culture-bound, and subject to change with political and moral environment. This attitude seems congenial to few men, immoral to some, and difficult to maintain by any man across the range of personal and social issues he confronts.

If one accepts this peculiar attitude called "scientific" as his preferred explainway (and its rejection has some interesting consequences),[7] he accepts, as corollaries, other concerns. One of the first of these is with the nature of his story-elements, "facts."

THE TROUBLE WITH "FACTS"

"Facts" are sentences; they are not to be confused with the phenomena about which they make declarations. Further, it is recognized that the reports of phenomena that constitute the substance of a factual statement are always channeled through some conceptual scheme.[8] Conceptual schemata reside in our languages and much of what is perceived of our worlds is interpreted through a prism of words. (Symbols other than words may be used, of course; but the essential point remains.)

The shaping of percepts by concepts has led some students to argue as if facts were nothing but constructions, nothing but subjective, and "real worlds" illusory. In such a view, "objectivity" becomes delusive, knowledge "personal," and the appreciation of scientific truths more a matter of conversion than of ". . . objective criteria of verifiability — or falsifiability, or testability. . . ."

This romantic attack on the hard world would make reality nothing but conventional illusion, and would, if accepted, prevent any serious attempt to explain behavior except through passionate vision. No statement of relationship or of the likely consequences of behaviors could be made, other than as opinion. Moral and political debate would reduce, as some have urged, to a matter of taste and, if carried to its logical extreme, "purely personal knowledge" would allow of no reasoned grounds of action.

A variety of answers may be given to this subjectivist argument. The answers are intertwined and support each other.

First, it is an error to assume that because "reality" can be variously conceptualized, it must, therefore, be nothing but idea. There are, of course, schools of thought that advocate action consistent with the notion that reality is nothing but concept. Such reasoning is exemplified in the doctrine that, since "disease" is a concept, one won't be ill if he thinks otherwise. Behavior consistent with this belief is difficult and the results unfortunate.

Similarly, students who learn about the conceptual structuring of "reality" find themselves arguing like Bishop Berkeley but behaving like his critic, Samuel Johnson. They never leave the penthouse seminar room by walking through those ideas called "walls" or leaping from those called "windows."

This error can be restated by saying that it is a mistake to assume that because factual statements are phrased with concepts there must be an equation of a concept with a percept. On the contrary, we perceive things, discriminate among them, without necessarily according the discriminations the status of word-notice. Some scholars have erroneously assumed that concepts embrace the totality of what is perceived. Gardner comments (1968:218):

> Anthropologists have yet to find a primitive society whose members are unable to count. For some time they assumed that if an aboriginal tribe had no words for numbers except "one," "two" and "many," its members could not count beyond two, and they were mystified by the uncanny ability of such people to look over a herd of sheep, for example, and say one was missing. Some anthropologists believed these tribesmen had a phenomenal memory, retaining in their heads a *Gestalt* of the entire herd, or perhaps knew each sheep personally and remembered its face. Later investigators discovered that the use of the same word for all numbers above two no more meant that a tribesman was unaware of the difference between five and six pebbles than the use of the same word for blue and green meant that he was unaware of the difference in color between green grass and blue sky.

Psychologically, the answer to the subjectivist is that, while perception is influenced by conception, this influence is partial. There are "native," that is, species-linked, determinants of perception as well as learned operants (Bower, 1966). Further, the ability of concepts to shape percepts is not limitless and varies with "ambiguity," that is, with the operation of other determinants of what one perceives (Hebb, 1949, Chapters 1-4; Segall *et al.*, 1966).

In short, perception is *not* determined solely by conception. The nature of the external stimulus *does* make a difference, and it seems wiser to operate with the assumption that there is a "real world out there" than to adopt the notion that it is "all in our heads."

Indeed, the idea of a "fact" carries this connotation—that what is predicated won't "go away" just because one doesn't believe it.

A philosophical answer to the subjectivist argument has been well phrased by Scheffler (1967:38-39):

A category system, within a limited context, may be described as imposing order in general and in advance on whatever experience in that context may bring. It commits us to ways of delimiting items to be recognized, as well as to modes of classifying them. Lacking such order altogether, we may indeed aptly be described as facing an undifferentiated chaos, since we lack the very recognition of things. . . . Yet having a category system, we do not thereby prejudge the future. Without a vocabulary and grammar, we can describe nothing; having a vocabulary and grammar, our descriptions are not thereby determined.

Categorization does not, in other words, decide the forms of distribution which items will in fact display, nor does it, in itself, determine the categorical assignments of any particular item or class of items yet to be encountered. Such special anticipations may, however, be expressed by suitable hypotheses. Categorization provides the pigeonholes; hypothesis makes assignments to them. It is crucial to see that alternative assignments stipulated by different hypotheses are yet possible with the same categorization. . . .

Observation may be considered as shot through with categorization, while yet supporting a particular assignment which conflicts with our most cherished current hypothesis. It may be critically independent of such hypothesis while retaining its full categoricity, for categorization is itself . . . independent of any particular assignment of items to categories. We have here a fundamental source of control over the arbitrariness of belief.

Scientific explanations depend, then, upon facts. The dependence in scientific explainways runs in both directions—facts support or test the scientific stories and the stories scientists tell require facts.

This dependence constitutes one of the criteria which, by degree, distinguishes scientific thinking from other modes. While other explainways may use facts, they do not depend upon them. One can test for story-style by noting whether he can conceive of any fact that would modify an explanation. When the explainway remains the same regardless of what happens, it is not in the scientific genre.[9] Empathy and ideology can be bent, without changing their stories, to many events; they carry immunity to disproof. Science does not share this privilege.

Factual dependence makes attempts at the scientific explanation of many social behaviors difficult because of the deficiencies in our social accounting. Regularities that would need to be known in order to construct a scientific explanation are lacking. Yet, some academic studies of man have labeled themselves "scientific" and have thus encouraged publics to seek from them answers that might be more sensible than common sense, less prejudiced and more accurate. Thus flattered, social "scientists" respond and, since their theories are pocked with data-holes, "interpretations" and "plausible assumptions" cover the deficiencies. Under challenge of expertise and the need to act, the interpretations themselves get organized as ideologies that move into the vacuum left by the failed aspirations of a "social science."

Facts are one thing; their explanation is another. Facts are beginnings of scientific explainways; they are not the totality. A scientific explanation refers the events to be clarified to a body of facts organized in some rule-ful way. The organization of what is deemed to be the relevant body of facts occurs with the aid of categories (constructs), operations (adding, including, interacting . . .), and assumptions (empirical, but nonfactual, propositions). Such an organization is called a "theory."

Scientific theories are inventions for the ordering of facts. The organization of facts implies principles (even when they are unstated) under which facts will be held to have "meaning" (relevance) for each other: meanings such as entailment, causation, inclusion, and independence.

The philosopher of science recognizes that these organizing principles are not closed, and are themselves subject to change. The philosopher has some sympathy for the lady who asked: Who makes the rules of logic?

ADDITIONAL DESIDERATA IN THE SCIENTIFIC EXPLAINWAY

The scientific style of explanation is characterized by preferences in the way in which facts are put together to produce "knowledge." Again, these desiderata are approached by degree.

(1) *A preference for propositions*

Some philosophers tell us that all science is a circle, a grand tautology, and that everything one says to explain anything brings one sooner or later back to his point of origin so that thinking man resembles the fabled Whifflebird that flies backward in a decreasing spiral until it flies up its own cloaca and becomes extinct.

Those of us who resist such intellectual extinction believe it possible to distinguish propositions from definitions. A scientific explanation aspires to be propositional. It is not to be confused with a definition nor a description, although it employs both.

"In principle," one can acknowledge that everything in the world may be "connected." [10] Yet we persist in acting as if some connections were more immediate than others and we establish relationship and distance by dividing the world into segments that seem, for our purposes, self-contained. (This "natural" process is today dignified by philosophers of science who speak of some conceptual segments as "systems.")

Definitions perform this dissection for us. But the scientific explanation would go beyond definition and beyond a semantic clarification that balances equations between symbols of equal value.

A scientific explanation is to be built with "propositions." These are statements of relationship between facts of "one kind" and those of "another kind." The "empirical regularities" that constitute the knowledge sought by science are regularities among such relationships. The *kinds* of regularity scientists invent and attempt to verify vary, as will be seen in Chapter Five. But in the beginning, there is categorization. Abstraction. Discrimination.

If there were no classification of events of "different order," then, by definition, nothing could be predicated and every statement would be redundant.[11] This is the trouble with regarding explanations as "nothing but" descriptions.

Descriptions define, and they can do so without relating the events depicted to any other category of happening. A description of the "psychopath" defines him, without "explaining" him. A description of a "revolution" tells *what* is to be explained, but, if there is to be a science of such movements, one has to look beyond the description to ascertain what *other orders of events* are associated. If there are no such regularities to be discerned, then there are no lessons of history and its study becomes, as some would have it, aesthetic and dilettantish.

It is true that descriptions are "compositional." It is sometimes said, then, that they are scientific explanations. They tell what goes with what and hence are themselves rule-ful. A "psychopath" is a person who does this-and-this-and-that, and feels so-and-so about the world, and is likely to respond to kindness thus. Knowing *what* a "psychopath" is like carries its own anticipations of his actions.

As with all explaining, the problem here is a matter of what one intends to achieve, if anything, by taking thought. The cachet of "scientific explanation" is reserved for statements that relate the *defining* regularities to *other* observables. This reservation serves dual purposes in man's itch to know: it satisfies his curiosity while it excites it, and it implements his attempts to control events. Both objectives are met by expanding the *scope* of knowledge. This means that descriptions are first steps, and just that.

The resistance to tautological explanation runs in parallel with the preferences for simplicity, clarity, and scope, and with the attendant suspicion of an explanation that satisfies out of induced sumpathy.

"Motives," for example, have been criticized as part of the empathetic explainway. It was held earlier that conferring motives often satisfied curiosity without adding information. It is not that such reference can never be part of a scientific explanation, but that motives are metaphors that can be invented endlessly as engines of action never observed except in the behavior to be explained.

For example, D'Arcy argues that we do not ascribe a motive to an action unless motive and action belong to different moral species; lust, he claims, cannot be a motive for adultery, nor the desire for money a motive of theft.

D'Arcy is well aware that a motive is not the same as a reason for action. . . . (Locke, 1965:139)

"Motive" may be useful in a scientific clarification of conduct when the term refers to observed or inferred behaviors *distinct "in kind"* from the behaviors to be "understood."

(2) *Clarity*

Scientific explanations require that the event to be explained be clearly defined and, hence, subject to classification.

Before a scientific explanation may be attempted, there must be agreement about *what* is being explained. If we cannot say *what* happened, we cannot explain it. If we keep redefining *what*-is-to-be-explained, as we often do in political debate, there can be no scientific explanation.

The what-is-to-be-explained requires description. Description is preliminary to scientific explanation, but it is neither *an* explanation nor *the* explanation. Further, everything that describes is not relevant. Only that description is necessary that allows for a taxonomy of events/objects in the explanandum and explanans. This parsimonious desideratum distinguishes attempts at scientific explanation from empathetic styles in particular since much descriptive material that builds identification with the actor-to-be-understood has no causal or predictive relevance.

Within the description, the concepts that a scientist borrows, or the constructs that he invents, are kept . . . as sharply delimited as possible [with] all borderline vagueness [reduced] to a minimum. (Feigl, 1953:12)

Utility in scientific theory and communicability among students are enhanced by the use of sharp concepts. These organizing terms become more exact as their indicators allow for measurement. The measuring devices usually also increase the degree of objectivity. This is especially clear when they are contrasted with purely impressionistic ways of estimating magnitudes or grades.

It should be noted that the choice here is not between measuring and not measuring, but between knowing when one is measuring, by which standards, and with what degree of error. The impressionistic language which, because of our conditioning, avoids the vapidity of numbers is nevertheless shot through with ranking labels — "rich and poor," "bright and stupid," "honest and deceitful." The scientific attitude prefers to make explicit the criteria for any such adjectival classification and to assign the ratings to a metric, if possible.

The fineness of a concept and the accuracy of its measurement need be attuned, in the scientific schema, only to the purposes at hand. The answer to many psychological and sociological questions may be given with coarse tools or, to use Feigl's folk metaphor: You need no razor to cut butter. (*Ibid.*)

(3) *Simplicity*

The history of attempts to know tells of the verbal traps into which thinking men have fallen. One response to this ubiquitous entrapment is the preference, in a scientific explainway, for simplicity.

Simplicity refers to "conceptual economy." It refers to restraint in the invention of constructs or hypotheses *ad libitum* for we are warned by man's intellectual past that futile explanations can be spun indefinitely out of metaphor. There are slogans to remind us of the scientific preference for simplicity:

Hypotheses non fingo. (I do not make hypotheses.) — Issac Newton

Entia (principia) non sunt multiplicanda praeter necessitatem. (Beings, or hypotheses, are not to be multiplied beyond necessity.) — William Ockham

There is no firm guide to how "simple" a scientific story ought to be except, first, that its constructs must be clear. Second, if a term contributes nothing to *taxonomic* description (and hence nothing to the other desiderata of a science: the facilitation of causal inference and prediction), it is suspect as excess intellectual baggage. Such excess "thinking material" militates against a science of human behavior, but it continues to characterize efforts to know man because, as will be detailed, we confound the *what* of social behavior with our moral evaluation of it. The "unsimple" terms that make thinking about man difficult are terms that praise or blame him while masquerading as descriptions.

(4) *A concern for the accuracy of the observation out of which facts are built*

The scientist assumes that untutored observation suffers from inaccuracy. The inaccuracy is engendered by the impact of desire and other preconception upon perception and by the limitations of individual experience. The chronicle of imperfect perception and faulty recording is a detailed one (Evans, 1954; Gardner, 1957; Jastrow, 1962; Rawcliffe, 1959).

It becomes part of the scientific chore to develop instruments and observational procedures that reduce the errors characteristic of simple experience.

Observational accuracy remains a thorny problem at one with Pilate's question about the nature of "truth." The best test of accuracy remains action. When actions from competing perceptions lead differentially to expectation, they are thus probed for accuracy. This is the "evolutionary reason" for observing and, in this sense, it is Nature's test. In societies the test is not always immediately available since social orders function to protect classes of ineptitude.

(5) *Objectivity*

The preference for objectivity refers to a regard for observations that are reliable in the sense intended by Feigl's phrase, "intersubjectively testable" (1953:11).

This phrase defines the ideal of "objectivity" where this abused term refers not only to efforts to control personal and cultural bias in inference and observation, but also to the formulation of propositions so that they are in principle falsifiable and capable of public test.

Hypotheses that recognize no observations which could, in principle, refute them are not scientific hypotheses. "Truths" that are known only through private vision are not scientific truths.

The scientific ideal of "public test" does not call for checking observations by a vote, but rather by submission to review by any person of sufficient intelligence and technical competence. One has to learn to use a microscope or a statistic.

"Objectivity" so conceived is a "regulative ideal" (Feigl, 1953:11). It refers not merely to the observer's "frame of mind," but more strongly to his acceptance of canons for the phrasing of propositions and the conduct of observations in interpersonally testable form.

Commitment to fair controls over assertion is the basis of the scientific attitude of impartiality and detachment, says Scheffler (1967:2). Indeed, he continues, one might say that it constitutes this attitude. . . . What is central is the acknowledgment of general controls to which one's dearest beliefs are ultimately subject. These controls, embodied in and transmitted by the institutions of science, represent the fundamental rules of its game. To devise fair controls for new ranges of assertion, and to guarantee the fairness of existing controls in the old, constitute the rationale of these rules.

This is a scientist's definition of "objectivity"—an ability to abide by procedural rules for the assessment of factual evidence. Philosophers who regard objectivity in this light would like to separate it from personality. The public and democratic tone of science resists the possibility that "being objective" may be easier for certain kinds of men in certain kinds of social circumstance. The credo holds that any man should be able to learn the procedures that give "objectivity" as he does the rules of chess. Thus Floud (1966:970) argues against Karl Mannheim . . . that he [Mannheim] builds into his theory the mistaken notion that objectivity is essentially a point of view, or frame of mind of thinking individuals, whereas we are now familiar with the idea that it is essentially a feature of organized inquiry and consists in the observing of the rules and procedures which govern it and which provide for internal controls and self-connecting checks.

Scheffler, who has given us a strong defense of scientific objectivity, would also divorce this commitment from personality and allow . . . scientific habits of mind (to be) compatible with passionate advocacy, strong faith. . . . (1967:4)

The arguments of Floud and Scheffler may be regarded as hopes and treated as hypotheses. The evidence of how scientists are (cf. Roe, cited on pp. 89-90) and of the impact of wish upon thought and "passionate advocacy" upon rule-following run counter to the probability that a man can abide by scientific canons when he takes up causes.[12] Those who support positions such as Scheffler's often maintain the plausibility of their argument by confusing the multiple roles each of us may assume. Thus the fact that a man behaves scientifically while he functions as a biologist does not mean that he will follow the public rules of evidence when he speaks on political issues. And, even *within* a discipline, passion perverts so that we do not assume that the clinician who objectively studies and treats familial relationships can be a scientist to his own domestic affairs.

The scientific rules that comprise "objectivity" can be taught, but some men are better suited than others to acquire these lessons and some situations abet their exercise.

(6) *An interest in enlarging the scope of reliable observation*

The most popularly impressive distinction between scientific and commonsensical knowledge is the greater range of scientific knowing.[13]

It is patent that each of us lives a limited span in a constricted environment and, while our experiences vary from the sheltered to the adventurous, even the most wide-ranging and vocationally checkered career can encompass but a trivial segment of human encounters.

The scientific enterprise is aware of this sampling bias, a self-consciousness that constitutes yet another contrast with naïve knowing. Science would reduce the bias by expanding the varieties of report, by facilitating the exchange of observations, and by developing instruments that extend our senses and enable us to "see" the astronomically large and the microscopically small.

(7) *Ability to abide with the selective and the abstract*

The quest for clarity in a scientific explanation is associated with an awareness that our procedures toward knowledge are partial and taxonomic.[14]

The ability to abide abstraction is not unusual; it becomes rare as it is combined with a preference for clarity and empirical reference. Here the guru and the scientist are separated.

The explicit use of selective, abstract, and taxonomic devices runs head on into the common humanistic complaint that a science of man "leaves something out," that it fails "to tell the whole story," and that it undignifies man by denying his uniqueness.

Some part of the answer to this complaint has already been given. All views of man are partial. Something is "left out" of every description. The scientific attitude is concerned with making self-conscious the fact of abstraction, and its level, and assessing the relative value of different taxonomies. Meehl says it well (1954:129-130):

No two individuals are exactly alike, and no verbal or mathematical characterization can do complete justice to their individuality. No two explosions are identical nor can any system of equations give a description of any of them which is exhaustive. As Thurstone has pointed out, those who object to assigning the same score to two introverts because their introversion is distinguishable should in all consistency object to saying that two men have the same income since one of them works and the other steals (1947:54). A cannonball falling through the air is "more than" the equation $S = \frac{1}{2} gt^2$, but this has not prevented the development of a rather satisfactory science of mechanics. The exhaustive description of an individual event is not aimed for in the scientific analysis of the world *nor can it be hoped for in any descriptive enterprise*. All macroscopic events are absolutely unique. It is a further mistake to exaggerate the degree to which this lack of concreteness reflects a special failing of the scientist, since there is *no* kind of human knowledge which exhaustively characterizes direct experience by a set of propositions. No set of percentile ranks, no graphical representation of personality components, and *no paragraph of characterological description* can contain all the richness of our immediate experience. The abstractive or summarizing character of descriptions is shared by differential equations, maps, gossip, and novels alike. So-called scientific description, however, abstracts those things which are most relevant in terms of causal-analytic and predictive aims; and, secondly, employs a langauge (mathematical when possible but not always!) which minimizes ambiguity. (Emphasis in the original)

Every science begins with a taxonomy, a classification of the realm of experience to which it attends. The difference in this regard between being scientific and "just human" lies in the degree to which one is aware of his criteria of classification and has made them definite.

The argument in the humanities against taxonomy holds that science groups "individuals" (note the word) and considers them the same to the disrespect of their differences. The answer to this is that while we can acknowledge *in principle* that anything observed may be unique, in practice we can "know" nothing uniquely. Our very instruments of regard are categorizing tools. When knowledge is defined as those propositions that can be communicated, it becomes the more apparent that unique matters are known only by reference to dimensions, classes, "kinds of things." There seems to be no escape from "calling names"; we can only try to make them clear.

Every noun, adjective, and adverb with which one describes his environment does so by classifying it. The question is not whether to use or refuse classification. The question is one of the clarity of categories, and the ends to which they can be put.

THE HUMANIST AND THE POSITIVIST[15]

Humanist: Your categories are crude. You take men and you lump them. Lump, lump, lump. By race, or age, or economic class. You talk about bunches where there are individuals.

Positivist: I may agree that some categories are crude. But that, to me, is a matter of purpose. Of what you're trying to do.

Humanist: But don't you see? *Everything* is unique. Every penny that comes out of the mint is unique. If you had sufficiently refined instruments, you'd observe that each coin is different from any other penny in weight, or shape, or texture. Certainly, if nothing else, it is unique in "time of birth."

Positivist: True. But for certain purposes, like the gum machine, any penny will do.

(8) *Sensitivity to the impact of language, construct, interest, and theory upon the observations included in the scientific explanation, upon the modes of measurement, and the styles of inference*

Scientific knowing is self-conscious knowing. This means that all the problems of "organizing reality" come to a focus when one adopts a scientific attitude.

There are limitations upon knowing with which the scientist grapples. His wrestling does not "conquer all," but is a further mark of the difference between folk knowledge and disciplined belief that the latter is aware of the difficulties of developing knowledge. The scientist, but not the commonsensical chap, confronts the imperfections in knowledge that may result from constructs used or sides taken. As an aspirant toward reliable knowledge, he even battles with possibilities of low probability, as when he considers whether his public forecasts may affect the predicted behaviors.[16]

(9) "Utility" of the regularity

Men take thought for a variety of "reasons." Some of the "reasons" we read are "purposes"—objectives the thinker can verbalize. Some of the "reasons" are "functions"—nonintentional objectives read into the thinking-act by some observer. Some of the "reasons" are matters of physiology. They are results of the way man is "wired."

Man, like his simian relatives, is curious. He will not "let matters be." His reaction to Pandora's box is predictable. He tinkers with his world and his instruments for knowing it. His search for regularity is grounded in his neural constitution. He seeks regularities for the same "reason" he climbs Everests. Because they are there. Or might be there.

This source of thoughtful search is usually what is referred to when one speaks of the aesthetic satisfaction in knowing. Many empirical rules may be constructed, and tested, for no other "reason" than this: One wants to see how things work.

The scientific histories, like the hypothesis of animal evolution through natural selection, may have no greater use. Nothing seems predictable from such an explanation (Scriven, 1959), although the *principle* of selection can be manipulated. The major test of such sciences of the past is the coherence with which they put data together and tell a story of their relationships.

But other constructions of regularities are built for purposes, the perennial one of which is a mapping of the jungle in which we live so that we will be less often taken by surprise.

This need to anticipate underwrites a powerful test, but not the sole one, of the adequacy of competing explainways and, within science, of competing visions of regularity. When faced with conflicting, and equally cogent, stories about how things are, the scientific thoughtway prefers the tale that increases foresight.

Any confirmed regularity increases the ability to predict, but there are variations in the tightness of the associations adduced as scientific explanations. These linkages vary with the *kinds of events* to be explained and the *kinds of rules* inferred.

NOTES

[1] There is an extensive literature recording popular conception, and misconception, of the scientific enterprise and its practitioners. Cf., for example, Beardslee and O'Dowd (1961), Calder (1964), Dooley (1959), Hirsch (1956), Jaques (1966), Mayer (1961), Mead and Metraux (1957), Michael (1957), and Withey (1959).

The gist of these papers holds the public to be uninterested in science and ignorant of its peculiar methods. Thus Lindeman (1954, p.26) claims: We have never accepted the scientific view of our universe. We seek from science more gadgets, not a *Weltanschauung*. Rocket ships, atomic bombs, and automobiles are the romantic end-products of the scientific mind.

And a committee of the American Association for the Advancement of Science (1957) reports: The public interest in, and understanding of, science is not commensurate with the importance that science has attained in our social structure. It cannot be said that society provides good conditions for the proper growth of science. The effort to explain the nature of science to the public is given to other less consequential areas of human activity. Interest in science as a career is so restricted that a serious and worsening personnel situation has arisen.

[2]Attest of the self-consciousness of scientific knowing is its attention to the tenuous state of "facts." In other explainways, "facts" are more readily assumed.

[3]Just as we expect cultural correlates of the scientific attitude, there are undoubtedly individual preferences for this explainway. Psychologists have studied some of these personal proclivities toward "sciencing" as will be seen in Roe's study. (Cf. pp. 89-90.)

A novelist describes the Faustian spirit thus: Knowledge is an attitude, a passion. Actually an illicit attitude. For the compulsion to *know* is just like dipsomania, erotomania, and homicidal mania, in producing a character that is out of balance. It is not at all true that the scientist goes out after truth. It is out after him. It is something he suffers from. The truth is true and the fact is real without taking any notice of him. All he has is the passion for it. He is a dipsomaniac whose tipple is facts, and that leaves its mark on his character. And he doesn't care a damn whether what comes of his discoveries is something whole, human, perfect — or indeed, what comes of them! (Musil, 1953:254)

[4]The debate about the effects of truth-knowing and truth-telling is distinctively Western. It reflects a culture-conflict between the praise of knowledge and the mythic requirements of personal integrity and social solidarity.

Since the debate is ethical (a matter of values), it is seldom soluble in facts, and one would predict that men who hold themselves to be in favor of "the truth" have difficulty maintaining a consistent stance. There are truths that are socially disruptive and personally sickening.

Truth and utility are not identical, the relationship fluctuates with circumstance, and we do not expect an absolute benefit or detriment from knowledge.

I. SOME EXPRESSIONS OF THE THESIS OF THE DIVORCEMENT OF TRUTH AND UTILITY

Nietzsche: Though there undeniably exists a faith in science, it cannot owe its origin to . . . a utilitarian calculus but it must rather have originated *in spite* of the fact that the inutility and dangerousness of the "will to truth," of "truth at any price," are proved to it continually. . . . (1954: 449, emphasis in the original)

Sorokin: If empirical truth is given an unlimited liberty for its development, it may prove exceedingly injurious to many "illusions" which are necessary for the existence of value in a group. (1937, v.2:120)

Parsons on Pareto: Hence society, so long as the value element plays a part, will always be characterized by the currency of untrue, i.e., nonscientific doctrines. These doctrines moreover partly manifest, partly constitute, elements essential to the maintenance of the social equilibrium. (1937: 275-276)

Auden: In politics, there is a distinction, unknown in science, between Truth and Justice. (1962:86)

Santayana: . . . truths that cannot bear the light of day; not that the light of day would disprove them, but that they, in their tragic horror, would extinguish the light of day in an unchastened spirit. Such truths must be conveyed with caution. (1963-64:25)

Wilde: If one tells the truth, one is sure, sooner or later, to be found out.

Bacon: He who follows truth too closely at the heels may have his brains kicked out.

Morgan: A fantastically false theory might well serve better than a true one, from a psychological point of view alone. (1958:32)

Wirth: The distinctive character of social science discourse is to be sought in the fact that every assertion, no matter how objective it may be, has ramifications extending beyond the limits of science itself. Since every assertion of a "fact" about the social world touches the interests of some individual or group, one cannot even call attention to the existence of certain "facts" without courting the objections of those whose very *raison d'être* in society rests upon a divergent interpretation of the "factual" situation. (1936:xvii)

Mencken: No normal human being wants to hear the truth. It is the passion of a small and aberrant minority of men, most of them pathological. They are hated for telling it while they live, and when they die they are swiftly forgotten. What remains to the world, in the field of wisdom, is a series of long-tested and solidly agreeable lies. (1958:19)

Pareto: As regards determining the social value of Marxism, to know whether Marx's theory of "surplus value" is false or true is about as important as knowing whether and how baptism eradicates sin in trying to determine the social value of Christianity — and that is of no importance at all. (1935:para. 1859)

Burnet on science versus man: A comment on the eve of genetic engineering: It is a hard thing for an experimental scientist to accept, but it is becoming all too evident that there are dangers in knowing what should not be known. (Sir MacFarlane Burnet, Nobel laureate, on the possibility of gene-control. Cited by James, 1968)

de Sade: It is a danger to love man, and a crime to enlighten him.

II. ON THE PERSONAL LEVEL: DOES THE TRUTH HEAL OR SICKEN?

Allport: It is not wholesome to live by illusion.

Eliot: Mankind cannot stand too much reality.

Smith: The golden virtues are . . . love, truth, beauty, self-realization . . . [they] conduce to psychological health.

Roche: Mental integrity may rest on the capacity for denial, for sustained repression of the truth. (1951:140)

Nietzsche: If you wish to strive for peace of soul and pleasure, then believe; if you wish to be a devotee of truth, then inquire. (1954:30)

Boring: Is it ever good for man to believe a superstition? Probably yes. . . . (1957:193)

Davis: Conducted research on parental responses to information about their children paralyzed by poliomyelitis. Suggests such knowledge may often be more "dysfunctional than functional." (1960)

Stryker: Measured accuracy of role-taking in cases where parents and their children did not get along. Found parents more likely to resist evidence of conflict. But when parents recognized the nature of differences separating them from their children, their problems of adjustment to them were *intensified*. . . . At least under certain circumstances, Stryker (1957) writes, knowledge of others can be maladjustive.

Feder: Ranked subjects along a bipolar dimension of characteristic reaction to threat: repression-sensitization. Those who respond to threat by "repression" deny unpleasant facts and rationalize; those who respond by "sensitizing" attempt to reduce anxiety by approaching or controlling the stimulus and its consequents. "Sensitizers" "intellectualize," ruminate, and are subject to obsessive-compulsive symptoms. Feder found the "repressive" style to occur more frequently among "adjusted" persons and the "sensitizing" mode to be more characteristic of persons judged to be "maladjusted." (1967)

Nettler: Tested the neo-Platonic association of truth, goodness, and psychic health through the assessment of the accuracy with which "good and bad men" view their worlds, their world-views having been gleaned from seven psychometrics. Found no relationship between being good and knowing the truth. Rather, found a slight tendency for the "evil eye" to be more accurate. (1961)

Decore: Tested Nettler's findings on samples of "normal" and "maladjusted" persons using two indices of "maladjustment" and a specially constructed measure of social reality. Found no significant difference between "sick" and "healthy" perceptions of reality. (1966)

III. ON THE SOCIETAL LEVEL: IS TRUTH USEFUL OR HARMFUL?

We can define truth one way. For example, Gletkin, the Commissar, to Rubashov, the Revolutionary, as told by Koestler: Truth is what is useful to humanity, falsehood what is harmful. In the outline of history published by the Party for the evening classes for adults, it is emphasized that during the first few centuries the Christian religion realized an objective progress for mankind. Whether Jesus spoke the truth or not, when he asserted he was the son of God and of a virgin is of no interest to any sensible person. It is said to be symbolical, but the peasants take it literally. We have the same right to invent useful symbols which the peasants take literally. (1941:227)

If we reject the Commissar's definition and employ independent criteria of truth, then some truths will be deemed harmful to some interests and censorship will be justified. Five instances:

(1) *Hopkins versus Hartley*

Hopkins: I consider it very fortunate and to its credit that Her Majesty's government has not as yet stooped to the practice of demeaning its minority subjects by providing others with discriminatory statistics over which they may gloat.

The United States is one of the very few advanced nations to employ this device. Such statistics serve primarily to establish non-whites . . . as pariahs among other Americans and as an ego support factor for our many bigots. (1967:109-110)

Hartley: We must recognize that statistical classifications of any kind are discriminatory.

Will the elimination of prejudice . . . be aided by withholding social facts?

(2) *The Shockley case:* In a series of papers, one of them delivered this spring to the National Academy of Sciences, Dr. William Shockley has asked for an "objective inquiry" to determine whether . . . there is taking place a "genetic deterioration in the potential for intelligence" among the lower strata of our population.

. . . Dr. Shockley hasn't been able to get a seconding voice in the National Academy for his suggestion of a careful, thoughtful and objective study of the genetic effects on intelligence, if any, of the interbreeding generation after generation of those at the lowest ends of the intelligence scale. . . .

Moreover, a recent symposium at Brooklyn Polytechnic Institute of nearly 500 scientists and humanists was canceled under pressure because Dr. Shockley was scheduled to deliver a paper asking for an "objective diagnosis" of the genetic deterioration theory. (Royster, 1968)

(3) *DeGré on Lindbergh:* In a speech made on August 4th, 1940 at Chicago, to the "Keep-America-Out-of-War Rally," the Colonel made the following points:

1. That poor nations, when they become powerful enough to do so, are liable to attack rich nations.

2. That there is a possibility that Germany might win the war.

3. That if Germany wins the war, then either the United States must adjust herself peacefully to that situation or make war against Germany.

4. That if the United States and Germany did go to war . . . then it would be difficult for either side to force a quick decision, and the war might last a very long time. . . .

It is difficult to see how, on a purely logical level, these statements could have been objectionable to anyone. They consisted either of statements of fact or of various alternative possibilities of action or of historical development. As is usually the case in these matters, however, Colonel Lindbergh's statements were attacked not on factual grounds, but primarily on moral and sentimental grounds. (1943:35)

(4) *Politics versus science: Schur on the President's Commission Task Force Report on Narcotics and Drug Abuse:* Prevailing policy often has been based more on emotion than on reason, . . . an exclusive concentration of enforcement efforts may be of limited value and may even produce positively undesirable results. . . . certainly it does appear that in assessing the drug problem the Commission was more responsive to political considerations . . . than to disinterested evidence and analysis concerning the existing drug situation and the drug policies currently in force. (1968)

(5) *Glazer on sociology as ideology:* From the point of view of the radical critic of society, numerous among sociologists, the mere accurate description of society (assuming it is accurate) can be seen as an effort to justify it; the account of how it works can also be seen as a rationalization that there is no other way it could work; indeed, scientific language itself can be seen as ideological: does it not conceal the true horror of society? (1967:68)

[5] This proposition need not be proved in detail here in order to be advanced. The research concerning the pull of expectancy upon perception is extensive. When human interests enter, pure reason is a figment of an abstracting philosopher, Jastrow tells us (1962:ix) as he chronicles *Error and Eccentricity in Human Belief.*

Rosenthal's work (1966) comprises a body of confirming evidence. But, lest one conclude from such investigation that seeing (and effecting) is nothing but believing, Zegers (1968) and Barber *et al.* (1969) provide tests of the limits of such influence.

The present hypothesis relating the ability to be objective (to be truth-seeking-and-saying) to *lack* of emotional commitment to results gains plausibility from studies that show the impact of ethicopolitical concern upon thought. Logical power tends to decrease with emotionalized content. (Abelson and Rosenberg, 1958; Lefford, 1946; Morgan and Morton, 1944; Thouless, 1959; Thistlethwaite, 1950)

Affect may infect judgment by at least these five processes:

Reducing the number of subjective categories of judgment available. (Bieri *et al.,* 1966:240)

Decreasing the ability to differentiate *among* dimensions, as well as *within* a dimension. (*Ibid.:* 241)

Limiting the range of cues used in judging. (Easterbrook, 1959)

Increasing response stereotypy. (Eriksen and Wechsler, 1955)

Reducing the width of "cognitive maps." (Tolman, 1948)

We are caught, then, in this predicament: As we become morally concerned, we become incapacitated for scientific procedure. This is no surprise to those who have noted the difficulties of maintaining a consistent logic in company with moral indignation. When we think about justice and power in particular, we suffer an oft-remarked tendency to dilute logic through the application of double moral standards:

"My policies are principled; yours expedient" constitutes a familiar conjugation. (Ross and van den Haag, 1957:614, fn. 5)

Historians excuse horror that succeeds. (Heilbroner, 1967:34)

[We note] . . . the political superstition that while absolute power is bad when exercised by the Right, it is in its very nature good and a boon to humanity once the Left, that is to say "our own people," takes hold of it. (Rahv, 1949:749)

A revolutionary group, emerging as a consequence of disgust felt against reactionary forces and determination to wipe them out, will lead the individuals involved to achieve deeds of genuine selflessness; a lynching party, instigated by reactionary ideology and groups, will commit beastly acts. . . . (Sherif and Cantril, 1947:281)

Finlay, Holsti, and Fagen (1967) provide case histories illustrating the apparently universal tendency to judge the actions of others, particularly those defined as enemies, according to standards different from those applied to oneself.

[6]All views of man are partial. It is recognized that a bias, a discrimination, may produce accurate, as well as inaccurate, perception.

"Distortion" refers to *errors* in expectation induced by a particular partiality. To call a view "distorted" is to say that acting according to its expectancies leads to disappointment.

[7]Fatigue with scientific explanation leaves one either seeking no explanations, but simply enjoying (if possible) the rush of sensation, or reverting to intuition, folk knowledge, or *ad hoc* explanations. Most of us, most of the time, operate with pieces of scientific explanation blended with larger fragments of "personal knowledge," ideology, and folk wisdom.

[8]*Fact:* An empirically verifiable statement about phenomena in terms of a conceptual scheme. (Henderson, 1932)

Fact: Any "fact" is the result of our interpretation of sense data by means of a conceptual system.

By sense datum we mean what is given as a result of the stimulation of our sensory organs. A sense datum pure and simple remains what it is and cannot be a fact. It becomes a fact, relevant or irrelevant, when it is given significance through its interpretation by means of a conceptual system. It is possible, therefore, for the same object to give rise to different facts because it gives rise to sense data which are interpreted by means of different conceptual systems. We have arrived at a result that sounds paradoxical—the sense data are the same, but the facts are different. (Kattsoff, 1947)

[9]A qualification is needed. The history of science is marked with instances of "men of science" refusing "facts." Today, for example, parapsychologists claim that behaviorists won't face their data. Two answers meet this qualification:

(1) "Being scientific" is a preference, characterized by the desiderata mentioned. As with other ideals, these are imperfectly realized.

(2) There is a difference between being dogmatic in refusing a fact and being uncertain about the evidence for the fact or knowing how to accommodate an uncomfortable fact within one's theory. If there are scientists, men concerned to *know*, they are open to ambiguity. By contrast, men concerned to *do* must make decisions. This urges earlier closure.

[10] The writer Lewis Brown used to illustrate this point with a story in which he "explained" his motor accident on San Vicente Boulevard in Santa Monica by a forest fire in India that resulted from an airplane crash that, in turn, would not have happened had there not been a drunken wedding celebration in London. All the events "really occurred" and all were related in the sense that "without one, not the other."

The theme that "everything is a web of relationships" is an old one, expressed as diversely as in the poet John Donne's preachment that No man is an island, entire of itself and as in the view of "causation" as a Rube Goldberg device. Scientists, like all practical men, operate as if some webs were more intimate than others. Without this assumption, anything may "cause" everything and rational action becomes a dream.

[11] Dissection of the world "comes naturally." It is built into our physiologies as well as our acquired concepts.

Susanne Langer (1962:72-73) cites evidence that the beginning of the process of abstraction is in the eye itself: The emphasis on the outline here is produced by elimination of the "redundant" portions of the image, or "abstraction" in the purest classical sense; the process is automatically determined by the structure of the organ (not only the eye, but the whole optic tract, including the visual cortex), and the abstraction is performed unknown to its performer. On this hypothetical basis, Pitts and McCulloch have worked out a further theory of intellectual abstraction briefly presented in an article entitled, "How We Know Universals." (1947)

The analogy between the hypothetical processes in the sensory mechanisms and the more elaborate and variable ones in the "interpretive cortex" serves to explain the element of pattern recognition that is evinced in the behavior of animals. As Russell Brain said (1950), it is essential to their survival that they should recognize not only a specific thing or creature again, but any other of the same sort; and, indeed, "what the animal reacts to is not a mosaic of all the individual features of the object perceived, but a pattern which constitutes an abstraction from any particular individual, but for that reason is common to all individuals of the group." This sort of abstraction, however, is still what Bouissou (1942) has called "abstraction implicite"; it is a selective response on the organic level, but not on a conceptual one. And Sir Russell makes a very precise statement when he says, "Pitts and McCulloch have attempted to describe in mathematical terms the physiological processes in virtue of which the brain renders possible the recognition of universals."

[12] Evidence has been presented in note 5, above.

A supporting study is reported by Hart (1947) who assessed the relationship between the proclivity to "passionate advocacy" and the tendency to state facts for a sample of authors of sociological papers. Hart found:

A close association between the authors' tendency to make "unsupported value judgments" and the utterance of "unsupported sweeping non-evaluative generalizations."

A negative association (−.34) between the authors' tendency to make "unsupported value judgments" and the utterance of "factual statements not involving values."

No relationship between the utterance of "factual statements about values" and "unsupported value judgments."

No relationship between the utterance of "unsupported sweeping generalizations" and "factual sentences when both are non-evaluative."

[13]Thus, without knowing the hows of it, we laymen have learned that the last century has witnessed an expansion of the conceived physical universe to the very large and distant and the incredibly small. Wheeler (1968), speaking of Marie Curie's work, notes: She gave us the projectiles to penetrate a new world of small distances. She did more than anyone to open the door to 10^{-13} cm, as her countryman Copernicus did more than anyone to alert us to movement and meaning at the previously unimaginable distance of 10^{13} cm. Today, thanks not least to these great investigators, we see in our mind's eye each decade of the distance scale alive with its own special activities, from the expansion of the universe at 10^{28} cm to the growth of a crystal at 10^{-1} cm, and from the collapse of a white dwarf star at 10^{8} cm to the form factor of the proton at 10^{-16} cm. Copernicus directed our gaze out to the domain of the unbelievably remote, and today we have come close to plumbing the greatest distances that we know how to conceive. The discoverer of radium by her life and work directs our gaze down to the world of the small. There, many new decades of the distance scale still wait to spring into life and meaning, all the way from 10^{-16} cm to Planck's 10^{-33} cm.

[14]The necessity of starting a science with a taxonomy of its subject matter is defended by a contemporary "Linnaeus of psychology," R. B. Cattell (1967:87), who holds that . . . the aims and values of a comprehensive, nonsubjective taxonomic scheme, expressed in concepts of wide theoretical or practical negotiability . . . are not merely to achieve academic neatness. On the contrary, as in the periodic table in chemistry, or, in the more abstract way, the covariation chart in psychology, we soon perceive that a valid scheme for ordering existing material or methods is commonly very fertile in producing new concepts and practical possibilities. It reveals underlying laws, suggests new principles, and permits extrapolation from existing limited elements to unrealized new combinations which would otherwise only be found slowly and fragmentarily by the course of merely random exploration.

[15]Once again, a reminder that all conversations and illustrations, paraphrased or verbatim, are actual.

[16]The possibility of "self-fulfilling prophecies" (Merton, 1949) is not so serious a social-science problem as some philosophers have assumed. For a discussion of "reflexive predictions," cf. Buck (1963) and Simon (1954).

The objectives of scientific thinking and its supporting attitudes and desiderata have produced a variety of empirical rules. At least five kinds of "law" may be distinguished. Allowing for the possibility of overlap, they are rules of: (1) Taxonomic relationship, (2) functional dependence, (3) development, (4) statistical regularity, and (5) causal connection.

(1) *Taxonomic rules*

Man is a categorizing animal. His categories change, but the cognitive procedure remains.

This thoughtway assumed that "things" of which the world is composed exhibit some "natural" clusters of similarity and difference.

The scientific explainway employs this common-sense assumption to refine the ordering of objects, people, or events. The procedure may be outlined as taking these steps:

(a) *Grouping* — objects, events, or people.

(i) Grouping requires some measure of similarity.

(ii) Similarity . . . can be established only on the basis of homologous, or corresponding, characteristics. Hence, it is not possible to compare the forelimbs of vertebrates without prior agreement on what to call a forelimb . . . . (Sokal, 1966:110)

(iii) Groups ("classes," "taxa") that differentially share some property not similarly distributed among other classes may be described "monothetically," on the basis of one or a few characteristics, or "polythetically," on the basis of many characteristics.

The latter is, of course, the more difficult procedure. Methods of determining similarity among polythetic, psychological taxa have been described by Cronbach and Gleser (1953) and by Mahalanobis (1936). One way of ordering such taxa hierarchically has been demonstrated by Ward and Hook (1963). These procedures, although developed by psychologists and biologists, are applicable to any study of human activity.

(iv) The achieved grouping of unordered objects, people, or events on the basis of some measure of similarity is called a "classification." "Identification" refers to the allocation of a previously uncategorized object, person, or event to its appropriate "class."

(v) "Typologies," systems of classification, may include "characterizations" — descriptions of variations within each "type" (Laughlin, 1966).

(vi) The ways of classifying will vary with the data and the definition of similarity chosen for the investigator's purpose (MacNaughton-Smith, 1965).

(b) *Building taxonomies*

(i) Taxonomies are systems of related typologies.

(ii) Taxonomies do not start "from scratch." They begin somewhere. It is popular to say that theories guide them, but it seems more accurate to hold that they are built from some hypotheses concerning how things might "go together."

If the taxonomy is to be more than a card file, it ought, in the process of construction, to reveal some unsuspected relationships.

(iii) There are many procedures for building taxonomies. "Hierarchial taxonomies," for example, are ordinarily developed by divisive or agglomerative steps (MacNaughton-Smith, *ibid.*).

(iv) Either divisive or agglomerative methods may be used with different ordering principles; that is, with different grounds for the perception of relationships among types. Sokal *(ibid.)* suggests such principles as the "phenetic," in which the relationships are based on "overall similarity," the "cladistic," based on common lines of descent (or process), and the "chronistic," based on temporal relationships.

The accompanying diagram, from Sokal *(op. cit.*:108), illustrates these ordering principles.

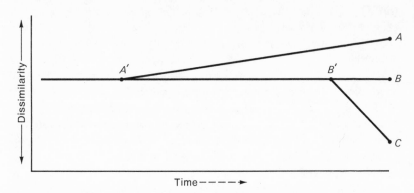

TAXONOMIC RELATIONSHIPS can be viewed from three distinct aspects. "Phenetically" organism B is more closely related to organism A than it is to organism C, even though C evolved much later than A as a branch of stem B. "Cladistically" organisms B and C are closer to each other than either is to A, since they have an ancestor (B') in common before either has a common ancestor (A') with A. "Chronistically" A, B, and C are closer to one another than any of them is to B', since they occupy the same time horizon. (From R. R. Sokal, "Numerical Taxonomy," *Scientific American* 215 (December, 1966):106 -116. Copyright © 1966 by Scientific American, Inc. All rights reserved.)

(c) *Testing taxonomies for their "goodness."* Two criteria of a "good taxonomy" are ordinarily used—"internal" and "external."

(i)   The favored "internal" criterion is stability. Stability is resistance to distortion by the addition of new information—either in the form of additional observations on the individuals in each class or by enlargement of the initial set.

(ii) The "external" criterion is a test of the taxonomist's purpose. It may include predictions that members of the final sets will differ on as yet untested behaviors ("success" or "failure," for example). Or it may involve predictions for as yet unordered individuals. The procedures for constructing predictive classifications are various (MacNaughton-Smith, 1965).

Thus constructed, a taxonomic rule is definitive, but it does more than tell what words mean. It states the highly probable associated properties of kinds of objects, people, or events. It builds anticipations and allows for an order of prediction, but it need make no *causal* claim although it may be useful to such assignment.

In the studies of man, the significant, modern taxonomic tool is the mathematical analysis of multiple factor clusters. Such analysis probes the way in which measures of behavior, performed on presumably single dimensions, are correlated. The "factors" thus revealed provide grounds for new definitions of the subject matter with, in turn, new procedures for their assessment and ideas about their theoretic implication.

As an illustration, studies of human intelligence have led to a new picture of the "vectors of the mind." In the work of Guilford (1967), for example, evidence is given for a three-dimensional structure of 120 factors of cognitive behavior. Such a model of the "kinds of intellect" is taxonomic: it defines similarities and differences and shows the regularities of relationship among them.

(2) *Rules of functional dependence*

Some regularities have been phrased as rules of "functional" relationship, when "function" is considered in its mathematical sense.

Such rules state the way in which measures of events or selected characteristics of objects co-vary. "Laws" of this nature are familiar in the physical sciences and rare in the social studies. They state the manner in which variables change together under certain constant conditions, as in the formulas describing the behavior of freely falling bodies in a vacuum or the interdependence of the temperature, pressure, and volume of ideal gases.

Such "laws" assert "if p, then q, if and only if r," where p represents "relevant variables" that remain constant.

A statement of this kind is not interpreted as a *causal* proposition in the strict sense since it says nothing about the *sequence* of events and since the functions described are *symmetrical*, variations on either side of the equation resulting in changes in the related function. However, in the lay usage of "causation," such a statement may suffice "causally" since *intervention* upon any variable *produces* changes in its correlate. Whether or not one calls "cause" in using such a rule, the regularity permits prediction.

Functional regularities are rarely described in the social studies and, when they are, they lack the quantitative exactitude that a law of functional dependence promises. An example of such an attempt would be the "law of supply and demand" in economics that states that price varies *directly* with demand as supply remains constant or, conversely, that price varies *inversely* with supply as demand remains constant.

A more recently devised economic rule of functional dependence is that described by the "Phillips curve" (Phillips, 1958). This rule describes a linkage, in industrial countries at least, between full employment, wage rates, and inflation. The rule depicts more rigorously and cites more thoroughly the empirical evidence proving "what everyone knows" — that there is a trade-off between inflation and full employment, that periods of a tight labor market are periods of more rapidly rising prices, and that the cost of price stability is some level of unemployment (Perry, 1966).

In the social studies there are difficulties in specifying the slope of curves describing functional dependencies and the conditions under which the curves may shift. This difficulty, in turn, stems from the problems of stating which variables are relevant to deviations from the rules, which is another way of saying that it is difficult to specify the constants and the limits beyond which the functional rules no longer apply.

Debate moves into this region of uncertainty and, with it, ideology. For example, the conditions under which the "law of supply and demand" is believed to operate divide men politically as does the value attached to the differential costs of such decision in uncertainty.

THE RIGHT ECONOMIST AND THE LEFT POLITICIAN: WARTIME U.S.A., 1942

Right: You can't put an effective ceiling on the rental of dwellings unless you are prepared to control the price of house sales as well and are prepared to pay a price for the ceilings in the costs of policing the rules and in the costs of deteriorated landlord services to tenants.

In short, you can't keep prices constant on commodities in short supply under conditions of rising demand without paying another kind of price elsewhere.

Left: We can't allow people to be victimized by conditions beyond their control and by the needs of the nation in wartime. We have got to make decent housing available at prices people can afford. Rent control is, in the short run, the most feasible procedure.

As to the costs you allege, they are unknowns and undoubtedly much less than the sacrifices that would result from your *laissez-faire* attitude. The costs you talk about assume an exactness in the "law of supply and demand" that is not there.

Right: Your use of the word "feasible" introduces other considerations into our argument—considerations of "values" and of "politics." I can't quarrel those with you. I can only predict that controls on rental units unaccompanied by similar controls on sales will drive a quantity of rental units off the market and will produce cheating of various sorts, particularly in landlord services.

I should like you to agree with this prediction, but your political needs won't permit that. If you would agree with the possibility I propose, then we might enter the difficult debate about relative costs and different means. Given the unknown, this, too, may be unresolvable, and time is short.

(3) *Developmental rules*

Another form of regularity that scientists use as an explanatory base describes the invariant ordering of events in time. These rules are of the form: If Alpha exhibits property *x* at time *T*, then it will exhibit property *y* at a specific later time.

These laws have also been called "genetic" and "historical." There is no need to quibble about terminology if it is recognized that the statement of regular development need imply nothing about sources or causes, as might the word "genetic."

While causal laws also specify sequences, they impute *sufficiency* to those antecedents that bear some *proximate* relationship to later events. A developmental rule may specify what is *necessary* if later events are to occur, but it does not state what is sufficient for the occurrence. Further, a developmental rule may describe sequences of distant order such that the satisfaction of "causality" is denied.

The facts that organisms develop and that the uniform patterns have been reliably described have led some writers to apply the analogy to societies. If society is to be regarded as an organism, however, it is not the same kind as botanical and biological systems, and the search for laws of societal development has not been fruitful.

Societies, unlike organisms that exhibit developmental regularities, do not change by timetables and they sometimes skip stages.

(4) *Statistical regularities*

The most common expression of rule-fulness in the behavior of the human animal takes the form of a "statistical regularity." A statistical law asserts that, in some "sufficiently long" series of events, the probability of a determinate occurrence can be known. In practice, such a law usually adds that "the probability can be known within such-and-such a range of contingent events."

The simple model of such a rule is the assigning of a probability of occurrence to such an event as the fall of a fair die or a balanced coin. The rule is not invariant, as is a developmental law. It does *not* say, "Every sixth roll of a six-sided die will expose a 'five.'" It does *not* say, "This must follow that," although some gamblers foolishly interpret probabilities in this manner. Such a rule tells what to expect "probably, in the long run," or it tells, "in a series of events *A*, thus-many will be *B*'s."

The model of a statistical regularity regards "probability" as Aristotle did and as most laymen do: . . . as that which happens for the most part. This "frequency interpretation of probability" is not to be confused with other notions of the "probable" — such as the definition that accords "probability" to . . . what it is reasonable on the grounds of this evidence to believe." (Braithwaite, 1966) A statistical regularity seeks to express the probability of a happening as a ratio.

In this sense, a statement of statistical regularity is predictive whether or not a causal nexus is conferred upon it. It is not in itself a statement of causation, but it provides a foundation for such attribution. Attempts to formulate causal rules in the scientific explanation of human behavior are ordinarily based upon statistical regularities. When they are not so grounded, they can be given little credence. When they are based on empirical probabilities, they share all the problems of these noncausal "laws" *plus* the difficulties peculiar to the more restrictive idea of causation, about which more later.

Thinking with probabilities has its own problems and its distinctive defense.

(*a*) *Apologies for probabilities.* It is popular to apologize for the employment of probabilities in the social studies on two major grounds, both of which have lay support and both of which are true: (i) We are ignorant. (ii) Humans vary. (Actually, these dual reasons for inexactitude can be reduced to one tautology: "We are ignorant because we don't have knowledge.") Our ignorance receives these justifications:

(i) Statistical regularity may be the closest approximation to rule-fulness that we can expect in the study of social behavior because such behavior is "complex." Calling behavior "complex" is another way of saying that our classifications of conduct are crude and that we can't specify the contingencies of these coarsely defined "kinds of behavior."

(ii) The argument from human variation in this context takes the form of an appeal to man's "essential unpredictability." This argument is clothed in varied verbal garb, but the different concepts symbolize a common referent. Thus whether one speaks of man's "free will" or his "unconquerable mind," the intent is the same: to posit an internal and independent mental motor that makes laws of human behavior at best only probable and at worst impossible.

The prevalent sociopsychological version of this apology asserts man's "freedom" to give similar events widely different definitions and hence to produce a gap of unknown dimensions between conditions and actions.

The attempted, and thus far failed, scientific response to this indeterminacy has been a search for regularities between circumstances, definitions, and behaviors. If beliefs intervene, says the scientist, let us put the possible determinants of belief, the dimensions of belief, and their consequences into a matrix and test for order. Thus the history of "attitude" research and the conclusions of page 67.

Beliefs make a difference. We are certain of this. Yet the *regularities* between believing and doing remain thin. The meeting of faith in belief with belief's low correlation in action serves as an apology for accepting ratios of low order as "scientific."

Into this uncertainty gap move two devices of men who think about men: *ad hoc* explanation and ideology.

If definitions of situations "cause" behavior and "ideas *are* weapons," and if the regularities between conditions, attitudes, and actions are of low probability, then license is given to construct "attitudes" that can, *post factum,* explain anything. With such *ad hoc* clarification, one moves "backward" toward empathy or "forward" into ideology.

When one would explain human behavior in order to judge it and change it, the system of its explanation tends toward one that puts the explicandum "in its moral place." It becomes not merely an event to be "understood" as recurring thus-frequently under such-contingencies. It is also something to be "for" or "against."

Systematized, such moral disagreement becomes ideological disagreement, a difference in the kinds of unproved and unprovable ideas to be used in constructing one's world and in responding to it.

A major dimension of ideological disagreement today divides those who see "conditions causing" and who would, hence, remedy circumstances, and those who believe "beliefs determine" and who would change attitudes. Since this debate is *moral* when ideological, we don't expect men *consistently* to use definitions of the situation as an explanatory intervening variable. Logical consistency is difficult enough; consistency in moral argument, *a fortiori* (Lefford, 1946).

Thus there is no surprise in the observation that fatalists choose and determinists exhort. Conversely, it is not surprising that, when symbolic interactionists engage in social reform, they may wish to change situations rather than their definitions according to "which side they're on."

Within an ideology, "attitudes" and "conditions" can be given different positions to protect in the moral war. Reference to the "intervening variable" of "mind" becomes a tool to be used when it serves. The service, good for some "things," need not be useful as a true map of the jungle.

However we appreciate these apologies for probabilities, they are there. They are uttered by explicators, and they seem valid despite our inconsistency in their use.

(*b*) *Difficulties with statistical regularities.* The problems of explaining by reference to rules of probable relationship are at one with most problems of knowing. An outline of the difficulties in thinking about human behavior on this elementary scientific level is no substitute for a text in epistemology. It can only be a statement of what would need to be known or assumed if one were to use this explainway. For the nonce, three difficulties loom: (i) Counting, (ii) relating a count to a base, and (iii) justifying induction.

(i) Frequencies depend upon counts. Counts depend upon things reliably identified for tally. This brings one full circle to the need for a reliable taxonomy, since without such a schema of definitions of *what* is being counted, no rules can be perceived. With too broad a classification system, everything counts and nothing specific can be confirmed or refuted.

An immediate deficiency in the study of human behavior is apparent: Our taxonomies of persons and acts and "social conditions" are too "open" and unreliable.

It is popular to attribute this measurement problem to the peculiarities of the subject matter — man. It would be more accurate, although perhaps no more helpful, to attribute the difficulties to the kinds of questions we prefer to ask about social behavior. We are accustomed, here, to think with high-level abstractions and, as we move up the abstraction ladder into the stratosphere of such powerful ideas as "freedom and democracy," "welfare and ill-fare," "prejudice, discrimination, and justice," the taxonomy becomes promiscuous. Many "kinds of events" may occupy it. And we debate without resolution what shall count as "improvement" or "crime" or "self-actualization."

Promiscuous classification permits the aspiring scientist of society to work with concepts that can prove anything. Since the loose abstraction will accommodate diverse measures, including indicators of the behaviors that are themselves to be explained by reference to the abstraction, we confront, once again, the perils of tautology and the fate of the Whifflebird.

"VALUING" AS AN EXPLANATORY ABSTRACTION

Homans (1961:55): The more valuable to a man a unit of the activity another gives him, the more often he will emit the activity rewarded by the activity of the other.

A critic (Skidmore, 1969): People do those things which they value, and shun those things they do not value. This simple assertion contains the whole of the explanation of normative behavior in the simplest case. (P. 62)

Since the propositions of the theory are stated in terms of "value" rather than in terms of something that could conceivably be ascertained independently of the associated behavior, it is possible to load the concept "value" with any substantive meaning one wishes . . . If the term "value" is to be a working term in the theory, it must be accorded an assumed substantive reference of some kind. (P. 71)

(ii) A statistical "law" would express the probability of an event as some frequency of its occurrence among other events.

The probability will obviously vary with the denominator chosen. The denominator of such a fraction is the class of attributes to which the event to be anticipated is referred. Such "reference classes" are used because the point of stating a statistical regularity is not to define something, but to predicate. Such a proposition, by definition, is connective. It says, "Whenever events of class *A,* then, over some sufficiently long series, events of class *B* will occur so many times." The events of class *A,* used here as the base for the computation of the relative frequency of the explicandum, class *B* events, constitute the "reference class," and varying that class changes the probabilities of the events of concern.

We usually require some warrant for choosing one base rather than another in calculating the probability of human acts. The suggested warrant is "relevance." "Relevance" is ordinarily, but not necessarily, sought through some theory of causation. Whether or not such a theory is used, the test of the "relevance" of a proposed reference class is whether its employment makes a difference. Pap (1962:188) gives this example: We unhesitatingly estimate the probability of throwing six with a symmetrical, uniformly dense die as equal to the probability of throwing six with a symmetrical, uniformly dense *and blue* die. . . . the reason is that a great mass of experience in the past has indicated that there is no significant correlation between the color of a solid object and its mechanical behavior.

In practice, the assumption of "relevance" requires a generalization from experience. "Relevance" remains an open question. It is not known *a priori* and there is no escape from "using one's head" when one would explain matters as instances of statistical regularities.

THE SPORTS-CAR STATISTICIAN AND THE SQUARE LEGISLATOR

Square: Speed limits must be legislated and enforced if we are to reduce carnage on the highways. You will note that Nevada, one of the two states with no maximum speed limit, has the highest death rate from motor accidents.

Sport: I know this will sound flippant to you, but in any series of "things," some "thing" is always "highest." (Unless there is a tie, of course). So, when one eliminates this year's "leading cause of death," there will next year's "leading cause."

A first question about your causal imputation — no speed limits equals higher death rates — is *how much* higher Nevada's rate is than that of states with strictly enforced speed limits. And, when we know this, we shall still have to agree *how much* difference will count as a causal difference.

Square: Well, I don't know offhand how great the difference in rates is, but my understanding is that it is considerable. Further, this difference seems consistent and it is common sense that the difference is due to speed.

Sport: All right. The differences in rates may be great or negligible. Right now, we don't know. But there is something more wrong with your reasoning. The rates are fake.

Square: What do you mean? They're based on official statistics.

Sport: Yes, but a death rate is a fraction, the number of deaths *per* something. What is the base for computing the rates you cite?

Square: It's the number of deaths per year per capita population.

Sport: But Nevada has very few people.

Square: That's just the point. They have a very sparse population, no maximum speed limit, and the most — no, the highest rate of — traffic fatalities.

Sport: That's not a fair statistic. The denominator in your fraction should not be the population of Nevada, but the population of all automobile passengers in the state per period of time. The "reference class" of your statistic is incorrect. It would be more sensible to use as the denominator in your rate "the population at risk." That is, *all those, and only those, who could have had an automobile accident in the state of Nevada,* not the smaller figure of the state's population. This more realistic base is not known, of course. And, since Nevada has a tremendous interstate traffic, particularly on the Los Angeles-Las Vegas run, your statistics are actually meaningless.

(iii) Explanation from statistical regularity entails induction. It has been argued that induction ought to be "justified," but can't be.

If one is to use a statistical regularity as the basis of inference, he must assume some continuity. He must "induce."

Mill (1866) called induction . . . the process by which we conclude that what is true of certain individuals of a class is true of the whole class, or that what is true at certain times will be true in similar circumstances at all times.

Induction seems a "native" predisposition. Particulars are noted and the running similarities among them observed. Generalization and anticipation follow. Most often, in the past, *these* cues have been associated with *that* kind of event; therefore, given signs $_{1,2,3}$, I expect event$_a$ (Ackermann, 1966).

Cicero (1963, I:118) told us that this was the way things are: Thus in the beginning the world was so made that certain signs come before certain events.

Who doubts Cicero? Yet we continue to debate which signs signify which events with what probability. The common logic of constructing general propositions, even if "only" propositions of probability rather than certainty, is inconsistently employed by philosophers and laymen alike. The layman abides with induction when it confirms his preference (experience has shown. . . .) and abandons it when his hopes or fears require (just because it always has been doesn't mean it always will be).

It is here that we find yet another split in man's mode of response to his world: He both denies and believes in the inductive thoughtway, and he acts inconsistently toward it. He doubts continuity while he bets on it, and he believes in continuity while he runs risks against it.

Everyman induces and thus "learns from experience." Confronted with the sadness of such lessons, though, he places faith against the odds, even when he knows them. (This is considered noble or stupid depending upon who judges whom taking which risks toward which objectives.) The "gaming industry," as it prefers to be called in Nevada, is evidence of hope denying history. In similar fashion, but with higher stakes, the "ideology industry" is counter-inductive.[1]

The hesitant use of induction has been abetted by philosophers who have questioned the legitimacy of making the "inductive leap" from particulars known to those as yet unknown. We are indebted to Hume for this doubt. It was he who denied the *necessity* of facts being connected, of there being any *necessary* relationship between the data at hand (all the cases of class X counted) and instances yet to be noted. He told us that (1758: Section IV):

All inferences from experience suppose, as their foundation, that the future will resemble the past, and that similar powers will be conjoined with similar sensible qualities. If there be any suspicion that the course of nature may change, and that the past may be no rule for the future, all experience becomes useless, and can give rise to no inference or conclusion.

Hume's doubt that the future need resemble the past is justified in a "changing world" by the arguments that generalization from particulars is forever susceptible to sampling error and that concluding constancy from a pattern with unknown contingencies involves a risk that the underwriting conditions may change.

In addition to the debatable assumption of continuity, inducing has been posed the problem of specifying how many disconfirmations of a statistical rule will be allowed before the "law" is abrogated. The answer to this problem becomes a matter of the values attached to the consequences of rejecting a rule when it is true or accepting it when it is false.

Thoughtful men have met these two classes of problems with different reactions. They have either abandoned the attempt to give reasons for induction, defected to a deductive camp (a stronghold of certainty), or have struggled to bridge the inductive chasm with some deductive principle.

As an example of the last response, Mill and others have proposed that we can induce *because* "nature is uniform." But this hope begs the question, for the "law of the uniformity of nature" would itself have to be established, and there seems no way to do this *independently* of data inductively correlated.

Einstein's famous phrase, I refuse to believe that God plays dice with the world, is lovely aphorism, and full of assumption.

Failure to justify induction by deducing its legitimacy from some Grand Principle has been popularly met among philosophers of science by a plea for deductive theories. In the social studies these have been advanced as producing the only "true" form of explanation and one that permits prediction from knowledge of "causes." This claim will be examined later.

There is a third style of response to the question of induction's legitimacy. A radical approach to the impossible demand for a deductive rationale to guarantee induction is to deny the demand (Braithwaite, 1966; Scheffler, 1963:232; Will, 1947). Such denial, and the consequent comfort with induction, has powerful implications for the explanations one seeks. If one rests with induction from statistical regularities, he explains matters *actuarially*.

(*c*) *The "actuarial explanation."* The actuary refines the procedures of common sense. This means that he moves self-consciously from taxonomy to correlation, to the assignment of weights to indicators, to predictive test, to revision of his measures or their values.

Once classes of behaviors, structures, people, or events have been delineated in the satisfaction of the investigator's interests, the intriguing and difficult step is taken of noting how these classes correlate with other objects or events. The other events may be those occurring on different levels within the taxonomic system or in other schema of ordered observations. They may also be co-varying or sequential events.

From this kind of knowledge, "experience tables" are drawn. Everyman functions with his own implicit "tables." The statistical rule-seeker differs only in the self-consciousness and rigor with which the taxa and their correlates are sought.

The construction of experience tables permits the substitution of verified expectation for that less probable combination of expectancies called "hope." The verified expectations run laterally, and backward and forward. That is, once such actuarial tables are devised, they can be read as indicators of the probabilities of concurrent events or conditions and antecedent and subsequent happenings. In contrast with those prophecies divined from less public procedures, like "listening with the third ear," forecasts made from actuarial tables deserve the title of "predictions."

An experience table, once built, need not be assumed forever. Continuities are counted. One observes how the concatenations of events, attributes, and correlations change or remain stable and, if possible, records the contingencies associated with such change or stability. Indicators and their weights are revised and, if necessary, abandoned.

The actuarial objective is to be able to state the probability of a class of human action from knowledge of the weighted cues given by other kinds of condition or event. In this, again, nothing need be said about causation although the actuary may seek that statistical refinement that reduces "spurious correlations" (that is, those relationships that disappear when other correlates are held constant).

Most men resist calling an actuarial inference an explanation since the "why" of the correlations and the continuities is unanswered. Thus additional stories are told as per a variety of models that are supposed to give "meaning" to the chains of events.

In a scientific story, the ideal model is usually conceived as a "theory": *a hierarchy of general propositions from which particular propositions can be deduced.* In the social studies, such theories are either nonexistent or of limited scope. The limitation is precisely that the experience tables from which the general propositions could be drawn are deficient or lacking. It remains debatable whether this restriction on knowledge of human social behavior will ever be surmounted with such scope and accuracy as would permit the construction of scientific "theories" of social relations.

In lieu of generalizations induced from such "experience," some theorists would have us start from "theory" out of which hypotheses are derived and tested for the agreement of observation with the expectation of the hypothesis. Thus Popper (1959:32):

> The method of critically testing theories, and selecting them according to the results of tests, always proceeds on the following lines. From a new idea, put up tentatively, and not yet justified in any way—an anticipation, a hypothesis, a theoretical system, or what you will—conclusions are drawn by means of logical deduction. These conclusions are then compared with one another and with other relevant statements, so as to find what logical relations . . . exist between them.

If this procedure is being applied to the study of social behavior, it remains uncertain whether its failure is to be attributed to: poor theories, poor logic, or poor tests which, in turn, may result from poor instruments, sampling errors, or the human "freedom" to evade tally.

Lacking such scientific theories, the studies of social man tell tales that vary with generalizations *assumed or redundant* and with the content of "things looked at" in the disorderly pyramid of hypotheses. The variety persists because of the many reasons for taking thought about man and because our generalizations about social behavior are weak. The generalizations are weak because the distinctive data-level (above folk knowledge) is low — time-limited and situation-bound.[2] The proof, and consequence, of weak generalization is flaccid prediction.

Despite this proof, some students contend that "theories explain" although they may not contribute to forecast ability. This has been granted for empathetic or ideological "theories" and it holds for those scientific stories for which there is warrant in public evidence but which explain with reference to rules the contingencies of which cannot be foretold.

An instance of such a scientific tale is the explanation of changes in plant and animal form through the hypothesis of natural selection. This explanation would seem to lend justice to Scriven's argument (1962:188) that

. . . we know something when we are called on for an explanation that we do not know when called on for a prediction, viz., that the event referred to has occurred.

This reasoning assumes that inferences from signs of the past are *necessarily* more reliable than inferences from signs of the future. At first blush, this seems sensible. However, Mayo (1968:292-293) is able to demonstrate that the supposed asymmetry between knowledge of the past and that of the future is illusory, a deception produced, in part, by our having memory but little precognition. Mayo holds that . . . "portents," so far from being few and unreliable, ought to be as pervasive and as reliable as traces, if not, indeed, more so. He goes on to illustrate the possibility of future states that can be inferred *more* reliably than past ones!

Mayo's demonstration has importance for the practice of social "science." For here recourse to the presumed asymmetry between explanations of history and prediction allows theoreticians to propound explanatory principles that render pasts plausible, but that are defaulted in action. In short, the social "scientist" becomes an expert in the reading of *traces,* but there seems to be little transfer of this interpretive ability to the reading of *portents.* It might be conceded that an expert so gifted with hindsight and myopic in foresight can be a dangerous guide.

One is alerted to the possibility of hoax, to the possibility of being persuaded that scientific theories may explain without incurring the probative liability of prediction. If the principles adduced to explain a past cannot be used in the anticipation of a future, then any plausible story will do and the test of the explanation remains the contentment of curiosity. If there is no *pattern* of experience to be described, then there are no "lessons of history" and its study becomes dilettantism. It seems to involve a contradiction, albeit a protective one, to maintain that scientific theories may explain without making a contribution to forecast. As an instance, note the turns of argument on one page of a recent social studies text in which Meehan (1967:60) claims that:

The basic goal of science is the explanation of observed phenomena — the organization of previous observations and experiences into general propositions and theories *whose effect is to lead us to expect* particular phenomena to occur in given circumstances. (N.B.) Ideally, the scientist is able to predict the occurrences of a given phenomena (sic!), under stipulated conditions, with considerable accuracy; but prediction is *not,* contrary to supposition, an absolutely essential prerequisite for scientific inquiry. (Emphasis supplied.)

Then he adds: Explanation . . . depends fundamentally on the capacity to stipulate relationships or linkages, on the availability of generalizations.

The actuarial response to this is that, if one can "stipulate relationships," under specified conditions, he can make predictions. If one finds that his forecasts go awry, the linkage he has assumed is incorrect, insignificant, or spurious, or the predictive contingencies do not obtain. The scientific "theorist" cannot have it both ways, however. He cannot claim that his story tells how things go together, and even "why" they do, and then opt out of a statement of "what will happen if . . . ."

A more satisfactory attitude toward the symmetry of explanation and prediction is expressed by Hayek (1967:9):

I assume that the prejudice of certain earlier positivists against the word "explanation" is now a thing of the past and that it may be taken for granted that prediction and explanation are merely two aspects of the same process where, in the first instance, known rules are used to derive from the known facts that will follow upon them, while in the second instance these rules are used to derive from the known facts what preceded them. For the purposes of this article it would indeed make no important difference if instead of "degrees of explanation" we spoke of "degrees of prediction."

Willy-nilly, everyman is involved in this game. Everyman who debates his fate or the quality of social policy is arguing for a favored view of connections and prophecies.

POLITICIANS EXPLAIN CRIME*

Humphrey: Crime rates are highest among the poor and disadvantaged who commit more crime but also suffer more crime. In the long run, we can only cut crime by getting at its causes: slums, unemployment, rundown schools and houses.

Nixon: If poverty were eliminated tomorrow, the violent and the criminal and the depraved would not disappear. The war on poverty is not a substitute for a war on crime.

Wallace: The permissive attitude of the executive and judiciary at national levels sets the tone for this moral decay.

SOCIAL SCIENCE IN ACTION

Moynihan (1969): I have sought to argue, by illustration, that social science is at its weakest, at its worst, when it offers theories of individual or collective behavior which raise the possibility, by controlling certain inputs, of bringing about mass behavioral change. No such knowledge now exists. Evidence is fragmented, contradictory, incomplete. Enough snake oil has been sold in this Republic to warrant the expectation that public officials will begin reading labels. This precaution, if growing, is nonetheless far from universal. In the late 1960's the circles in New York that a decade earlier had conceived community action as a cure for delinquency, came forward with the notion that a slightly different form would cure educational retardation on the part of minority group public school children. Community control *might* improve the school performance of slum children. It might *not*. No one knows. It might have other effects that are quite desirable, or undesirable. It is a perfectly reasonable proposal to try out. But at this point in time it is almost unforgivable that it should be put forth as a "proven" remedy for anything. About the only forecast that could have been made with any confidence would have been that the effort to impose community control would lead to a high level of community conflict, which in New York City it has been doing, and which will presumably be the case elsewhere. (P. 191, emphasis in the original)

This is the essential fact: *The government did not know what it was doing.* It had a theory. Or, rather, a set of theories. Nothing more. The U.S. Government at this time was no more in possession of confident knowledge as to how to prevent delinquency, cure anomie, or overcome that midmorning sense of power-

*Reprinted from the San Francisco *Sunday Examiner and Chronicle,* November 3, 1968, Section A, page B.

lessness, than was it the possessor of a dependable formula for motivating Vietnamese villagers to fight Communism. At any time from 1961 to 1964 an afternoon of library research would have established that the Cloward-Ohlin thesis of opportunity structure, though eminently respectable, was nonetheless rather a minority position, with the bulk of delinquency theory pointed in quite a different direction. (P. 170, emphasis in the original)

"Science" attempts to improve the playing of the anticipation game by making conscious the grounds of prediction, by keeping score, and thus bettering the bases of forecast.

To state this effort is not to belittle it. There are good reasons, to be discussed, why being scientific about social behavior is difficult. There are additional reasons, including the preference for ideals over knowledge, why one may not wish to adopt an actuarial stance. Both preference and difficulty permit men to assume the mantle of "science" without behaving scientifically and to lend the cachet of "science" to explanations that are more empathetic or ideological.

It is proposed here that, if there were to be a social science, the inquiry would have to proceed from taxonomy to the counting of statistical regularities. If the regularities are themselves to be explained by being embedded in a hierarchy of generalizations, then such an additional story deserves the title, "scientific theory," *when it increases the power to predict other happenings* (as, for instance, the consequences of intervention among the variables described in the table).

Lacking such theory, the nearest approximation to scientific behavior for the student of the social scene involves the laconic outlook of the actuary, in defense of which the following points are noted.

(i) A DEFENSE OF THE ACTUARY

(*a*) *Those who bet their money (and sometimes their lives) on the behavior of others use an actuarial system.*

The use of such a statistical schema may be quite conscious and mathematical or implicit and vulgar. It holds for insurance underwriters, parents, vote-seekers, policemen, con-men, and students of the horse race.

(*b*) *The actuarial method is applicable to the prediction of individual as well as group behavior.*

The behaviors of a single person can be classified and counted for recurrence in a life history. Conditional rates can be estimated for a single actor and a class of actions as for a collection of actors. The logic, is identical. It has been argued (Lundberg, 1941; Sarbin, 1944) that this is what is done implicitly even by those clinicians who assume they are using other thought-ways.

(c) *Any longer, scientific story that would explain events theoretically (and the style of the scientific theory is irrelevant) must include the actuarial tables.*

If one will not rest with the predictive use of base expectancy scores as explanation, then these, in turn, become data for explanation. We have thus returned full circle to the question of the meaning of this additional story, the "theory." If it contributes nothing to conditional forecasting from the experience tables, it has no status as a scientific account. It may, nonetheless, give comfort, mollify a moral judgment, or provide an impetus to action as an ideology.

(d) *In the social studies surely, and in psychology also (but perhaps less strongly), there seems to be a Gresham's law at work such that the "more theory," the lower the predictive power.*

By "more theory" is meant the number of assumptions made "above" the experience tables. Such assumptions include postulates (indemonstrable propositions), hypotheses of fact, and hypotheses of relationship among facts. The use of "more theory" here is compatible with Skinner's definition of "theory" (1950:193): . . . any explanation of an observed fact which appeals to events taking place somewhere else, at some other level of observation, described in different terms, and measured, if at all, in different dimensions.

Skinner argues that emphasis upon "theorizing" frequently has the effect of stopping the search for the variables upon which behaviors are contingent, and that it may prompt unimportant study:

Research designed with respect to theory is also likely to be wasteful. That a theory generates research does not prove its value unless the research is valuable. Much useless experimentation results from theories, and much energy and skill are absorbed by them. . . . this could be justified if it were true that productive research requires a theory, as is, of course, often claimed. It is argued that research would be aimless and disorganized without a theory to guide it. The view is supported by psychological texts that take their cue from the logicians rather than empirical science and describe thinking as necessarily involving stages of hypothesis, deduction, experimental test, and confirmation. But this is not the way most scientists actually work. It is possible to design significant experiments for other reasons and the possibility to be examined is that such research will lead more directly to the kind of information that a science usually accumulates. (*Ibid.:*194-195)

It is not necessary at this juncture to engage in the endless quarrels about "the place of theory" in the study of human behavior. Rather, the present proposition about the inverse relationship between "more theory" and predictive power should be regarded as a hypothesis. Although the suggested negative association seems to follow from the definition of "theory," it is advisable for a scientist to be suspicious of "things that *appear* logical." Data would be more satisfying than debate or continued presumption. Investigation of this topic has been meager; however, such research as is relevant corroborates the hypothesis. For example, in psychology, Fancher's work previously cited (Chapter Two, note 10; Chapter 3, note 43) shows how "theorizing," in the sense considered here, does reduce predictive accuracy. It is distracting.

Similarly, Sargant (1964), among others, has demonstrated how psychoanalytic theory, and its domination of North American medical schools, has frustrated attempts to improve the unsatisfactory arts of psychotherapy. Such a therapy, if it aspires to be a medicine, must include a conception of who will "get well" under what conditions. The predictive powers of the psychoanalyst continue weak.[3]

In the field of social psychology, Levonian (1968) provides an interesting illustration of the negative association of "theorizing" and knowing. He reviewed eight studies addressed to the test of hypotheses concerning the influence of personality upon opinion change in response to mass communication. He found that . . . although 40% of the results emerged in the direction opposite to that predicted, and although none of the studies showed an overall significant result, the authors generally interpreted these results as support for their theoretical positions. (P. 388)

Levonian himself conducted an *atheoretical* study on the relationship of personality to opinion change that yielded different results (1963). He was able, then, to describe some of the thoughtways that produce erroneous conclusions when theories are developed beyond the facts they are supposed to explain.

A principal confounding factor is the confusion of prediction with precognition. Prediction of results serves the purpose of formalizing hypothesis evaluation. Prediction does not imply precognition. (1968:388)

Levonian means that a scientific prediction is made, not to prove oneself right, but to assist in the evaluation of a hypothesis. A significant hypothesis predicts a distinctive result, but the experimenter need not "know" how the results will turn out.

When one accepts a theory, however, he is apt to develop an anxiety lest an experiment refute the favored formulation and this anxiety is relieved, Levonian shows, by such devices as:

Using one-tailed tests of two-sided hypotheses.

Emphasis on hypothesis confirmation, rather than on hypothesis evaluation.

Ignoring significant results that emerge in the direction opposite to that predicted (For example, in one study . . . the personality-opinion-change relation for the control group was simply not reported despite the fact that the control group showed as much opinion change as the experimental groups). (P. 389)

Failure to reinterpret hypotheses when results emerge in the direction opposite to that predicted.

If theories of human behavior often seem to distort the individual man as they move beyond experience tables that describe his actions, this applies, *a fortiori*, to the explanations of societal phenomena. The vulgar question is, "What are theories of society good for?" If one applies the *scientific* test of distinctive forecast to political studies or sociology, his reply cannot be encouraging.[4] The scientific status of economics may be less questionable, although also of relatively low calibre when compared with the physical sciences (Morgenstern, 1963; Postan, 1968; Zarnowitz, 1967). Heilbroner summarizes the "science" of economics thus (1968:8):

How successful has been this audacious intellectual effort? On the face of it, the achievement has been astonishing. Models of the economy are now so complex that they require the facilities of a computer and the techniques of difference equations, matrix algebra, LaGrangian multipliers, and the like. Sophistication, elegance, rigor — the criteria by which mathematics has traditionally been judged — are now the standards of economic theorizing. Not least, the success of modern economics can be read in the flattery of imitation paid to it by its sister disciplines of sociology and political science which now seek to build models similar to those of the economist. Certainly, when the intellectual history of our times is finally written, the creation of the edifice of modern "neo-classical" economics will occupy a central chapter in it.

The only question is, what will that chapter say about the usefulness and relevance of this extraordinary enterprise? Here I suspect the appraisal of the future will not be uncritically admiring. The theory of economics, magnificent to behold, is considerably less impressive to use. It is true that it has given us a rough picture of how the market system works. . . . But beyond this conception, which can be taught with ease to a college freshman, the ramifications of economics have produced singularly little. A rococo branch called welfare theory, for example, has not, to my knowledge, yet resulted in a single substantive proposal that has added significantly to the welfare of mankind. The beautifully finished portion called price theory fails to explain the pricing operations of the great corporations. International trade theory does not adequately account for the most important single fact about international trade — to wit, the failure of an international division of labor to shed its benefits on poor countries and rich countries alike. The theory of economic development does not tell underdeveloped countries how to grow.

Even the central achievement of twentieth-century economics — the elucidation of the forces that determine prosperity and recession — fails when we seek to foretell the fortunes of the economy a few months hence. . . . Kenneth Arrow [sums up] the collected papers of Paul Samuelson, the most brilliant theorist of our generation, with these words: "A careful examination of the papers both on theory and on policy yields only the most oblique suggestion that neo-classical price theory is descriptive of the real world."

In sociology, a prime case of the irrelevance of theory to prediction (and, hence, to reasoned action) is that of the Parsonian schema. Berger, in a review essay "On Talcott Parsons" (1962:510), remarks:

One of the going clichés in sociology is the view that theory is a "tool," justified insofar as it encourages and guides "fruitful" research. On this criterion, of course, the Parsonian theory is a conspicuous failure. Available in its main outlines for at least 15 years, it has so far failed to produce a body of research of really impressive substance. In an otherwise excellent discussion of the general theory, Robin Williams, a sociologist, alone among the critics represented, chooses to defend Parsons' utility in this respect; but all he can cite are three or four research reports scattered in the professional journals, an unpublished study in Kansas City, and a much over-praised book on the analysis of roles.

(e) *Accepting the actuarial explainway does not close the door to "theorizing."* Such acceptance asks, however, that theories remain close to data. It assigns priority to observation, counting, categorizing, continuity-noting, correlating, and predicting. It agrees that provisional, quasi-theories may guide observations, but it suspects that emphasis on "theorizing" militates against the development of experience tables. It is congenial to the lay accusation against "social science": that many professional explanations suffer from "theoretic overload," a heavy burden of story upon a slim foundation of fact.

A preference for the actuarial explainway can afford recognition of the ideal of a scientific explanation as set forth in the hypothetico-deductive model described by Hempel and Oppenheim (1948) and revised by Hempel (1965). But such recognition does not confuse a *definition* of a scientific explanation with a *description* of how scientists proceed. Luchins argues that (1968:112) . . . the logical foundations as read into a particular science by logicians or philosophers of science, are not necessarily isomorphic to empirical foundations of the science, and are not likely to be the bases on which the science was actually built.

The question is one of first steps and whether explanations of human behavior should aspire toward the exacting requirements defined for "science" by philosophers of science or whether, in this "natural history" stage of observing matters social, scientific theory is "good enough" when characterized as *a set of verified propositions, of probabilistic nature, inductively derived, and organized in a matrix of logical relationships that aspires toward simplicity and predictive increment.*

The question gains relevance in the context of point (iv) above that the yearning after theories of social behavior of the "covering law" form distracts the student from the "dirty work" of building generalizations upon reliable observations. "Inexact science," stumbling after an exactitude that may forever be beyond its grasp and waylaid by demands to explain "why," neglects what it might do better, and that is answer some empirical questions, count some consequences, and enlarge the scope of verified generalization about the contingencies of human action.

This point is put in different language by Helmer and Rescher (1960:13) who define an "explanation" as something more than a prediction, in the popular sense of an "explanation" telling "why" the predicted facts occur. With this distinction in mind, they go on to say:

The epistemological asymmetry between explanation and prediction has not, it seems to us, been adequately recognized and taken into account in discussions of scientific method. For one thing, such recognition would lead to a better understanding of the promise of possibly unorthodox items of methodological equipment, such as quasi-laws, for the purposes of prediction in the inexact sciences. But more generally it would open the way to explicit consideration of a *specific methodology of prediction* — a matter that seems to have been neglected to date by the philosophers of science. . . . it becomes pertinent to investigate the possibilities of predictive procedures autonomous of those used for explanation. (Emphasis in the original)

To start a science from this actuarial ground is not to prejudge the utility of any style of construct that may be employed to produce relationships among the data of the expectancy tables. Given a factual basis, scientific theories may be constructed without prejudgment as to the relative values in that theory of such popular concepts as "motive" and "purpose," "causes" of whatever class, "beliefs" and "definitions of situations," intrapersonal constants, and interpersonal environments.

The difference between the scientific orientation and the empathetic and ideological outlooks, however, lies in the criteria of conceptual utility. In the latter explainways, terms are maintained as they serve the explicators' purposes of building empathy or justifying ethico-political causes. In the scientific schema, any concept or construct is, in principle, dispensable regardless of these empathetic or ideological effects. All terms are regarded as borrowings or inventions whose efficacy is to be tested against the objectives of reliable knowing, the main measure of which is accurate mapping through the maze of competing perceptions of how-things-are and what-will-work-if . . . .

To argue thus is not to assume that there *can be* a "science of society" or that such a science would "save us." It is only to distinguish what might be involved in the construction of scientific explanations of human behavior from other explainways.

Given the difficulties of behaving scientifically, we usually explain matters in other ways. This "choice" of explanation, it has been argued, is a function of cultural climates (what is available) and personality differences. However, there are distinctive results of such "choices." Being as laconic as an accountant in one's explanations of human behavior has consequences of a personal nature as well as effects on one's presumed expertise in public policy.

(ii) A SUGGESTED CONSEQUENCE

On the personal level, one becomes attentive to what people do. Talk tells, but deeds have a louder voice. With this emphasis goes a lessened optimism concerning the possibility of revelation, change, and the therapies that would transform lives.

We found evidence for considerable consistency of several variables, in spite of fallible tools and a time span of nearly twenty years. Absolute changes in personality scores tended to be small, but similar in direction and magnitude for men and women. (Kelly, 1963:680)

With context reasonably constant, the best predictor of what a man will do in the future is what he has done in the past. (Owens, 1968:782)

"Everybody" knows this, but the actuary *believes* it.

A CORRESPONDENCE — THE PSYCHOLOGIST-AS-ACTUARY VERSUS THE SYMBOLIC INTERACTIONIST ON THE "COME-AGAIN" OF "DIRTY-DO"

Dear Bill:

I should appreciate your comments on some observations that have been occupying my recent attention and that, I think, may well constitute a Newtonian discovery in social psychology. (I'm only half-kidding since the psychology textbooks don't come near telling us "what people really are like.")

If you don't mind, let's call this "discovery" Doc's First Law of Human Relationships. This rule may be phrased, in the vernacular, thus: "He who does you dirt a first time will do so again, if you stick around long enough."

I can, of course, clean up this canon for academic purposes, but I think the popular phrasing says it well.

This law is an empirical one. That is, it is based, not on deduction from theory or web of premise, but "merely" on noting and counting. It is, in short, inductive.

I think this law has no exceptions. At least, pondering it at my desk and wrestling with it in my tossed sleep, I can think of none such in my life. How about yours?

There are certain difficulties that the law confronts. The rule runs counter to hope, but this, of course, does not make it false. It runs counter to "theory" — learning theory, for example, or some learning theories, at least — but this, again, does not invalidate it. It "just" means we have to look again at this question of learning. People *do* learn, but what? And how much? There is no quarrel with the fact that one can learn to speak French, prepare Irish coffee, or dance the boogaloo, but can one learn to be a "different person"?

While the phrase "different person" is now vague, it can be made clear and you know what I mean and that I doubt the probability (and even the possibility?) of becoming "different." (We grow older, and fires die, but you won't argue that *this* is the issue?)

Well, as I say, this rule is an empirical one and, perhaps, without exception. Do we need examples?

Case #101: AE has had "trouble with his wife" for some 14 years. He has hope, however, and he tries ("trying" is an approved American pastime). But she continues to do him dirt — flights of mood, complaints, criticism of his alleged ineptitude, and swings between love and hate, peace and battle, sobriety and drunkenness. And AE, good man, runs her through the gamut of "cures."

I'm saying that it doesn't matter whether his wife gets her tubes blown, her sinuses dried, her hormones balanced, her colon cleansed, or her psyche probed, she is going to continue to be an interesting neurotic. (Which is a nice way of saying an intelligent and rude bitch.)

Case #102: IW is impotent. He feels, therefore, inferior and compensates for this feeling by talking romantically and grandly when in the company of good-looking women. He has no men friends that I know of, a function of his being jealous of the interesting men he has known and bored with the lesser chaps.

If you become a "close acquaintance" of IW's, and an opportunity arises for him to demonstrate his verbal potency with a challenging woman, he will do so at your expense — by gossiping about you and running you down. He will then apologize, there will be excuses, and he will do it again. . . . if you wait around long enough.

Case #103: ST is not a lady. She has never really wanted or needed to be until a recent romance and her hopes for marriage led her to aspire in this direction. But, "Du glaubst zu schieben, du wirst geschoben." She can wish, she can want, but she does not have the "free will" to be a lady . . . (Pygmalion notwithstanding).

And the kinds of rudeness that are comfortable with "her class" are the kinds she will repeatedly demonstrate. She will then cry, beseech, and promise, and if you reconcile with her, you will, again, be confronted anew with some facet of her class-linked vulgarity.

Case #104: EHO, spoiled "son-of-the-rich," at 19 years showed his inclination to respond to stress with the bottle. That, too, is probably a psychological cliché; he *liked* to get drunk, with or without stress.

It is no surprise to learn, 25 years later, that he is a loyal member of Alcoholics Anonymous.

Case #105: KWM is a "mama's boy." He talks big, looks big, and swings big deals. He gets involved with women with whom he finds it impossible to behave responsibly. He lies. He breaks dates. He just can't get there. There are "mix-ups."

"Why" does so much happen to KWM that doesn't happen to others? Does one need to listen to his justification? Or can one reasonably predict that his future will be an extension of his past?

Case #106: JA is a beautiful woman. She is very sexy, very intelligent, and very talented. She runs through men the way Killy takes a slalom course. She has been multiply married. She goes to psychoanalysts. She is assured that the difficulty is that there are "no men"; they are all weaklings. But when she confronts a likely possibility, she finds herself lying, cheating, and "having problems" (always with reason, of course).

She then proposes to her "spouse" that *he* "needs help" and that, if they both seek such psychoassistance, all will be well. Meanwhile, her so-seeking-help gives her license to continue as always, a marital muck-up.

Well, enough. The point is clear and the law has implications:

(a) There is no excuse.

Unless one is stupid or ignorant of our canon, he cannot protest that he was not given signs of the other's inclination to hurt. The man who sorrowfully tells us, after marriage, "I didn't know she'd turn out that way," is, as I say, either stupid or ignorant. For *we all give signs,* and quite early in a relationship. The person who cannot be prompt, who is a liar, or an irresponsible, or a heller . . . these people show us soon what later to expect. As my black friends used to say, "Man, he signifyin'."

In short, people don't disappoint us. They live up to their early promise.

(b) There is a defense.

If the law is true, and if one doesn't enjoy being dirty-done, then one may respond to the law (not all are able, of course) by adopting its corollary, "You get one turn only."

Now I'm interested in your own observations. Is the law valid?

Cordially,

Doc

Dear Doc:

. . . the focus of the law is on the individual doing the dirt. It says, in effect, "behaviors of a certain kind are liable to be repetitive." Nobody argues with that.

I would ask of Doc's law to explain why individual A does dirt to individual B, or others like individual B, but not to individual C? I am assuming here that A "makes choices" as to who is a "deserving" target. I think I can show that criminals "specialize" and that neurosis is not "completely" a generalized stance, but varies with the situation and the others in it.

Let's look at, not people (one-by-one) . . . , but *relationships* as the unit of analysis. Let's ask "What's with #103's relationship with #106 that allows, leads to, encourages . . . his doing-dirt, and why not with #109?"

I would propose, in this connection, a notion we've discussed before: that central to a person's choice of behaviors, from those open to him . . . is the consideration of *self-interest*, as that may be seen psychologically by the actor. Without going into explaining "Why" it may be in a person's conception of his own interest to do dirt, can we develop, say, typologies of relationships in which some actor's performances will be to bite — or to kiss?

Pardon my role theory.

Cordially,
Bill

Dear Bill:

Be my guest. Develop your "typologies of relationships." But I question the *economy* of your acting upon Laing's logic.* How much time do you have?

The interpersonal axioms of role theorists are defective. They assume behavior is *nothing but* a function of experience. It isn't!

Further, interpersonal assumptions of role theory deny "character," by which is meant a morally evaluated *consistency* of response. And "everybody knows" there is character, yes?

Oliver Wendell Holmes, Jr., is said to have remarked that "even a dog knows the difference between being stumbled over and being kicked." Well, so too with human beings. We can tell the difference between a dirty-do that is an "accident" and that which flows from "character." If *you* can't, you're in trouble!

You ask "why" some people get done more dirt than others. That's easy. Some don't know Doc's First Law, and others don't believe it. You think, vis-à-vis a psychopath, let's say, that *you* will make a difference. Ha!

Talk about "empty vessels" and "blank slates"! Interactionists assume the actor brings nothing to the situation. *It* makes him. You remind me of what Marion Magid said about Tennessee Williams (1963:42) . . . that he suffered ". . . that curious American aversion to facts: the view that somehow or other people are different from what they do or say, from what experience has turned them into — that a man is defined by something other than his actions.

*A reference to Laing *et al.* (1966).

America is after all the home of the new start, the second chance, and there is a kind of gloomy, adolescent optimism, reflected in the culture, which clings to the possibility that people may change—that with enough love (which means forgiveness) they may one day become beautiful, good, and happy. . . . Like America, Williams lacks ultimately the conviction of his own neurosis."

In addition to all this, there is emotion. I need not know "why" there are masochists to accept the idea that there are such people: La mujer abnegada. The suffering sister. The mom-mangled grown boy. Given the wonderful permutations of people, it's not surprising that sadists continue to find their masochists, con-men their pigeons, and, in sum, every dirty-doer some victim.

As with typhoid, so with evil. There are carriers.

Protectively yours,
Doc

Optimism and pessimism about the way in which worlds and individuals change have cultural connections as well as psychological roots. Western man, living in the world's bloodiest century, this one, still resists the assumption of the easterner's Bhagavad Gita that "the world generally grows worse."

Without intruding upon this cultural quarrel, it need only be noted that any man who would organize his realm and act upon his vision of how things are (Is that not all of us?) will forever be in the dilemma posed by induction. Each knower stands between the uncomfortable horns of "ubiquitous continuity" and "chaos." Most of us vacillate between these points. It is doubtful whether any Western man regards his social scene as nothing but a logically linked parade of human events, each future deducible from a perceived series of past occurrences. Nor, at the other pole, does any modern function as if all were haphazard—nothing causing anything, no event a precursor of any other, everything at random.

The lively questions, then, are:

Where one is placed on this continuum of perceived continuities in the behaviors of himself, others, and societies. That is, *how much* continuity does he see?[5]

How this placement varies with particular classes of event.

From which cues one infers continuity when he does.

The answers to these questions distinguish the "theoretical schools" that would explain human conduct, whether the theories aspire to be scientific or are more empathetic or ideological. In short, the answers one receives flow from different models of man, and the varied images of man encourage the appreciation of different sets of cues from which to predict his behavior. It is notable that, even when one attempts to construct explanations as a scientist, he may pour different kinds of behavioral reports and hypothetical constructs into the mold of his theory. The scientific way to evaluate these many stories has been set forth.

(5) *Causal laws*

The principal dissatisfactions with inducing from a statistical rule are that:

(*a*) Knowing *how* things go together does not, for many people,[6] explain *why* they do.

(*b*) Unless the "why" is known, the inductive inference may be falsified by a change in the contingencies that underwrite the actuarial regularity.

Knowing the "causes" of the regularity expands experience so that we need be less often surprised by vagaries of the rule with changes in its context.

The "causal law," then, is intended to act as the major premise from which particular explicanda are *deduced,* and we may thus be spared some of the embarrassments of appearing as "inducers."

(*c*) To act efficiently in the resolution of personal or social problems may require action against "causes" as opposed to the correlates or consequences of undesirable behaviors. This is a popular, and largely unexamined, belief.

These dissatisfactions themselves involve assumptions. The assumptions are built into popular thought about human behavior and into attempts to be scientific about it. Despite their vogue, these ideas remain presumptive, and worthy of assessment.

The idea of "causing" has its own history and peculiar difficulties.[7] One can agree, for the most part, with Hume that causation is *attributed to* relationships rather than known intuitively despite the experiments of Michotte (1963) that show some specific and narrowly limited spatio-temporal features of events to . . . unleash [directly] this impression [of causality] in us. (Oldfield, in Michotte: vii)

Operating even as a Humean, we can ask many questions of causation:

(*a*) There is the *psychological* question: "Under what conditions do people of a particular age-time-place assign causation?" (Leifer, 1964; Piaget, 1930; Schiffman and Wynne, 1963)

(*b*) There is the *causal-historic* question: "What are the causes of thinking causally?"

(*c*) There are the *philosophic* questions:
    (i) "What is meant by a causal connection?"
    Which can be translated to ask: "What informational conditions ought we to aspire to meet before we accord causal warrant to an association between events?"
    Which raises its converse: "What conditions, commonly assumed to deny causality, need not be met?"
    (ii) "What problems of logic and morals arise in attributing causation?"
(*d*) And there is the *sociopsychological* question: "What are the behavioral consequences — the utilities and deficiencies — of the use of the idea of causation?"

These inquiries are entangled, of course; they help to answer each other. Here, in explication of "explanations," some of these questions need only be addressed in outline.

(*a*) *The comforts of "causes":* There are good reasons for thinking causally, however difficult it may be to define causation. Two of the reasons lie in our pasts; one, in our futures.

Causal thinking is ingested with our language and our ethico-legal beliefs. Once learned, and thus-supported, we sometimes find causal thinking efficient. However, the limits of this efficiency have not been well described as we move from making causal connections between inanimate events to imputing such relationships to human acts.

(i) The conventions of our language require thinking with causes.

There are critics of "causes" who would rather do without them because of our reliance in social "science" upon regularities that are "only" probable rather than certain. Since some strict definitions of causation opt for a *necessary* bond between that which is called cause and one type of effect, it has seemed presumptuous to such critics to talk about causation. They find it discomfiting to refer to causes in indeterministic systems, like the scenes of all human action, in which *plural causes* operate so that different sets of causes may produce similar effects.

Nonetheless, we are addicted to "causes," however much, metalogically, we might wish to abandon them. It would, indeed, take a devoted positivist to be able to speak for a week without reference to such terms as "the sources of . . . ," "the reason for . . . ," "production," "effect," "control."

Thus, in one recent critique, Scriven (1968*a*) is able to show that those who doubt "causes" use them, as when one such skeptic who has alleged the incompatibility between probability and causation relapses into the convenient language of "the probable effects of a course of legislation" and, i∎ another place, describes the human body as . . . a highly complex system [in which] the glands, genes, DNA, exercise control in a most efficient manner. To which Scriven asks: And what does "exercise control" mean if it does not involve "bringing about"; and "bringing about" if it does not involve cause and effect?

It seems clear that our language is, as Scriven puts it (1966b:240-241) "cause-impregnated," and that descriptions of our worlds form a *continuum* of causal and noncausal terms with no sharp divide, but with . . . clear cases of each that are not cases of the other, so [that] we are dealing with a continuum and not a confusion.

If language, as well as experience, habituates us to causal thinking, it would seem wisest to handle our habit by acknowledging it and aspiring toward moderation. Such temperance would require knowing what we are doing, and that is working with assumptions. It would require a wariness of overdoses of "causes" and a pragmatic willingness to test for the efficiency of thinking-with-causes, or without them, under different circumstances. The "different circumstances" are defined by variations in the purposes of thinking and the information available.

(ii) Causal assumptions have legal and religious roots.

Western religions and the legal systems that have grown with them prescribe that "one be held responsible for his acts." To be "responsible" is to be judged as the "cause" of an act and, within some limits, the chain of events that "results" from that act. Even those moderns who deny the religious sources of their morals continue to respond with a morality that sees justice as the balance between one's acts and his deserts (Kelsen, 1957). When society "does justice," it intrudes upon this balance.

The conditions under which "responsibility" may properly be attributed vary and, within Western societies, are in dispute, a reflection of the infiltration of religion and law by psychiatry. But, however these limits are defined, to be held "accountable" is to have been assigned causal efficacy. It would seem impossible, then, to waive causal thinking without abrogating our morality.

There is a pedagogical wisdom in this thinking insofar as behavior is shaped by its consequences (Skinner, 1953). The sanctions we apply to each other are not always merely vindictive. We intend also that moral and legal codes shall *change* behavior. We seek to do this by allowing, or forcing, the actor to experience the consequences of his acts. And if the "natural consequences" are not sufficient to mold behavior as desired, societies *attach* consequences.

"Spoiling a child" is recognized as the process of protecting the learner against the usual consequences of his acts — again, beyond some limit. This recognition leads to a related societal possibility: that social orders prosper or suffer as they permit or remove significant areas of consequence from the experience of their agents. Political philosophies are engaged in this sociopsychological and moral debate as to who should be "spoiled," how much, with what justification and expected effect. Whichever side one takes, he assumes causation.

(iii) Causation is part of the vocabulary of intervention.

Some positivists have argued that one need not assume causation in order to act effectively. They have been answered by laymen and some philosophers who hold that every act taken to change or maintain course assumes a cause-and-effect relationship.

This debate has received several translations. A common meaning assigned to the quarrel alters the question slightly. It asks, "To what extent must one know the causes of the conditions or behaviors he is to respond to (or cure) *if* he is to act rationally?" Here, "to act rationally" means to select consciously the most economic means toward one's end.

The popular response to this emended question *assumes* that knowledge of causes promotes efficient cures. Common sense is joined in this assumption by the folklore of social work and some social "science."

No one knows to what extent knowledge of the causes of human behavior promotes rational action in response to it. Present purposes require only that this assumption be noted for later challenge (pp. 167-170) where it will be argued that some rational response, and "cure," does *not* entail confidence in causes.

However this issue is decided, the fact that some evidence and much popular belief support knowledge of causes as requirements of cures constitutes yet another comfort of causal thinking.

The discourse of personal and social policy is laden with causation. This is so *a fortiori* as one seeks to intervene in his fate. Says Nagel (1961:75):

It is because some things can be *manipulated* so as to yield other things, but not conversely, that causal language is a legitimate and convenient way of describing the relationships of *many* events. (Emphasis supplied)

(*b*) *The meaning of causation.* The difficulties of using the notion of causation in scientific explanation become apparent as one attempts to define the concept. A definition of causation might be approached by listing the conditions that many philosophers of science consider warrant the conferring of causality upon a verified relationship between facts. These causal guarantees will vary as one attempts to behave scientifically as opposed to humanistically, however, and as one moves from "models of causal logic" to the practice of attributing causes.

Those who would think about *causal laws* of social behavior (those, that is, who would behave as social "scientists") usually invoke a popular trinity of causal criteria: the "necessity, sufficiency, and sequence" of an association. But these warrants have themselves been under attack and variously used, abused, and abandoned. To these trembling three criteria, some scholars have added "asymmetry" as definitive of causation.

Briefly, the criterion of "necessity" usually refers to the warrant for causality given to condition or event C if effect E never occurs without it. "Sufficiency" refers to one kind of "invariance" or "uniformity" criterion: whenever C, then E, under conditions $_{1,2,3}$. "Sequence" acknowledges the commonsensical definition of a "cause" as preceding its effect. This trio of guarantees, but particularly "necessity" and "sufficiency," gives to "cause" its popular imprint of "force," or ability to produce.

The criterion of "asymmetry" is not so frequently mentioned by laymen or social "scientists," although it is acknowledged implicitly. The asymmetry requirement refers to the perception of unidirectional and irreversible relationships. We observe, and call "causal," the ordering, "Ample rain → large wheat crop." We also allow an inference in reverse, "Small crop, therefore there must have been inadequate rain." But, although the first sequence is "causal," we do not accord causality to the second.

Simon (1965:160) gives this example: . . . deficiency of water in body tissues → reduction in salivation → dryness of tongue and palate → stimulation of nervous system (sensation of thirst).

It is difficult to think or write of these functional relationships as symmetrical, or as asymmetrical but running in the opposite direction. For example, if there is normal salivation but the saliva is prevented from reaching the tongue and palate, thirst is produced, but this neither reduces salivation nor produces a deficiency of water in the body tissues.

Simon shows that, at least for "causal models," if not for the "real world," the asymmetry criterion is more important than the sequential. In his words (1968:II, 353), the asymmetry criterion . . . imposes no requirement that the cause precede the effect. It moves us away from thinking about temporal sequence and toward thinking about the "direction of influence."

It may not be "helpful" to the student of social relations — although it may be sobering — to be told that all these conventional criteria of causation have been challenged. Scriven (1968*b*), for example, argues that "causes" cannot be identified as "sufficient conditions," "necessary conditions," nor even "contingently necessary conditions." Further, he gives reasons for agreeing that . . . causes need not be separated in space or time from their effects, [nor] logically separated from [them].

Much of this continuing debate is definitional and open. However, logicians seem agreed that, whenever causation is imputed, it is assigned within a context. The very idea of causation implies boundaries to the "system" within which it applies. This might be translated by saying that, although everything may affect everything in our web of human relations, men who think about causes think only about certain classes of condition or event with reference to other classes of condition or event. What interests the inquirer determines the context in which he assigns causes and selects them.

For instance, the . . . classical dynamic principle of causality [attributes causation to a system if] there exists a law by means of which from a given initial state *all* of the subsequent states of the system can be predicted. (Hillinger, 1968:144, emphasis in the original) This definition would restrict causation to contexts that are . . . stable, closed, or conservative. It would require an unambiguous specification of the state of a system and its isolation from unknown influences.

When one asks questions about systems that are unstable, where the boundaries of the system change, and where system-isolation cannot be assumed — as is the case in thinking about social systems — this definition of causation cannot be used. In its place, a weaker form of causal construct is applied, one that leans upon probabilities. A system is causal if there exists a law by means of which from an *approximately* given initial state all the subsequent states can be predicted *approximately*. (*Ibid.*, emphasis in the original)

One is returned to finding statistical regularities before he can propose causal laws of human behavior.

The debate about the meaning of causation has been largely semantic, an argument about how the term *should* be applied. Apart from some attention to the uses of causes in historical analysis (Dray, 1966; Hook, 1963; Scriven, 1966*b*), neither the psychological question ("How *do* people use the idea?")[8] nor its pragmatic cousin ("What are the consequences of its use or neglect?") has been adequately studied. Relevant to the debate, it has been argued that the search for causal connections has led some students into the employment of "false criteria" of causality.

Ducasse (1960) has addressed himself to an aspect of the psychological question and, in so doing, has shown the hazards of an absolute application of causal criteria—Hume's, in particular. Ducasse demonstrates that the Humean notion of causality as "empirical constant conjunction" itself underwent change at the hands of its author from . . . that constant conjunction, on which the relation of cause and effect *totally* depends to that on which it *chiefly depends* to that from which the *first* idea of [the causal relation] is derived.

Worse, Ducasse reminds us that there are constant sequences to which we do *not* attribute causality and that there are singular events upon which we *do* confer a causal nexus.

Examples of the first are common (1960:223): The succession of day and night; . . . the fact . . . that in infants the growth of hair is regularly followed by the growth of teeth; or that in human beings birth regularly follows the tenth return of the moon since conception. Beginning students of the social readily learn that "correlation is not to be confused with causation" as they wrestle with such "findings" as George Marshall's classic correlation of +.86 over some years between membership fluctuations in the United States' International Association of Machinists and the death rate in the state of Hyderabad, India.

Ducasse illustrates the second fact with experiments in which a single sequence, rather than a "constant conjunction," may be sufficient to elicit judgments of causation. These are characteristically stable situations into which some perceptible change is introduced. Ducasse concludes (p. 224): By the *cause* . . . they mean the only change introduced into the situation immediately before the [event] occurred.

If one applies Ducasse's "false criteria" of causation, he narrows its definition. Regularities may not be causal (but we knew that), and singularities may suffice where a changing intervention is perceived.

Hirschi and Selvin (1966) add other "false criteria" to Hume's erroneous "constant conjunction." In so doing, they tell us something about how the term is to be used by students of social behavior. They would confer causation upon those associations between empirical variables that are *sequential* and *nonspurious,* a spurious association being defined as one that disappears as other antecedents are held constant. For them, it is *incorrect* to impute causation:

(1) Only to perfect correlations. There are none such.

(2) Only to variables "characteristic" of the effects to be explained. By "characteristic" is meant "found in most cases." To Hirschi and Selvin the "importance" of a "cause" is the amount of variation in the dependent variable it accounts for, whether or not it is "characteristic" of it.

(3) To correlations for a "single value of a situation," to the neglect of that situation's possible causal impact. For example, if some personality variables are found to be related to juvenile delinquency in different social situations, one should not thereby conclude that the differences in situation are not themselves of causal significance.

(4) To intervening variables, to the exclusion of antecedents further down the causal chain. Thus, if a correlation is found between X and Y, and if a psychological variable intervenes between these, it ought not be concluded, say Hirschi and Selvin, that X is not a "cause."

(5) To abstract concepts (like "anomie") rather than to measurable variables (like "home ownership"). The preference for abstract concepts over measured data is supported by the vogue of calling the measures "indicators" (there must be something "behind them" that is "indicated") and by the greater difficulty of falsifying a high level abstraction.

(6) To unconditional variables. If there were such, we might find perfect correlations. However, even some conditions/events that are *necessary* to produce an effect do so only under certain circumstances. Hirschi and Selvin deplore the tendency to eliminate such variables from the roster of "causes."

> The discovery that a variable has no intrinsic pathogenic qualities has often led to the conclusion that it has no pathogenic qualities at all. (P. 267)

Their point is illustrated by the statement of a researcher on tuberculosis who commented: After years of study, I am often of the opinion that the tubercule bacillus is the least important element in the disease.

Here a "least important" factor is the necessary one, and nonetheless a "cause" for being conditional.

Hirschi and Selvin conclude: The researcher who would grant causal status only to unconditional relations will end by granting it to none. *(Ibid.)*

To this, some scholars would retort, "And good riddance." For, despite our bondage to "causes," their definition is difficult and their use hazardous.

(c) *The trouble with causes.* The difficulties with causes are related, as might be expected, and are five in number: (i) Defining causation, (ii) choosing causal criteria, (iii) choosing causes, (iv) keeping causes free of ideologies, and (v) applying causes to cures. (This moves one into the problem of the failure of "knowledge" to produce the effects that sometimes justify it.)

(i) The definition of causation: Thus far, causation has been discussed in the context of *scientific* explanations, the characteristic of which is an attempt to infer particular propositions from general rules. In the much debated "covering-law" model of a *scientific*, causal explanation: To give a *causal explanation* of an event means to deduce a statement which describes it, using as premises of the deduction one or more *universal laws*, together with certain singular statements, the *initial conditions*. (Popper, 1959:59, emphasis in the original)

Men who would be scientists of human actions and social events aspire to assign causality with this reference. This meaning of causation, however, is not its only one. Although we lack a catalogue of common usage, we do not lack an inventory of the uses of causes among thoughtful men. Philosophers and historians describe a continuum from those who deny the utility of the idea of causality for their purposes (Oakeshott, 1966) to those who see the causes of human events only in decisions (Donagan, 1966) to those who give causation a humanistic and unscientific ("unlawful") meaning when applied to human behavior (Scriven, 1966*b*).

Oakeshott: These causes either explain too much, or turn out to be no causes at all. And when we pass from these causes and pseudo-causes to the more general conception of cause, we shall, I think, be obliged to conclude that it also has nothing to offer of which history can make use. What, I take it, is fundamental to this conception is that we should be able to separate the cause and its effect, and endow each with a certain degree of individuality; but it is just this which is impossible while we retain the postulates of historical experience. It cannot be achieved by selecting some single event and attributing to that any subsequent event or the whole course of subsequent events. No single event in history is isolable in this manner, and if it were there would be no more reason to isolate *this* event rather than *that*. (P. 198)

The strict conception of cause and effect appears, then, to be without relevance in historical explanation. (P. 199)

The historian, in short, is like the novelist whose characters (for example) are presented in such detail and with such coherence that additional explanation of their actions is superfluous. (P. 208)

History accounts *for* change by means of a full account of change.

The relation *between* events is always other events, and it is established in history by a full relation *of* the events. (P. 209, emphasis in the original)

Donagan: Although historians are not, as such, committed to any particular view of human action, they practice a methodological scepticism which resembles the scepticism of traditional Western morality. (P. 148)

This methodological scepticism may be formulated as what I shall call "the presupposition of individual choice." By affirming this possibility historians allow that the traditional moral doctrine may be true that a man ultimately has an unconditional power to choose how he will act. . . . according to it, a man simply chooses the ultimate principles on which he will act, and he may choose them either in accordance with or against his own inclinations, either reasonably or unreasonably. Most choices are explicable, because they are conditioned by prior choices; but the only explanation of a man's ultimate choice of principle is: that is how he chose. (Pp. 149-150)

Scriven: The search for causes does not require . . . *universal* laws, [but only an] appeal to some general proposition which *(a)* applies reliably to the present case, and *(b)* is founded upon other cases. But knowing a universal C-E [Cause-Effect] connection, qualified or not, is only one means to this. Another is knowing a *possible* C-E connection, combined with an *elimination* of other possible connections. And a third is the trained judgment of the historian, which requires no knowledge of laws at all. (1966*b*:245-246, emphasis in the original)

. . . a cause is one of several alternative factors the presence of one (any one) of which is necessary in order that a set of conditions actually present be sufficient for the effect. (P. 249)

. . . causes [are] selected on pragmatic grounds from conditions which are *(a)* known to be possible causes, *(b)* known to be present in the case under consideration, and *(c)* not known to operate in a way contraindicated by known data about the case. (P. 258)

Further, Scriven says we cannot define the "possible causes" of human action through some combination of necessary and sufficient regularities. Ideas of "causes" are built up from cases in which the idea is applied and these cases are themselves thought of in causal terms so that a specification of the extracausal definiens of causation is impossible. Types of such cases, according to Scriven, include:

The Basic Experimental Case. Suppose that whenever and however we produce C, E occurs, and that E never occurs unless C is produced . . . then C is the cause of E. (P. 258)

The Basic Observation Case. Suppose that C just occurs on various occasions and is accompanied by (perhaps followed by) E, and E never occurs on any other occasions. C is the cause of E if (but not only if) we can conclude that C would always be accompanied by E, no matter how or when it was produced. . . . (P. 259)

Compound Causes. Suppose that we need to bring about not only C but also D in order to get E (and that D alone is not sufficient). We may call C and D *causal factors* or *co-causes* of E. (P. 259)

Multiple Causes. If C and D are each sufficient to bring about E, and nothing else is, then whichever occurs is the cause. If both occur, one of them may not have had any effect on this occasion, a possibility which we check by examining the situation for the presence of known intermediate links which characterize the *modus operandi* of C and D, i.e., any sets of conditions "C_1 or C_2 or . . ." (or "D_1 or D_2 or . . .") which are necessary for C (or D) to act as the cause of E. This test does not apply where no such links are known, and since it is not logically necessary that there be any (C and E may be adjacent links in the chain, or differ only from a certain descriptive standpoint, or represent "action at a distance"), the test is not part of the meaning, of course.

If one has brought about E before the other could, although it would have in time, we have a case of *independent overdetermination,* but only one cause.

If both occur, both may have been effective, bringing about E simultaneously, or essentially simultaneously for the purpose at hand, which gives the case of *simultaneous overdetermination*—for example, a firing squad—and neither factor can be identified as *the* cause. . . .

. . . *linked overdetermination* [refers to the cases in which the multiple causal factors] are not independent; the circumstances are such that the very act of preventing C from occurring will bring about D which will itself cause E ("Damned if he does and damned if he doesn't").

LINKED OVERDETERMINATION IN CURRENT EVENTS

Dove: If one acts to repress the rioters, he hardens their intransigence.

Hawk: If one does not respond firmly and quickly, the rioters win positions and consolidate their gains. You cannot reward violations of the rules of the game.

LINKED OVERDETERMINATION AGAIN

The last dilemma I want to mention . . . is difficult to label. It probably comes under the heading of "no matter what you do you can't win!" And this goes both for the students and the groups and institutions against which they are struggling. On the one hand, the students do want a confrontation. They want something definite and unyielding against which to resist . . . . At the same time, of course, if a college president, for example, takes a firm stand, such as Pusey at Harvard or Wallis at Rochester, the students view him as a perfect example of the entrenched establishment. (Rubinstein, 1969:136)

To these cases of *compound* and *multiple* causation, Scriven has added (1968*b*) the possibility of *plural* causes, cases in which several factors, in differing combinations, can produce the same effect.

The flow of definitions described leads one toward the murky province of the sociology of knowledge where the question is raised, "Among all these possible views of the causal process, from 'Causes are useless, since all is a web,' to 'He did it because he chose to,' to the humanist's variety of causal possibilities to the scientist's search for causal laws, how is it that, in this situation, puzzled by that set of events, philosopher$_1$ accepts this idea of cause$_1$, philosopher$_2$ that notion, and philosopher$_3$, none?"

This sociopsychological question will not be answered here. It is pertinent only to indicate that *the very model of causation is open* and that, as with any explanation, the choice of model is in the service of personal histories and present purposes.

Scientists, however, are ingenious and they have tried to incorporate some of these causal possibilities within the framework of their search for regularity. Their task is difficult, perhaps insurmountable, but, like Bruce's spider, they persist. Modern examples are to be found in the applications of multivariate statistical analysis and in the causal presentation suggested by Burt and others. One of Burt's students, Mace (1965), has described this research effort thus:

Cyril Burt . . . has gone around collecting data for causal propositions of the form

$$p = f(a + b + c + \ldots) \text{ or } f(b + c + d + \ldots) \text{ or } f(c + d + e + \ldots),$$

where p denotes the probability that a given child (say) will become delinquent, neurotic or educationally backward; a, b, c, etc., stand for conditions or causal factors actually observed; and f denotes that p is regarded as a function of the group of factors specified in the equation, with each item given its due weight and the whole appropriately combined. The special implication of the formula is that (in Burt's own words) "the result to be predicted (as a probable, and not an assured, deduction) springs, not from a single universal cause, but from a multiplicity of converging influences, often differing widely in their nature, their grouping, or their relative importance from one group to another." . . . This is the sort of causal proposition which is most characteristic of psychology. Psychologists do not establish laws of the kind: "All delinquents come from broken homes," or "All broken homes produce delinquents." They do what Burt has done with such elegance: marshal evidence that delinquency, for example is the consequence of a large number of alternative combinations of factors, $(a + b + c)$ or $(b + c + d)$ and so on to the end of an almost endless proposition.

Burt has not attempted . . . [as did Charles Spearman] to formulate a few general laws from which all the facts of mental types could be deduced and presumably predicted. He is a psychologist in the tradition of Francis Galton . . . in showing Galton's interest in *answering the question* rather than in formulating laws or methodological principles. (Pp. 26-27, emphasis in the original)

Burt's resolution of the causal search can proceed without attention to causal laws. It is empirical and pragmatic, only minimally theoretic and, for these reasons, unappealing to men who would have more assurance in their knowledge of human action.

For such men, the pursuit of causal laws runs into an obstacle related to their choice of "model of causation." It is the hazard of selecting criteria of causal regularity and justifying the rigor, or its lack, with which such criteria will be applied before causation is inferred.

As Thurman Arnold told us (1937:47), definitions may get in our way as often as they help us. Defining the requirements of a causal law restricts us so much that, in practice, we abandon some portion of the desiderata of causation while clinging to the idea.

(ii) The choice of causal criteria: In application, behavioral "scientists" ignore "necessity," attend to "asymmetry" only when they have to, and work with a limited sense of causation. Recall (p. 148) Hirschi and Selvin's elevation to causal title of associations that are sequential and nonspurious.

One apology for this limitation lies in the possibility that students of the social scene are observing networks of plural causes that bear only probable relationship with their similar effects — which vitiates "necessity." Despite Ducasse's examples of the attribution of causation to singular interventions, collective behaviors are known through statistical regularities, which are usually of modest order. The social "scientist," then, suffers all the difficulties of trying to "know" from such conditional regularity plus the added pains of verifying the rules by which causation is reliably to be ascribed. With such an epistemic burden, "necessity" becomes an unbearable load.

Similarly, the *plurality of causes* and the possibility of *interaction* in social affairs militate against the use of "asymmetry" and "sequence" as causal criteria.

On the other hand, the reduction of causation to sequence and nonspurious association attenuates the moral and legal meaning. The historical sense of a "cause" as that of a *force* is not entirely contained by *any* nonspurious antecedents. It is conceivable that some nonspurious correlates of some events that interest us do not seem sufficient to produce the explanandum.

CRIME AND BAD CAUSES

Van den Haag (1968:283): Even though its effectiveness seems obvious, punishment as a deterrent has fallen into disrepute. Some ideas which help explain this progressive heedlessness were uttered by Lester Pearson, then prime minister of Canada, when, in opposing the death penalty, he proposed that, instead, "the state seek to eradicate the causes of crime — slums, ghettos and personality disorders."

"Slums, ghettos and personality disorders" have not been shown, singly or collectively, to be "the causes" of crime.

The crime rate in slums is indeed higher than elsewhere; but so is the death rate in hospitals. Slums are no more "causes" of crime than hospitals are of death; they are locations of crime, as hospitals are of death. Slums and hospitals attract people selectively; neither is the "cause" of the condition (disease in hospitals, poverty in slums) that leads to the selective attraction.

If it be allowed that slums bear a nonspurious antecedent relationship to certain kinds of crime, van den Haag's argument demonstrates that we seek *more* from "causation." Otherwise, one meets the paradox of "causes" without causal force.[9]

Looking backward over this shambles of causal criteria, it is apparent that the noncausal datum that appeases one philosopher is ignored by another. The social "scientist" who would talk about causes is thus "free" to defend shifting criteria of causation or to remain, as is more customary, vague.

CAUSAL CRITERIA AND THE SUBJECTIVE PLUS

Calhoun (1942:715): . . . the central theme of MacIver [in his *Social Causation*, 1942] is that causation is something more than "mere" correlation and observed "regular sequence," and that causation in the social realm is different from causation in the physical realm because of the presence of subjective factors.

. . . although MacIver maintains that causation is correlation plus something more, he fails to tell what the something is, save implicitly by reference to the feeling people have when they think of one event's "causing" another.

The problems here seem twofold. A minor difficulty is that of working in fields of probability. When social "scientists" think about collective behaviors, they are involved in a "probabilistic" system in which events seem only tenuously connected to their "causes." According to Simon (1968:II, 352), formalization of theories about such systems . . . shows that the causal relationships implicit in them hold between probable distributions of events rather than between individual events.

In this situation (the Markov process), disconfirming a theory requires not just simply disconfirming an observation but rather a sufficiently large set of observations to show that a predicted distribution does not hold.

Economists have moved further with such thinking than sociologists, a result in no small part of their more developed taxonomy of events. Before one can talk about "distributions," he must be able reliably to count homogeneous classes of acts.

A more difficult problem in the choice of causal criteria is that of justifying assumptions about the nature of the "system" in which one thinks with "causes."

It bears repeating that causation is a context-bound concept. . . . no mere consideration of the physical facts about an event can identify anything as *the* cause of it, or even settle the question whether it has a cause. Reference must be made to the context of the discussion in order to identify the *type* of factor which is of interest, but type-selection often leaves several equal candidates and further contextual considerations must then be used as discriminators. *(Ibid.)*

Contexts, in both everyday usage and in science, are given by some "theory," some set of assumptions about "related" generalizations. The notion of a "related" generalization is itself dependent upon the definition of the "system." It is uncomfortable, but necessary, to suggest that we don't "know" what to call exogenous to a social system, except at some extreme like the conjunction of stars and planets.[10] For example, we assume "interdependence" of social institutions, but we don't know *how much* interaction occurs. We recall that our measures are modest—behaviors, beliefs, and conditions, reliably counted, are loosely linked. Does this slippage reflect "how things really are" or the coarseness of our measuring net? Perhaps, too, we are not even looking at the finer variables that would tighten imputed causal bonds.

Suppose one were trying to decide for a political system whether causal attribution should employ "sequence" or ignore it. One reads this recommendation (Simon, 1968:II,353):

If almost all the variables in a dynamic system are directly interdependent, so that the value of each variable at a given time depends significantly on the values of almost all other variables at a slightly earlier time, the causal ordering provides little information and has little usefulness. When the interrelations are sparse, however, so that relatively few variables are directly dependent on each other, a description of the causal ordering provides important information about the structure of the system and about the qualitative characteristics of its dynamic behavior. For this reason the language of causation is used more commonly in relation to highly organized and sparsely connected structures — manmade mechanisms and organisms with their systems of organs — than in relation to some of the systems described by the partial differential equations of chemistry and physics, where the interactions are multitudinous and relatively uniform.

But how is it in "society" (itself an ambiguous word)? The interrelations measured by sociologists are "sparse," but the assumptions preferred and used in justification of policy are otherwise. Namely, that the . . . value of each variable at a given time depends significantly on the values of almost all other variables at a slightly earlier time, and that . . . no man is an island, entire of itself.

The search for causes is an exploration for forces, but we are not clear about what "determining," or "forcing," or "producing" might mean as we move from observing the collision of billiard balls to asking "What made Mike do it?" or "Why mob violence?"

The criteria of a causal bond should be defined in noncausal terms if we are to avoid the traps of redundancy and the fate of Whifflebirds. But it does not appear that we have done this in the explanation of social behavior. Whichever set of criteria is selected as justifying the attribution of causation is a set that is itself cause-impregnated. It will satisfy the inquirer curious about "causes," but not the logician who studies his inferences.

If one probes for the criteria that might do justice to both the ethicolegal intention of causation and that conception with which social "scientists" work, it seems that, in these contexts, causal agency *is* attributed to those statistical regularities among variables that are sequential and "sufficient to produce" the explanandum. Notice that "sufficient to produce" begs the question, but it is the shibboleth of causes in these contexts.

This set of criteria — regularity of association, sequence, and sufficiency — describes what laymen and professional policy-makers seem to have in mind when they talk of causes. They are criteria that can accommodate Ducasse's test of causal attribution (that which is changed in a stable situation) and Hirschi and Selvin's requirements of sequence and nonspurious association. Yet, in application, this popular notion of causation takes various forms.

In the historical, physical sciences, as in aspects of geology, "sufficient to produce" is warranted through a taxonomy of traces and contemporary observations *supported by inferences* from the regularities revealed by the "compositional" sciences: chemistry and, at times, biology. If similar conditions prevailed in the social studies, and they do not, human history might become scientific.

Among experimentalists, the search for sufficiency is satisfied by holding constant other hypothesized causes, allowing the "cause" under test to vary, and observing the fit between predicted consequence and outcome.

For statisticians of social behaviors, the notion of "sufficient to produce" takes the form of seeking to eliminate "spurious correlations" and observing how much variance in the effect is "accounted for" by the assumed causal complex. For historians and humanists, the procedure is something like that described by Scriven (1968b:19-20):

Perhaps one might sum up the model of causal explanation in this way. We begin with a context which determines the *type* of factor amongst which we are hunting a cause, e.g., physiological or ecological, and the *kind* of factor within that type, e.g., childhood variation, proximate causes, whatever accounts for the contrast with the result in a certain other family of cases, etc. We also begin with a box full of basic causal connections, established or confirmed by direct experimentation . . . or by inference from theory: if the effect is E, we can say that this is the box labelled "Possible causes of E, type . . . , kind . . . ." Each basic piece in the box has a label on it which says C (or C' or C", etc.). The initial circumstances of the investigation are represented by a big pile of pieces of data on the table. Our task is to develop the piece representing one of the possible causes until it incorporates the effect. We can do this in two main ways: We can find the pieces of data to fit in the jagged notches fully around one of the primary causes, which excludes all other possible causes. Or we can find one piece that fits against one notch and build onto it until we finally reach a piece with E on it. The second strategy involves dipping into other boxes labelled "Possible causes of X; type . . . , kind . . ." where X is an intermediate event in the chain from some C to E, as well as adding extra pieces of data. The whole task is a pattern-recognition task: We are trying to find some configuration of the facts which meets certain constraints represented by the jigsaw edges. The crucial difference from the *prediction* task is our reliance on *knowing the outcome E in advance*. It is only that knowledge which enables us to find the boxes with E on them and get a starting point: It is only that knowledge which enables us to tell whether one of the many possible causal chains beginning with a given factor is the explanatory one. The prediction game requires entirely different pieces with both more and less information content. Only in very rare cases can the two be combined. The outcome of the explanatory game is that we can see what must have happened (the X's) and why (C and other X's); but we cannot assert that given C, E had to happen. In the prediction game, the *only test of success* is showing that a particular, heretofore unidentified E *must* come about. (Emphasis in the original)

In sum, the related problems of defining causation and of identifying noncausal criteria of the style of cause chosen show us in a modern way what Aristotle told us long ago: There are "causes" and "causes" — sequential and simultaneous; proximate, distant, and in-between; multiple, compound, and plural; efficient, formal ("dispositional"), and final (telic); overdetermined simultaneously, independently, or interactively; and recognized from singular experiences or patterns.

The style of cause chosen, like the style of explanation preferred, seems to be an effect of the interaction of personality and purpose in a specific cultural context. The result, and measure, of this interaction is a preference among the various tests of knowledge.

PURPOSES SIFTING CAUSAL STYLES

Mills (1942:171-172): Another element that tends to obviate an analytic view of structure is the emphasis upon the "processual" and "organic" character of society. In Cooley . . . one gets a highly formal, many-sided fluidity where "nothing is fixed or independent, everything is plastic and takes influence as well as gives it." From the standpoint of political action, such a view may mean a reformism dealing with masses of detail and furthers a tendency to be apolitical. There can be no bases or points of entry for larger social action in a structureless flux. The view is buttressed epistemologically with an emotionalized animus against "particularism" and with the intense approval of the safe, if colorless, "multiple-factor" view of causation. The liberal "multiple-factor" view does not lead to a conception of causation which would permit points of entry for broader types of action, especially political action.

Hirschi and Selvin (1966:268): Mills has suggested that accepting the principle of multiple causation implies denying the possibility of radical change in the social structure. Our analysis suggests that rejecting the principle of multiple causation implies denying the possibility of any change in the social structure — because, in this view, nothing causes anything.

Neither conclusion need follow. Both Mills and Hirschi and Selvin are right and wrong.

Versus Mills: One *can* "accept the principle of multiple causation" and yet propose radical social change through action against available (or disapproved) select causes.

This acceptance may make one less than rational. It involves working with an ideology that tells which "causes" to attack or defend, and it accounts for the slippage between reformist intention (where that is known) and outcome. But this is *how* we behave. It seems man's fate. Mills' argument is a call to arms against this destiny.

Versus Hirschi and Selvin: One *can* reject multiple causation, and men do, without holding that "nothing causes anything." Such men, like Mills' meliorists, opt for *this* cause rather than *that* one. Purposes and morals select causal style.

The trouble with causes does not end here. There is the difficulty of choosing among *styles* of causation and criteria of them, but there is also the problem of causal *content,* of selecting the things to be looked at from the range of possible determinants.

The choice of causes is itself caused.

(iii) The choice of causes: Kierkegaard posed the problem: Life can only be understood backwards, but it must be lived forward.

In different words, this is Scriven's point about the difference between making the causes of the past understandable and predicting. It is this problem, and this search for some continuity in knowledge, that drives some thoughtful men to be "scientists" of societies. If what suffices to "know" the past will not do as a way of "knowing" the future, then the expertise of scholars who would counsel governments and rationally change worlds must be of a different order from that of the humanist and everyman. In an attempt to develop this special wisdom, the aspiring scientist of man has fitfully sought causal laws—without much success, of course.

The current thesis is that such seeking is beset by all the difficulties that characterize knowledge of the probable relationships among behaviors *plus* the added difficulties of assigning causal guarantees.

These troubles are compounded by the fact that many questions posed by and to the social "scientist" are asked out of moral concern. (These are usually considered to be the "significant questions." Problems without moral meaning are defined as trivial.)

Given, then, that moral preferences are entwined with most men's thoughts about other men's behaviors (to the approval of most judges and the dismay of some), the choice of causes becomes ethically saturated.[11] This moral impregnation biases causal thinking about man. It determines what may properly be thought of as "causing" behavior. Since the regularities that might give credence to causes are many and modest, the variety of bias that can find causal warrant is great.

There would be "nothing wrong" with such a marketplace of prejudices if the sounder preconceptions were as free to gain guarantee as those biases based on weaker generalities. The trouble with choosing causes is that, outside of methodology textbooks, one does *not* seek for the highest order of correlation upon which to base his causal judgment about social behavior. He seeks, rather, the most congenial assortment of causes.

The search for causes is channeled by the moral segmentation of the world. It has already been remarked that the moral tincturing of causal thinking is visible in the tendency of explicators to assign "causes" to bad behaviors and "purposes" to good acts (Leifer, 1964). Additionally, when an explicator perceives an "influence" exogenous to the actor to be explained, he is more apt to call the influence "causal" when it is disapproved. When the influence is approved, self-determination is more likely to be assigned the actor (de Charms *et al.*, 1965).

In the current use of causes, evil acts must have evil roots. We should find it uncomfortable, if not immoral, to assign bad effects to good causes, and vice versa.

GOOD CAUSE, BAD EFFECT

One of the few hard pieces of information presented concerning education in the Report [The Report of the National Advisory Commission on Civil Disorders, 1968] is that rioters were better educated than those classified as uninvolved, but less educated than counter-rioters. Thus, if the Commission's goal is to forestall disorders by minimizing participation, it would seem that they should have proposed programs to *decrease* educational opportunities for black Americans since the non-involved were the least educated group. Obviously such a suggestion is preposterous, yet it illustrates the unclear connection between specific findings and policy recommendations. (Light, 1968:762, emphasis in the original)

BAD CAUSE, GOOD EFFECT

Senator R. Kennedy: Going into some of these areas and looking at the faces of the children between the ages of 6 and 12, and then comparing, walking along Fifth Avenue and seeing the faces of children between the ages of 6 and 12 who come from very wealthy homes, my impression, strong impression, is that the ones who come from these ghetto areas are much, much happier than the ones who are being pushed along in their programs. Do you think that is true or not?

Dr. Coles: This is a very touchy point and one, of course, immediately runs the risk of being called a romanticist and everything else, but this has been the most puzzling kind of experience for me, because I treated upper middle class children.

How do you tell the contented American middle class that craves every kind of new method of child training — and that has elevated us [psychiatrists] to a position of secular lay priesthood — that their children need suffering and stress? No, you don't tell them that.

Anna Freud, Sigmund Freud's daughter, at times I think has a little more sense than her father, particularly these days: I think that (after she had worked) with children facing the blitz in London, (she) commented . . . that perhaps the mind under suffering develops strength, that the mind that is in luxury not only does not develop but cannot develop, and progressively loses its ability to develop this kind of strength. . . . I think the objective at times of school administrators and even teachers, certainly I know people like me, is to kill that, to say we don't want that. It is inappropriate. It is too much for us. There may even be envy there. . . . (Coles, 1967:45, testifying before the Ribicoff Senate Subcommittee, Hearings on Urban Problems; emphasis supplied)

GOOD CAUSE, BAD EFFECT

A. Smith, Marx, Freud, Jung suggested that at times good comes of evil. More recently, analysis has indicated that evil may come of good: the virtues of white Southerners constitute a burden for the Negro. . . . racisms are demanded by the "decency" of the perpetrator. More villainous persons find such rationalization unnecessary. . . . because men are as "good" as they are, prejudice and discrimination are given additional nourishment. (Schneider and Brodbeck, 1955:150)

Labeling the "evil-causes-evil" notion a "fallacy" is one way by which sociologists have acknowledged that morals intrude upon causes. Another style of acknowledgment is that suggested by LaPiere (1938), but never adequately tested. LaPiere proposes that people think about human conflict in terms of causal explainways that take the form of a "dramatic triad." Social events are personalized and trichotomized as a contention between heroes, villains, and heroines. Good guys, bad guys, and innocent victims.

To the extent to which LaPiere's drama does characterize both lay and professional thought about the causes of social events, there is an obstacle, but not an insurmountable one, against the choice of the more effective causes in competition with the "right" ones.

CAUSAL DRAMATICS APPLIED TO CIVIL DISORDERS, U.S.A., 1964—

The National Advisory Commission on Civil Disorders (1968:10-11): Despite these complexities, certain fundamental matters are clear. Of these, the most fundamental is the racial attitude and behavior of white Americans toward black Americans.

Race prejudice has shaped our history decisively; it now threatens to affect our future.

Additional factors contributing to the disorders include racial discrimination in employment, education, and housing, the growing concentrations of impoverished black ghettos, and ... a widespread belief among Negroes in the existence of police brutality and in "double standard" of justice and protection.

Critic₁ (Friedman, 1969:61): One of the less fortunate results of the black revolution has been the development of a by now familiar ritual in which the white liberal is accused of racism and responds by proclaiming himself and the entire society guilty as charged; the Kerner report was only the official apotheosis of this type of white response to the black challenge of the 60's. No doubt the report has performed a service in the short run by focusing the attention of great numbers of Americans on the degree to which simple racism persists and operates throughout the country, but in the long run its picture of an America pervaded with an undifferentiated disease called "white racism" is unlikely to prove helpful. And even in the short run, the spread of the attitudes embodied in the report may have had a share in helping to provoke the current backlash.

Reviewer₁ (Yinger, 1968:145): The difficulty is not that the report fails to spread the blame, but that it does not go far enough in its search for causes. White racism is a fact, but it also requires explanation. It is an intervening, not an independent, variable. We are not served by continuing a rhetoric of praise and blame . . . . The need is for a careful examination of racism as a system, isolating its causes in the life conditions, the training, and the fears and hopes of various parts of the population. Only then will we be in a position to modify the system effectively.

Of Yinger's proposals, two things: First, he advances causes of the causes and, in so doing, he tells where to look for the roots of racism. His suggested search is itself selective and probably unnecessary. It can be expected to yield no greater knowledge than that difference is disliked. (Compare Giddings on "consciousness of kind.") Second, his reason for research, that *"only then* will we be be in a position to modify the system," commits *non sequitur.* Knowing is not always power, and knowing *these* causes (his) need not resolve *this* difficulty.

Reviewer₂ (Light, 1968:762): Most of the "Recommendations for National Action" . . . are not clearly related to the findings reported in the earlier sections.

It appears that the proposals for action offered in the Riot Commission Report are essentially the best ideas of a large group of informed, dedicated, and thoughtful men. They are well-explicated and justified by common-sense arguments but do not follow in any methodologically clear way from data presented earlier in the Report.

The isolation of the "causes" of civil disorders by the Presidential Commission, and the criticism by some reviewers, illustrate Oakeshott's theme: What is being told in response to "Why did it happen?" is the history of everything that happened and a partial description of what is.

No causal laws need be invoked, except under the pretense of being scientific, and no specific policy based on scientific *knowledge* of its probable consequences ("causes and effects") need follow.

As per LaPiere's model, villains and victims have been named and the role of hero is open in a contest between men of politics and men of "knowledge."

CAUSAL DRAMATICS CONTINUED — SCHOLARS AMONG THE STUDENT REBELS

Rubinstein (1969:134) asks . . . what have been the factors which produced student protest? He finds the following themes in the current literature:

Sampson (1957:1): Discusses a number of "activism inducing contexts" that are multiple and interrelated: The affluent family, the unresponsive university environment, the political and social climate, the ever-present mass media, Vietnam and the draft, and the usual problems of adolescence.

Halleck (1968): Divides causes into "critical hypotheses":

(*a*) Activism as personal pathology, a result of permissive upbringing, affluence, or some family disturbance.

(*b*) Activism as justified crusade — against Vietnam, the "quality of life," or civil rights issues.

(*c*) "Neutral hypotheses" which include increased technology, the mass media, and "reliance on scientism."

Rovit (1968): Traces the history of the "metaphor of the Apocalypse" and its influence upon the new-radical thinking.

Keniston (1968:242): The most important variable influencing rebellious behavior is the threat of violence. . . . the issue of violence is to this generation what the issue of sex was to the Victorian world.

Morality affects the selection of causes, but so also does practicality. When one would apply his knowledge to remedy social affairs, his choice of causes is influenced, not merely by what is morally acceptable as a "cause," but also by what is amenable to intervention. Thus Gouldner notes (1957:96): The applied social scientist inspects his independent variables to determine the extent to which they are accessible to control. Since his ultimate objective involves the furtherance of some kind of change, not all independent variables are equally suitable for this purpose, nor is the one with the highest correlation coefficient always the best.

Insofar as practice affects thought in the studies of man, it may be expected that the most forceful determinants of behavior will be passed over in deference to those congenial to our sense of costs and morality.

If, then, there are these boundaries upon the choice of causes, in addition to those limitations posed by our ignorance, what counsel can one draw?

Given the comforts of causes, we shall not abandon them, but we might aspire, with our ancient Greek cousins, to moderation. If one prefers the scientific explainway, he shall have to build his causes upon the actuary's foundations. If one leaps to causes ahead of the actuarial construction, he is bound to find himself in the arms of the ideologist. This, it seems, is where many social "scientists" land as they move from performing as societal accountants to performing as societal engineers. (Glazer, 1967)

(iv) Causes and ideologies: Where actuarial thinking is aseptic, causal thinking becomes infected by morals, powers, and sides taken, and one is moved from explanations with evidential rules toward beliefs with weaker bases.

It is here contended, as hypothesis for test, that attempts to infer causes from statistical regularities push one toward ideology.

The argument can be proposed by phrasing it as two questions: (a) "Who can best afford to think without causes?" and (b) "Who needs them?"

The man without causes, it is suggested, may be described as:

The man who, on *this* issue, need not take a side.

The man who will not be hurt by knowing how things are. Truth does play favorites; some sides can stand more truth than others.

The fellow who is idly experimental, who can tinker.

The person whose environment seems adequately controlled *for him.*

The man who has a faith or a belief system that precludes certain kinds of questions. This faith may itself be causal or it may define the problem away.

By contrast, the idea of cause and effect is more important for the interventionist in the social arena than for the truthseeker. It is for this reason that all ideologists speak of causes and some scientists do not. The man who needs causes need not be of one piece. He seems to be:

The one for whom old answers no longer suffice.

The man for whom present truths will not do. Painful knowledge can be rejected in the search for the "more fundamental causes" of sorrowful truths. "Are all the data in?" is not so much a question as an expression of hope that things won't be as we now know them.

The man mystified and urged to resolve his mystification with answers in deeds rather than with the answers in words that often lead to doubt and despair.

Hence, the man who would move himself and others to costly action. This requires a promise, dependent upon a picture of what makes the world horrible and what will make it better. The road to heaven need not be as clear as the way to hell; it usually is not. But he who would salvage sad lives talks as though he knew the way.

Cure, it is assumed, will follow from causes accurately known.

(v) Cures without causes: A slogan advanced in justification of knowing the causes of social behaviors is that such knowledge is a necessary step toward the more effective reform of unwanted conduct. The slogan has respectable forebears and today wears varied garb. We have seen it cloaked in the psychoanalytic doctrine that "knowing 'why' we do X frees us from its necessity." It appears in the robes of political scholarship where causal knowledge is a presumed requisite to rational action.

THE CASE FOR CAUSES

Somers (1959:1): If we are to deal intelligently with the medical care problem we must first understand it. We know a wise doctor who, with tongue in cheek, has said, "I often make a mistake in diagnosis, but never in therapy." In social policy, as in medicine, effective therapy depends upon the accuracy of the diagnosis.

SOME CONTRADICTIONS

Rogers (1946:421): Diagnostic knowledge and skill are not necessary for good therapy.

Patterson (1948:158): Since all maladjustment is similar in origin, diagnosis in
terms of symptomatology or etiology or dynamics is not essential to therapy.
Mainord (1962:91): There has never seemed any logical necessity for psychotherapy to be determined by theories of the development of psychopathy.
. . . if we can control the behavior, we believe we also control the feeling.
Camus (1948:189): One can't cure and know at the same time.

The question of the efficacy of causal knowledge in the promotion of rational social action is open. It is enough to challenge the cliché with an
outline of its weaknesses:

(*a*) To regard behaviors to be explained as "symptoms," behind which
"causes" must lie, is itself an interpretation of those behaviors. Unless one
is merely to *believe,* every such interpretation is subject to the terrible question, "How do you know?"

(*b*) Positing cure upon cause requires the ability to defend a choice among
styles of causation. Those who suppose that knowledge of causes is needed
for cures find themselves searching for the "real causes" as opposed to the
proximate correlates and treating the "deeper sources" rather than the
"symptoms."

(*c*) Urging that reform "go to the roots" assumes that one knows where
they are. In addition to the problem of causal style, there is, then, the problem of *causal content.* Any man who enters the political arena and there engages in a search for cures among the causes is bound to have *his* causes
attacked (and his motives as well). Purity of heart will provide only weak
defense. For one example, see Rainwater and Yancey's account (1967) of
what happened to Moynihan.

(*d*) Knowing the cause need not provide a cure. The cause may not be
"available" for intervention. Even when, in principle, it is "available," one
may not have the *power* to intervene. And, too, the cause(s) of unwanted
behaviors may be valued conditions. Thus there is a tradition in criminology
that sees the "root causes" of crime in the social conditions that foster freedom, ambition, and aspiration toward equality.

(*e*) It may be possible to cure without knowing the causes. The allegation
that "symptom treatment" does not effect cures is questionable and, for
certain categories of behavior, false (Eysenck, 1966; Lange and Melamed,
1969; Wolpe, 1966). If this is true for certain classes of individual conduct,
it may apply also to collective behaviors.

Histories have been written of man's successful action in the control of
unwanted behaviors where the "cures" did not depend upon causal analyses.
As a recent example, Bruce (1969) documents the suppression of Thuggee

in nineteenth-century India through the resolute police work of Captain William Sleeman. Prior to Sleeman's untheoretical "cure," Thuggee had flourished for hundreds of years as a secret hereditary religious sect whose members (Thugs) "earned a living" and propitiated their goddess Kali by robbery followed by ritualized strangulation. Thuggee was extinguished without a study of its causes.

It is popular today to argue that controlling actions such as Sleeman's carry implicit theories of the sources of human behavior. This may be true, but it is not the same as claiming that the change of undesirable behaviors requires knowledge of *their* causes.

(f) The search for the "real sources" of action distracts attention from what can be done now, even if the treatment appears "merely symptomatic." It opens the door to special pleading for a preferred program in lieu of a feasible or efficient one.

As illustration of these dangers, the penchant of presidents of the United States to meet behavioral crises with cause-finding committees has been criticized on grounds that are both unfair and just. These criticisms include the allegations that:

The committees are composed of "representatives" rather than experts.[12] It is as though causes were somehow to be delineated most accurately if "points of view" are represented. Thus today's commissions are carefully composed of the right balance of ethnic, religious, and occupational interests.

Committee action temporizes (there may be "good" reason for doing this, of course).

The connection between the facts described and the causes imputed is flimsy. That is, the causes "discovered" are as often wisdom-based as fact-founded. Even some social "scientists" who criticize such committees for their lack of expertise can, in the same breath, say that the "causes" are known without the additional research. So Etzioni (1968b) tells us,

. . . there is very little new in the recommendations of the Kerner Commission (e.g., more jobs, education, houses and welfare for Negroes). Nor need we await the Eisenhower Commission's report to know the close connection between domestic disarmament and the level of serious crimes, between alienation of Negroes and youth and rebellions, between education and respect for authority, law and order.[13]

The causes found are the ones looked for, including the ones we dare say to each other.

The relationship among "causes known," policies recommended, and policies enacted is slim.[14]

(g) The intensive and persistent looking-for-causes may itself become a sickness as debilitating as the one originally to be cured.

(h) The assumption that knowledge of causes enhances efficiency of action incurs the risk, but not the necessity, of confusing *being reasonable* with *being rational*. It confounds amenability to reasons, including those embedded in information ("knowing$_1$"), with behaving rationally ("knowing$_2$" how to get what one wants). Here, the rational man may be such *because* he behaves "unreasonably." When behaving unreasonably is rational, knowing causes may be unnecessary.

(i) Given the variety of causal content and style, the lack of causal laws of human behavior, and the modest statistical regularities upon which causal assumptions are built in practice, "muddling through" or thinking inductively and noncausally may be as rational (applying economic means toward empirical ends) as thinking-with-causes.

LAST WORDS ON CAUSES

Katz and Lazarsfeld (1955:189): The present study should be grouped with studies into the "causes" of crime and accidents, the "reasons" for suicide, voting, etc. In all such researches, a final act is traced back to some earlier point and the "causes" or "reasons" or "determining factors" are singled out. From the beginning there is a *necessary arbitrariness* in such efforts. A woman commits a crime or she chooses to buy a certain brand of coffee; in both cases, her whole preceding life has in a way contributed to this final event. If she had not been born so many years ago, or if the weather had been different that morning, the final act might not have come about at all. In this sense, the general question why doesn't really make sense. It has to be translated into a series of more specific questions aimed at discovering whether a specific set of factors did or did not play an important role. What factors we will need to study will be determined partly by the purpose of the study and partly by the general nature of the area under investigation. (Emphasis in the original)

Pope (1966)

In vain, the sage, with retrospective eye,
Would from the apparent what conclude the why,
Infer the motive from the deed, and show
That what we chanced was what we meant to do.

THE USES OF SCIENTIFIC EXPLANATIONS OF HUMAN BEHAVIOR

The empirical devotion and truthful attitude that characterize the scientific explainaway is for some students sufficient justification of its employment. But it would be false to history if one were to divorce these strange commitments from the hopes they have carried. Science has been "ideologized" by the *philosophes* and their descendants who have wished from knowledge of man more than it has given and more than it may be able to give. The Enlightenment motif has not been truth for its own sake but truth to make us free to build a "rational society." Empiricism was to have killed supernaturalism, pragmatism would be the death of superstition, knowledge of man would humanize him, and the New Jerusalem would be built on factual grounds.

Inheritors of this assumption can scarcely live in the twentieth century without questioning it. Knowledge has not been enough and science will not save us. If, by the science of human behavior, one means a thoughtway such as has been described, two conclusions as to its uses follow:

First, beyond providing instrumentation for the more reliable counting of conduct, beyond, that is, developing techniques for tallying statistical regularities that are largely time- and culture-bound, behavioral science has not moved far enough to fulfill the promise, or the threat, of human engineering.

Economics knows some rules of functional dependence and may be able to prove some causal laws. But political "science" works under a false title[15] and sociology texts are not noted for their causal proofs. Having mined its lore of preliterate folkways, cultural anthropology seems enroute to becoming a social philosophy and a form of social work among "native peoples." Psychology has been described by one of its disappointed disciples as knowing . . . many trivial things certainly, and important things doubtfully.

Second, knowing man scientifically is not only difficult, but it may not provide the answers men need when they ask for explanation. Today's significant questions are moral questions, not the technical ones that science might satisfy. The needs are of *that* moral nature, that some empirical truth is immoral.

In response, men move toward other styles of explanation. They seek not "whatsoever things are true," but "relevant" belief. This search reflects Ortega's *Revolt of the Masses* and underwrites Benda's *Treason of the Clerks.* It betokens, not *The End of Ideology,* but its continuity.

NOTES

[1] Students of the sects that promise better worlds have noted that such ideologies are, in their denial of history, counterinductive. In this vein, Ortega's description of the "mass-man" (1932), the man for whom there is no history, has been prophetic of 1969.

[2] Mazur (1968) calls sociology "the littlest science" precisely because it has added so few new facts to those commonly known. The disappointment results, in some part, from the fact that the inventory of folk generalization about man is so large that novelty must have a low probability. Nevertheless, in response to those who would argue as if behavioral science had discovered nothing true, of value, about man (e.g., Louch, 1966), cf. the sample of questions in Chapter Seven.

[3] The weak predictive power of psychoanalytic thoughtways is variously recorded and may be read in the dubious accounts of psychotherapeutic (largely psychoanalytic) outcome. *Inter alia,* cf. American Psychological Association (1953), Bergin (1966), Cross (1964), Eysenck (1966), Goldberg and Rubin (1964), Hoch (1948), Schwitzgebel (1967), Stollak (1966), and Walsh (1961).

The psychoanalytic defense against this criticism is to hold that the results of psychoanalytic therapy do not test the theory. Thus Weitzman claims (1967:307) that . . . Freud's intention [was] to consider analytic theory and therapy as distinct endeavors. Further, Weitzman argues, psychoanalysis is essentially a postdictive system: It can rationalize events after their occurrence, but cannot predict these events.

To a scientist, a theory that explains everything that has happened but is unable to offer a statement of what is likely to occur becomes "just" aesthetic, or intellectual play, or a nuisance.

[4] A summary of some of the pertinent research may be found in Nettler (1968b).

[5] It seems a safe bet that, within any culture, the perception of continuity will vary with age: The older one is, the more he sees things that have happened before. Hence, too, the "idealism" of the young.

[6] The qualification, "for many people," denotes the probability that individuals differ concerning the issues about which they will permit the question, "How does it happen?" to suffice for (or coincide with) "Why does it happen?" The range of difference and coincidence by personalities across issues has not been plotted.

[7] The literature is large. Students of human behavior will be interested in the debates to be found in MacIver (1942; revised 1964), one of his reviewers (Calhoun, 1942), in Bunge (1959), Michotte (1963), Hirschi and Selvin (1967), and in the symposium edited by Lerner (1965).

[8] Excepting Piaget's studies (1930) among children.

[9] In defense of Hirschi and Selvin's proposed criteria, it might be argued that such apparently impotent, antecedent, nonspurious correlates of an effect *would* prove to be spurious if we knew which additional antecedents for which to control. This, again, involves knowing the boundaries of one's "system," otherwise we are lost in an endless causal regression.

Spurious correlation can *only* be detected within the context of a scientific theory. Simon notes (1968, II:354): To interpret the correlation between variables x and y in causal terms, either here must be added to the system other variables that are most closely connected with x and y, or sufficient assumptions of independence of x and/or y from other variables must be introduced to produce a self-contained system. . . . all causal inference from correlation coefficients involves, explicitly or implicitly, this procedure.

[10]And even here, we who "know better" are challenged by the astrological forecasts syndicated in our daily newspapers.

[11]The religions out of which our morals have grown have been, as indicated, causal-thinking. The Judaeo-Christian ethic assigns blame. The assignment is impregnated with causation. The culture of prepsychological eras had a more limited repertoire of loci upon which to fix responsibility, a "defect" that has been remedied in the age of psychologies by our "knowledge" of the effects of birth trauma, birth order, infant socialization, parental discipline, socioeconomic status, ethnic membership, and school experience upon ego development and adult behavior. (For a satiric jibe at such promiscuous inventory, hear the song "Officer Krupke" from the musical "West Side Story".)

Given this change in the "open-ness" of causal repertoire, it has been hypothesized (Ezer, 1962) that children from intensely religious homes and those who have had more formal religious training would be more likely to think with animistic and anthropomorphic concepts ("pre-causally"). This hypothesis was, in general, confirmed.

[12]If a major corporation faced a sharp and continuing drop in the demand for its products or a prolonged crisis in its labor relations, it might well appoint a high-level, inter-divisionary task force to study the problem and suggest new policies. If the issue involved highly technical matters, experts would likely be appointed to the task force.

When the nation faces riots, political assassinations and a crime wave, the President appoints a commission too. But the members of these national task forces are neither part of his Executive agencies, nor are they experts. (Etzioni, 1968b).

[13]One cannot read Etzioni's list of the "causes" of civil disorder without questioning whether such professional knowledge is any sounder than that produced by the non-expert task forces.

(a) To speak of the relationship between the "alienation" of Negroes and youth, and rebellion, is not to describe a cause of unrest but, rather, a correlate. To be thus-rebellious is to be thus-alienated. Here, another circuity has been posed as a proposition.

(b) What is the relationship between education and respect for authority, law, and order? It may be doubted that it is the linear association among unidimensional categories assumed by Etzioni's statement. There is education and education, and respect for this law but not that one, and for the authority of Che or Mao but not that of Nixon or Hayakawa.

[14]The Riot Commission Report is the third major research effort in this country dealing specifically with issues of race and education. . . . [it] is the only document of the three which proposes a specific sequence of action programs. Thus, although I happen personally to agree with nearly all of the Report's proposals, I think it is important to make clear the relation between the descriptive findings of the earlier sections of the Report and the specific program suggestions offered in the final chapter.

Most of the "Recommendations" . . . are not clearly related to the findings reported in the earlier sections. This, of course, does not necessarily invalidate the proposals offered, nor does it indicate that these proposals are inefficient or not constructive. But this lack of a clear relationship does require that readers of the Report realize that many of the proposals for national action offered in the fields of employment, education, welfare, and housing are not developed directly from the findings of the surveys discussed throughout the Report.* (Light, 1968:762)

[15] For one demonstration, see the plenary session papers of the 1966 meetings of the American Political Science Association collected by de Sola Pool (1967).

A reviewer (Zonis, 1969:427-428) comments: These essays illuminate the essential intellectual anarchy of the discipline.

Moreover, the essays illustrate how the increasing pervasiveness of the scientific ethos is both a symptom and a cause of that anarchy.

. . . Pye reminds us that political science was virtually irrelevant to the problems of the new states — even less useful than the other social sciences.

[These essays] . . . illustrate that "the discipline" of political science is unified neither in terms of concepts nor in theories or methods; . . . and that its relevance to the policy process is questionable.

---

*In his careful analysis of the Plowden Report, David K. Cohen found a similar lack of direct linkage between descriptive data and program development for educational reform in England. *Harvard Educational Review*, 38 (1968): 329-340.

CHAPTER SIX

IDEOLOGICAL EXPLANATIONS

Explanations have been described as the stories we tell each other in attempts to produce some order in our lives. There are other reasons for thinking, or at least for making thinking-sounds, as in the achievement of Malinowski's "phatic communion," the verbal embrace that assuages sullen silence. Whenever men think "systematically, to put two and two together" (and this is always a matter of degree), whenever they give *argument* to their thoughts, they produce orderings of their experience. Even to label life absurd is to define it and argue for an attitude.

Needing to explain has been seen as a joint function of what one's culture asks, part of which is contained in past explanations, and what one's ego sees as problematic. Spinoza's questions are not Scarlett O'Hara's. Where a trivial question receives no sure answer, it can be forgotten. Where a more important question demands response, explanations are invented. The empathetic explainway has a long history and a currency in new mintage, the psychological.

The scientific explainway also has an ancient lineage to which varied application and value have been accorded. It has proved successful in mapping reality and it is identified by its peculiar preference for truth and one distinctive test, among others: The agreement between the map (the explanatory tale) and one's arrival at his destination when he follows it. There is good reason, etymologically and philosophically, for regarding the explanations scientifically derived as *knowledge*. By contrast, all other explanations express *beliefs*. The distinction is in the purposes served by the ideas and their consequently differing tests.

We do not take thought only to draw maps of reality. We symbolize our worlds also in order to judge them. Evaluation is a principal dimension of linguistic use (Osgood, 1957), and it is a dimension that confounds the description of human behavior (Peabody, 1968). It follows that the request for explanation is satisfied by knowledge only in special circumstances. When directed toward conduct, it is more frequently a request for a judgmental ordering that will be answered by placing the explicandum in its niche of matters valued or deplored.[1]

Upon such premise, one need not expect the uncertain regularities of a scientific explainway to satisfy many of the questions we ask about each other. Another style of story is substituted, a story that may not be true but that is "good enough." Such stories may be untrue, not merely because of the deficiencies of knowing but, more to the point, because the calls for explanation ask questions of preference for which facts are no answer.[2]

"Truth" is a good word that everyone claims for his side and only reluctantly abandons. The man who asks ethical questions wants them resolved in "truth."[3] If facts will not do as answers to moral doubts—and ultimately they must fail by definition of what is moral—then "truth" is translated from the empiric and declarative to that which is prescriptive and coherent. Thus one speaks of "moral truths," or "poetic" ones, whose referent is not a statement about how things are, but a statement in prescriptive and nonreferential language that "makes sense" because it strikes chords of conditioned abstractions.

Myths may tell coherent stories as they order the world morally, and they may be judged satisfying because of this, but they may not be used as maps of reality without high cost.

All such explanations with diminished concern for the factual can be defined residually, for present purposes, and grouped under the convenient yet risky rubric of "ideology." The theme common to ideological explanation is its *group-supported patterning of beliefs of inadequate empirical warrant, where such beliefs are energizing, in attack or defense of values, and comprehensive.*

Such a definition, and criteria to be added, raises the hobgoblin of the sharp delineation of explainways, a specter to be downed. Modes of explanation are offered in a mix of thought-styles as we pique ourselves about human behavior. The procedures here characterized as distinctive represent a gradient of thoughtways. We think *more or less* empathetically or scientifically or ideologically about conduct *x* in circumstance *y* as opposed to behavior *b* in situation *c*. Just as science is known by its peculiar desiderata imperfectly achieved, so, too, ideology is recognized by criteria that need not apply uniformly.

CRITERIA OF IDEOLOGY

It is always dangerous to use a word with an emotional history. The twists of meaning assigned "ideology" have certainly been dramatic, the remaining meanings are heavily connotative, and to borrow such a term is to hazard others claiming their property.

Ideologie was a neologism coined by Destutt de Tracy toward the end of the eighteenth century. The turns of the word's history tell us something about the legitimacy of its present employment as both a descriptive term and a pejorative label. The word as invented meant much that twentieth-century students have in mind when they aspire toward a "social science." "Ideology" was to have been a means of cleansing thought of the contaminants of religious faith, ancestral authority, and the biases of self-interest. It would do this by reducing ideas to their atoms of sense-perception. Hence, a "science of ideas" would discover "reality" and lead de Tracy and his *ideologues* to the "rational society" built firmly on knowledge as opposed to faith and constructed by means of education.

The naïveté is familiar and persistent. It has not been cured by Marx and his followers who stood this term, like much else, on its head. Where ideology for de Tracy would be a science of ideas and a road to truth, ideology for Marx came to mean, among other things,[4] "false consciousness." Ideas of the world, the Marxist knows, are socially conditioned, bound in the service of class interests and, unless freed of such bondage, inevitably prejudiced and false. But to speak of another man's ideas as false implies a stance from which truth can be known. If one's . . . social being . . . determines

consciousness . . . (Marx, 1950:363) how can one speak, with Marx, o
what "mankind" needs or does? The answer reverts to the hopes of the
ideologues: "Consciousness" is false because society is "irrational." Thi
historical defect will be overcome when men attain power over their fate
In Lichtheim's words (1967:21): Consciousness is ideological because it i
powerless. When it becomes the determining factor, it sheds its blinkers along
with its dependence on material circumstances. *A rational order is one in whicl
thinking determines being.* Men will be free when they are able to produc
their own circumstances. . . . When this state has been reached, it will n
longer be possible to speak of historical "laws," for history is subject to "laws"
only insofar as it is unconscious. . . . The mature consciousness which in retro
spect comprehends the necessity of this lengthy process of "prehistory" wil
not be an ideological one: it will be shared by all men, and will mark mankind'
understanding of its own past. (Emphasis in the original)

To accept this Marxist story about the conditions of false belief is ir
itself to think ideologically insofar as the tale invokes unproved and unprov
able propositions. It is not necessary to accept or reject the Marxian proph
ecy about the destiny of "false consciousness" in order to accord Mar>
principal responsibility for giving ideology its contra-Tracean, moder
meaning. However the term is disputed in the twentieth century, and how
ever it is evaluated, it carries this kernel of Marx's definition which we have
translated more generally: *The hallmark of the ideological explainway is tha
it rests on statements false, unproved, or unprovable through reference to empirica
rules.*

This definition in no wise makes such explanation unnecessary, "ground
less," or unworthy of subscription. It does not make ideology "nothing bu
lies," nor does it hold that ideological bias cannot be productive of truth
Bias may be fruitful.

Such a definition does say that the propositions of an ideological expla
nation are more assumed than known and careless of the verification of em
pirical declarations. Ideology persists despite the facts. Careless of truth, i
changes the meaning of truth (pp. 88-92), and it does so in satisfaction o
its distinctive motives that are not those of the scientist.

Ideology, directed toward evaluating the world and correcting it, is les:
concerned with knowledge than with justice. This characterization rests or
our ability to distinguish facts and values, although ideologies would fuse
them (Bergmann, 1968). Justice remains a valued state, and knowledge, a
matter of fact.

Ideological explanations, then, become operative as they are believed, rather than as they are verified. They are defensive of human needs, including some needs those beliefs may have themselves created. They become, therefore, immune to factual disproof, and subject to zeal.

This is not necessarily to speak pejoratively. Believing what cannot, or has not, been proved is a condition of life, a result of imperfect knowledge and of our asking some kinds of question, like the moral ones, for which empirical consequence (apart from personal satisfaction) is no answer.

Where the scientific explainway is good for reality-testing, the ideological mode serves other ends. It is useful as a societal cement, collective motivant, and personal integrant. To borrow Mannheim's distinction (1936), "ideologies" legitimize the way things are; their counterparts in "utopias" justify their change. Ideologies[5] define "our poor" and "our kind." They identify the forces against which our ideals must struggle, and they point to what is or should be rewarded in this or later worlds. Life is no longer absurd. Ideology tells the point of it all. It describes the forces of light and darkness and names the innocent to be saved. Men who "know" ideology "believe in that something greater than themselves" that makes their lives meaningful. They are joined with others and are themselves "made whole."

The beliefs that thus unite men divide them, but this paradox does not deny these functions.[6]

The theme of ideology is doctrine, and there are variations on it. Ideology can encompass empathetic explanations; it usually does, although, in their everyday form, empathetic appeals lack that system that deserves such a title. Ideology includes the interwoven explainways called "magical," "mythical," and "religious." It prevails in the moral beliefs we need and in the political and juridical perspectives invoked in their name. Ideology resides in the explanatory principles of "luck," "fate," and "God's will." It is the prevailing way of explaining collective behavior and it combines with empathy to clarify individual action.

With such functional foundation, we shall not abandon ideological explanation. Its persistence is both what ails us and what cures us and a good reason why science will not save us.

At the antipodes, the explanations that are scientific and ideological can be distinguished by what satisfies them, and what satisfies them may be read as the other face of what moves them.

The scientific explanation will satisfy curiosity and, where applicable, improve prediction. The ideological explanation may also allay curiosity while it answers outrage and personal interest. In application, its predictive record is ambiguous. Both thoughtways are engaged to describe futures, the difference lies in their methods. Where the scientist would forecast by extrapolation or by inference from replicated observations of regularities or through derivations from theories that connect series of such replicated observations, the ideologist would prophesy from authority and less empiric theory, both of which provide reasons that favor his side.[7]

Scientific truth is assessed by the concordance of facts with the expectations they arouse. Ideological truth is weighed morally; what is true is what is "socially useful," as per Gletkin (see p. 107). As a consequence, the scientist seeks objectivity; the ideologist denies its possibility. As a corollary, the scientist's preference is for statements that can be falsified; the ideologist's, for those that cannot.

The ideologist assures us that every description of the social world is distorted and that, therefore, sociologies, political "sciences," and histories are to be judged, not by their adherence to fact, but by their service to moral causes.

TRUTH AS UTILITY, AGAIN

Zinn (1967): In a world where justice is maldistributed, historically and now, there is no such thing as a "neutral" or "respresentative" recapitulation of the facts. (P. 180)

Truth only in relation to what is or was is one-dimensional. Historical writing is most true when it is appropriate simultaneously to what was in the past, to the condition of the present, and to what should be in the future. (P. 181)

There is an immense intellectual energy in the United States devoted to inspecting the past, but only a tiny amount of this is deliberately directed to the solution of vital problems: racism, poverty, war, repression, loneliness, alienation, imprisonment. Where historical research has been useful, it has often been by chance rather than by design, in accord with a kind of trickle-down theory. (P. 176)[8]

Another full circle has been turned in the career of a concept. From a "science of ideas" that would allow man to build a "rational society" upon sensate truth, "ideology" has been converted to an empiric-appealing theology that devalues objectivity and substitutes interested interpretation.

There are other litmus tests that distinguish the ideological explainway.

Ideologies are marked by chains of reasoning that have a high mixture of facts and value and which, therefore, permit the masquerade of values as facts. Bergmann (1968:129) holds that the disguise energizes the preference: The motive power of a value judgment is often greatly increased when it appears . . . not under its proper logical flag as a value judgment but in the disguise of a statement of fact.

Tests follow. One is syntactic. It is possible to construct an "ideology sentence-ratio," the proportion of hortatory-prescriptive sentences[9] reliably identified in an explanatory thesis compared with the proportion of declarative sentences. With some cutting-points adopted as defining the borderland between ideological thinking and other modes, the ratio would allow a test of the correlated distinctions of an ideology here advanced.[10]

A related test is logical. If values and facts *can* be distinguished, and if ideology serves values by coloring them as facts, logical power should be reduced as one moves into ideological areas. A test of illogic can be constructed, such as the use of neutral and value-loaded syllogisms to be judged for validity. The discrepancy between one's neutral logic and his valued logic is a measure of ideological distortion (Lefford, 1946).

It is also possible, although tedious, to read a student of the social for his logic, rather than his content, and to illustrate, as Bergmann has (1968:135-137), the infection of logic by values. Pareto's *Mind and Society* is an encyclopedia of such distortion.

It has been suggested that the ideological impulse toward illogic can be discerned in the contrasting explanatory modes applied to the actors in the dramatic triad. In the context of contemporary "liberalism," for example, Minogue holds (1968:8-10) that environmental determinism "explains" the bad behavior of victims but not that of villains or heroes. The victim, when delinquent, is seen as morally conditioned, but his oppressor and his savior are assumed to be morally free. Such logical inconsistency permits the exercise of moral indignation and the differential assignment of blame.

Again, such logic-failure is subject to test, as through a content analysis of quarrels. In ideology, the generator of this failure is assumed to be the tension between explaining and persuading.

A third test for ideology involves weighing an explanatory tale for its nonfactual load. This test must correlate with the "ideology sentence-ratio," but it is not the same. Following Bergmann's suggestion, it is expected that, the higher the ideological content, the heavier the burden of sentences that *appear* descriptive, but that say nothing truthful. It is important here to distinguish between statements offered as hypotheses and assumptions written as facts. This test calls it "ideology" as the explicator confuses his unverified assumptions with facts of life.

The test is applied by reading an essay's *declarative* sentences with two questions in mind: "What does the sentence mean?" and, if that seems clear, "How is what is declared known?"

Much of what we read in current literature pleases or angers us because of the sides taken. By contrast, it is not known how many people read how much for *information*. Such reading seems difficult. The difficulty can be illustrated by citing some declarations of contemporary social "scientists" that have had an appeal as "true" to many of our students in sociology. In fact, many, but not all, argue in favor of the validity of such propositions, all of which are unproved, unprovable, or false. Worse, some of the statements below are not "merely" false; they are the *opposite* of what seems known as true.

The point here is not necessarily to impugn in total the theses from which the appealing statements are drawn, but, rather, to corroborate for expert testifiers what the philosopher Morris Cohen said of professors: No one can get up in front of a class and refrain from saying more than he knows.

TRACES OF IDEOLOGY AMONG THE "SCIENTISTS"

Menninger (1968:204): Being against punishment is not a sentimental conviction. It is a logical conclusion drawn from scientific experience.

Moynihan (1967:38): The simple fact—it's a basic rule of social science—is that people by and large do their best. People do not cheat. (With reference to what people might do with their "family allowances.")[11]

Krech and Crutchfield (1948): To reduce widespread aggressions which can readily be channeled into war, the general level of frustration of all the American people must be alleviated. This means raising the standard of living of all classes of Americans.[12] (P. 609)

The businessman who sees a depression just around the corner must be shown that extending democratic practices to the economic, racial, and political field might avert a malfunctioning of the economic system.[13] (P. 527)

Just as the provision of an adequate standard of living for all people is the major economic task of the world today, so the provision for adequate participation and representation of all people in their governments is the prime political task of the world today. Both are indispensable to enduring peace.[14] (P. 610)

Sherif and Cantril (1947:593): It is obvious . . . that a young man who is economically secure enough either to marry or to have girl friends is not nearly so likely to get tangled up with problems of sex as is a young man similarly motivated biologically but who cannot afford the normal sexual outlets of our society.[15]

This game can be played endlessly with the words of social "scientists." It does not vitiate every attempt to know about social behavior. It points to a vulnerability: That writing what is not true, or what is unprovable, *as* social "science," is everyman's possibility as he thinks to move his world. The thesis, again, is "only" that wanting corrupts knowing, and we call him "ideologist" who can't see the difference. (Not all the men cited above suffer this myopia.)

There are additional marks of ideology.

Since ideologies invoke the dramatic triad, it is to be expected that they be characterized by "conspiracy theories" of history in which causes are framed as good and bad forces, usually personalized, contesting the fate of some heroine.

Cynicism follows. The cynic attributes baser motives to his opponent's actions, including his antagonist's allegations of intent, than he would allow. The ideological explicator, who today has usually read some Marx, "knows" that the *other* man's religion, *his* law and *his* science, are smokescreens camouflaging the interested position of a class-man. Seeing beliefs as weapons, rather than as hypotheses subject to test, he evaluates statements by "tele-psyching" the group interests they supposedly serve. Arguments are met, not by disproof, but by reference to the "interests" they advance or betray. The ideologist agrees with Mao (1967:9): We should support whatever the enemy opposes and oppose whatever the enemy supports.

Necessarily, the ideologist finds it difficult to see the error in the genetic fallacy. For him, *argumenta ad hominem* are tools, not logical errors. Identifying "who said it," and, hence, the "social location" of an argument, becomes, for the ideologist, an important test of a statement's validity.[16]

Again, language tells. The ideological explanation—evaluating as it describes, but more concerned with the first function; seeing "causes" personified in good men and bad ones; testing propositions by their sources and prone, therefore, to thoughts *ad hominem*—such explanation finds it satisfying to "call names." "Calling names" refers, of course, not to the use of descriptive labels but, rather, to the placement of emotionalized tags on the moral assignments given the "forces of history." One recognizes ideology as the ratio of "names called" increases.

The ideological explainway has been distinguished from the scientific by its opposed attitude to truth and objectivity, by its use of unproved and unprovable premises, and by its high saturation with ethical judgments of the matters to be explained. Other distinctions follow.

The practice of both ideological and scientific thinking may unite men and thus add purpose to their individual lives. However, where a science provides an empirical ground upon which differences can be resolved, an ideology, rooted in belief and value and less concerned with fact, divides men as it unites them and permits no mode of reconciliation other than its acceptance. The slogan "No compromise" is that of the believer, not the knower.

Sceptical of social knowledge, since it always takes sides,[17] ideological explanation is advanced authoritatively. It rests heavily upon exegesis ("what the founder really meant"). It can be recognized by its compulsion to conversion and its closure to variant interpretations. Its sure sign is emotionality in its defense.

Ideology is action-oriented. The sterile descriptions read from the actuary's tables do not tell "what is to be done." Ideologies do. The urge to act with one's explanations is energized by the tendency to evaluate what one describes. It may be partly measured in explanations by the ideology sentence-ratio. (P. 181)

The title of "ideology" is reserved for such patterns of belief that have been given group-approval (an idiosyncratic world-view doesn't count). One need not have formally joined the group creative of an ideology to enjoy its perspectives. Membership may be added but, with or without it, there are signs by which the profession of ideology can be discerned.

The story style of the ideological explainway is not only highly evaluative, it is also repetitive and comprehensive. Much is reduced to little. A few principles cover great territory. "Causes" are invoked, but they are not many.

Marxism and Freudianism, to take two modern examples of powerful ideologies, address themselves to questions beyond their origins in economics and psychology. They "explain" social change and stability, familial and religious associations, war and peace, crime and conformity, manners, morals, and the source of laws. Thus the author of a large work on Marxian thought interprets the Marxist philosophy as . . . *a complete system of man, nature, and history.* (Calvez, 1956, emphasis his)

The repetitive theme of a few principles widely applied is facilitated by jargon. The difference between the special idiom of a science and that of an ideology is in its use; the former is preserved as it points to distinctive operations or processes observed; the latter as it organizes emotion, expresses sentiment, and serves *cultus*.

Cultus refers to the practices that a believing group develops as its distinctive mode of "meeting the world," which includes establishing right relations with its unseen powers when these are part of the belief system. Cultus does more, however, than tell its participants how to orient themselves toward the values defended by their ideology. Ideologies affiliate, while they separate. Cultus attests commitment to a way of life and one's colleagues in it.

Idiom is one such sign, a potent one. So, too, are salutes and uniforms (including the anti-uniform uniforms), colors and odors, foods and drinks, postures, musics and dances, arts, and modes of manners and toilet.

Believing, taking a stand, communing with the right ones and disdaining the wrong, all these activities are signified to ourselves, and our friends and enemies, by the cultus we practice.

In this, the ideological explainway is again comprehensive, as it is in its reduction of many questions to few answers.

To explain matters ideologically is to become a "whole man," precisely like the religious one. Ideology, like religion, invests the totality of one's life with *this* meaning. By contrast, the man who aspires to think scientifically is segmented. He thinks scientifically only in certain provinces, about some kinds of question, and his religion, like his politics, can be a matter apart. The great biologist need *not* be a scientist of politics.

As one thinks ideologically, and finds it satisfying, spheres of activity that might once have been autonomous, enjoyed for their own sakes, now "have meaning" and are embraced by the commitments defined in the belief system.

For the man who has discovered psychoanalysis, all of his life becomes explicable from a few principles — his taste in food and women, his choice of career, club, and car, and why he got drunk last Saturday night. Dimensions of conduct once left unexplained are drawn within the orbit of matters to be clarified. Questions are asked, where once there were none, because answers are available.[18]

Similarly for the man who finds his religion in political vision. It becomes incomprehensible to him that others will not devote all living to the mandates of his explanatory construction. Everything becomes political —

painting, sports, and the cinema, work, architecture, anthropology, and the relations between man and woman. For him, bastions of ideological independence, like the university, become immoral.[19] One does not seek truth, dispassionately. One asks, instead, "Knowledge for what?" and seeks beliefs that are "relevant."

In summary, objective tests of the ideological explainway have been suggested that, by degree, distinguish it from other styles of explanation. These tests are applicable through a content analysis of competing explanations, oral or written.

(a) The ideological explanation is recognized with an increase in the proportion of nonfactual sentences offered as declarations. ("Nonfactual" means ambiguous and unprovable or without empirical warrant.)

(b) Such explanation employs a high ratio of hortatory-prescriptive to declarative sentence.

(c) A difficult test to apply is that for logic-failure. One touches ideology as the logical power of an explicator, known for neutral subjects, decreases comparatively with its application to interested topics.

(d) Ideologies prefer "conspiracy theories" of history. (This does not always make them false, of course.)

(e) Ideological explanation denies the possibility of "objectivity." It cites facts where they suit, but it holds all explanations of social behavior to be distorted. Its "cure" for this distortion consists of: (i) Stating one's own motives (Myrdal, 1942: Appendix II). (ii) Locating the "social position" from which the competing thesis allegedly originates. Both these "methods" are alien to the scientific explainway.

(f) As a consequence of (e), the ideological explicator is prone to employ argumenta ad hominem as a test of the validity of propositions. He has difficulty, therefore, seeing the error in the genetic fallacy. Correlatively, he has difficulty describing this fault, and he is likely to "call names" as part of his argument.

(g) By comparison with other explanatory modes, the ideological explanation resorts to authority and is concerned with exegesis.

(h) The group-integrating function of ideology is exemplified by the practices of: Seeking converts, responding to criticism with "excess" emotion and an abuse of the critic's motives, and developing cultus.

(i) The ideological explanation calls its auditors to action.

WHERE IDEOLOGY ENDS

There is no end to ideology, but there are consequences.

When men explain men without reference to the observed regularities of their behavior, they do so in two ways that may be one: They do so "ideologically," that is, with false beliefs or unprovables, many, but not all of which, are founded on empathy. Allowing for overlap, it might be said that ideologies serve as explanations of collective behaviors as empathetic ones do in the clarification of individual action; they fill the needs of curiosity left by the gaps in knowledge.

Knowledge of human behavior, we have seen, is difficult to come by. But curiosity will not wait, nor will our problems, and both are answered with uncertain facts and more certain faith. The question, then, that looms from our discussion concerns the results of acting in ignorance. The question is ancient and doubtfully answered, except in minute contexts. There are disadvantages to ignorance, we assume, and there are benefits, we have been assured (Moore and Tumin, 1949).

The counsel that derives from our explorations is advice against arrogance. It suggests that the desire to do permits preference to masquerade as fact and belief as knowledge.

This causal asymmetry assures some continuity to human history.

NOTES

[1] This sentence should be read as a hypothesis. Some evidence for it has been presented in Chapter Three. However, there has been no research that would definitively support the contention "more frequently."

[2] Moral questions are the major kinds of such preferential query. Men who would save us with knowledge cannot accommodate the possibility that moral conflict will not dissolve when saturated in facts.

The debate has a long history and it continues. Modern critics of "naturalistic" ethics trace their ancestry to Hume who, it is believed, showed the impossibility of deducing prescriptions from descriptions (1874:1): There has been an opinion, very industriously propagated by certain philosophers, that morality is susceptible of demonstration; and though no one has ever been able to advance a single step in those demonstrations, yet it is taken for granted that this science may be brought to an equal certainty with geometry or algebra.

Hume notwithstanding, the connections between moral opinion and factual belief remain in dispute. Foot (1958:505), for example, argues that "objective relationships" between facts and values do "exist" in at least two senses: logical, in that . . . factual premises might *entail* evaluative conclusions, and evidential, in that facts . . . might count as *evidence* for moral judgments. (Emphasis in the original)

The latter of Foot's contentions is not at issue here; the former is. For a sample of recent arguments on the factual entailment of morals, see Ayer (1936), Bennett (1960), Cohen (1959), Edel (1955), Glassen (1959), Hare (1952), Hudson (1959, 1962), Humbert (1963), Kerner (1962), Kolenda (1958), Lawrence (1961), Nicholson (1960), Stevenson (1963), Stigen (1960), and von Mises (1956: Chaps. 25-26).

Many religious men, in contrast with those "merely" moral, have not needed facts to substantiate their ethics. This modern penchant seems, again, a contagion spread from the success of science and from the Enlightenment urge to be "rational" about nonrational matters.

Wittgenstein, among other religious men for example, *restored the boundaries between facts and values.* The Nature of the Good, he wrote in 1930, has nothing to do with the facts, and so cannot be explained by any proposition. (Cited by Toulmin, 1969:69) Toulmin describes Wittgenstein as . . . feeling that the world of facts is *inherently valueless* . . . . Whatever exists in the world of facts, and can accordingly be "stated" or "represented" by the regular use of language, must *on that account alone* be dismissed as irrelevant to the deeper questions of ethics and religion. So, at this deepest level of all, the realm of facts and the realm of values were — for Wittgenstein — completely dissociated. (*Ibid.:*64, emphasis in the original)

[3] Thus Bergmann notes (1968:129) that the American Declaration of Independence would have less impact if it read . . . "These we hold to be self-evident value judgments" instead of the clarion call "These truths we hold to be self-evident."

[4] "Among other things" because Marx was not unambiguous as to the reference of "ideology." Whereas it might be "ideological" to be unaware of one's "true role" in history, it might also be "ideological" to represent self-consciously the "meaning" of an epoch. (Lichtheim, 1967: Chap. 1)

[5] Unless otherwise indicated, the present use of "ideology" includes both of Mannheim's senses.

[6] Note that "brother" is an effective term of unity insofar as it separates "us" from "them." It is used selectively.

[7] Gottheil (1966) provides an interesting exercise in testing the logical fit of Marxian theory with the predictions derived from it. Although Gottheil's objective is not to . . . pronounce judgment on the accuracy of the predictions in the historical sense . . . (p. 4), his work can be read as a chronicle of both the *aperçus* given by an evaluative "character-reading" of capitalism and the occlusion of foresight generated by hate and hope.

[8] In reply to Zinn:

(*a*) A "neutral" or "representative" recapitulation of the facts may or may not be possible *regardless* of the distribution of justice.

(*b*) Calling history "most true" when it is "appropriate" begs all questions and opens the door to such rewriting of histories as Orwell foresaw in his *1984.* It is a sentiment to which Commissar Gletkin would assent (cf. p. 107).

(*c*) When Zinn calls for historians to devote more "intellectual energy" to the solution of vital problems, he should be advised that other students of like legislative persuasion, but further to his left, hold applied sociology . . . to be sell-out sociology because it aims to provide the agencies of social control and their client power centers with solutions to problems which constitute a threat to existing social arrangements. (Molotch, 1969:51)

[9] Two kinds of prescription may be distinguished. The one is *instrumental:* "Given goal *x*, this is the most efficient means. The other is *moral:* "This is the goal to be sought."

Only the second type of prescription is to be counted in calculating this ratio.

[10] The test would parallel Hart's study, previously cited (Chapter Four, note 12), on the correlates of evaluative thinking.

[11] If that is a "basic rule" of social science, it's one without adequate test. The uses of "family allowances" are not known, but the inclusion of the statement about cheating is unfortunate. Much depends on the context:

(*a*) All employees of a chain store were run through his (Keeler's) polygraph when the company complained it was losing more than one million dollars annually through petty thefts. Polygraph records indicated that fully three out of four employees were pilfering funds. This and subsequent experiences led Keeler to pronounce a rather cynical dictum generally held by lie-detection experts today: "65 per cent of people who handle money take money . . . ." (Deutsch, 1950:154-155)

(*b*) Lie-detector tests of employees of certain Chicago banks showed that 20 per cent had taken money or property, and in almost all cases the tests were supported by confessions. Similarly, lie-detector tests of a cross-section sample of the employees of a chain store indicated that about 75 per cent had taken money or merchandise from the store. (McEvoy, 1941:70)

(*c*) The Comptroller of Currency reported that about three fourths of the national banks examined in one period were violating the national banking laws and that dishonesty was found in 50.5 per cent of the national bank failures in the years 1865-1899, and 61.4 per cent in the years 1900-1919. (Cressey, 1953:185)

(*d*) Undersecretary of the Treasury Fred A. Scribner, Jr., reported that a Treasury examination of 1956 income tax returns discovered that taxpayers had failed to report almost $4,500,000,000 of interest and dividends received during that year. (Sahlman, 1959:447)

(*e*) Investigators carefully dropped stamped, addressed postcards, letters, and letters bearing a lead coin simulating a 50-cent piece in various cities of the East and Midwest. Seventy-two per cent of the postcards were returned; 85 per cent of the blank letters; 54 per cent of the "coin-carrying" letters. "We conclude . . . that the public at large is very strikingly altruistic, manifesting obligingness, consideration, and responsibility. A sharp decline in the reliability of the public sets in under the effects of suggestion of financial gain. One third of the altruistically minded are converted to selfish behavior. It is probable that an even larger proportion of the public at large is unreliable in such a financial matter. (Merritt and Fowler, 1948:93)

(*f*) Hume said one could be sufficiently sure about certain aspects of human nature to predict with accuracy what would happen to a quantity of gold left unguarded in a populous place. On the basis of human experience in a free society one can now say the same of anything, of however little value, that is portable. For in all our centers of dense population any possessions left unguarded on the doorstep — trash receptacles and the like — disappear as if by magic. (F. Lundberg, 1954: 289)

(*g*) *Reader's Digest* Survey, 1941:
Of 347 garages visited, 63 per cent were dishonest.
Of 304 radio shops, 64 per cent were dishonest.
Of 462 watchmakers, 49 per cent were dishonest.

(*h*) The diary of a vandalized car in a middle-class residential neighborhood, New York City, as recorded by psychologists (*Time*, 1969:62-65): By the end of the first 26 hours, a steady parade of vandals had removed the battery, radiator, air cleaner, radio antenna, windshield wipers, right-hand-side chrome strip, hubcaps, a set of jumper cables, a gas can, a can of car wax, and the left rear tire (the other tires were too worn to be interesting). Nine hours later, random destruction began. . . .

. . . most of the car stripping took place in broad daylight. All of the theft was done by clean-cut, well-dressed middle-class people. Furthermore, the major theft and damage was always observed by someone else.

[12] The relationship between level of living, improvement of it, and individual aggression is neither so direct nor in the direction stated.

The relationship between individual frustration, individual aggression, and warring has not been demonstrated. The history of wars makes one question it (Wright, 1964; Sorokin, 1937).

[13] The relationship between the practice of democracy in industry and the viability of an economic system is not known.

[14] The relationship between popular representation in government and that government's international belligerence is not as stated (Sorokin, 1937).

[15] "Girl friends" can be variously defined. As regards opportunity for heterosexual experience, the Kinsey studies (1948), among others, show that, at the time of the Sherif-Cantril allegation, the *reverse* association held true between socioeconomic status and heterosexual activity. By now, the "new morality" may have moved "economically secure" lads toward greater sexual equality with their "underprivileged" contemporaries.

[16] Students of societies exhibit difficulty in learning the genetic fallacy. They are so habituated to evaluating the validity of a "social" proposition by its authorship that *defining* this logical error is itself a task. This habituation renders learners vulnerable to ideologies.

The characterization of the ideologist advanced here is open to test. We should expect that people who explain social events with a high ratio of hortatory to declarative sentences (who score "high" on the "ideology sentence-ratio") are also more likely to commit the genetic fallacy.

[17] Truth "takes side," not out of partisan intent, but because sides taken are not equally favored by what-is-so.

In areas of social policy, facts are simply not neutral. . . . In social science, data are political. Most social arrangements rest on assumptions about the "facts" of a given situation. To challenge such facts is also to challenge those social arrangements. . . . Walter B. Miller has suggested that because this is so there may even be a "direct incompatibility between careful evaluative research and the political process." (Moynihan, 1967:37)

[18] Bell (1966a:712) has defined an ideologist as a man running down the street shouting, I've got an answer! Who's got a question?

[19] Cf. Chapter Seven, note 17.

Men think, sometimes, but not always, about improving their lives, and those of others.[1]

Their attitudes toward improvement have taken on a lopsided polarity. Nineteenth-century notions of progress, leaning on the promise of a societal evolution, "knew" that things would automatically get better. Nature guaranteed it. "Better worlds" need not be enacted; perhaps they could not be. They were crescive. They "just grew" that way.

"Progress," in the twentieth century, remains a battered hope, not yet abandoned. The engine of progress has been changed, however. Social Darwinism is reactionary. Today's progressives are activists, and occasional rationalists.[2] They believe that matters do not improve by "letting them be," but that more decent worlds can be made, a result of human intention, organization, and plan.

The contrast is between *letting* the world improve and *making* it do so. There is a second axis to this argument, the way of *yoga*. Depending on its interpreter, it says either that making worlds better is an irrelevant task or, in its more Western version, that the world may improve if each man improves himself — particularly, if he improves himself in his relations with me, and I with him.

This is the debate between Koestler's *Yogi and Commissar* (1945). Among "intellectuals" throughout the world, the debate has been won by Koestler's "commissars." Within professional associations of social "scientists," *laissez faire* or the improving of "you and me" is a denigrated minority position, if it can be called a "position" at all. Intellectuals, professionally incorporated or solo, would be physicians of the body politic.

The majority attitude in support of the purposeful betterment of the world itself takes on many hues. At the infrared end of this spectrum are those who see betterment in destruction, the "reasoning" being that the achievement of justice (an improvement) requires revenge[3] (perhaps the oldest idea of "being just"), and that the destruction of "the worst of all societies"[4] leaves the world a better place.[5]

This side of the spectrum calls most violently for action. Problems are to be solved. People are to be polarized and neutrality "neutralized." He who is not with us is against us. The hypocrisy of objectivity and innocent study (Cohn-Bendit *et al.*, 1968) is to be exposed and denied. Social thought is to be politicized.

Social "science" will be revealed as ideology, masking economic interest. The concepts of a sociology will themselves be analyzed as "static" or "dynamic," as with the revolution or against it, as taking the side of "underdogs" or of their oppressors.

Examples of this argument are common. They range from Myrdal's early attack on the idea of "the mores" as a conserving concept (1942: Appendix II) to the Nanterre declaration of the proper uses of sociology (Cohn-Bendit, 1968; Brooks, 1968).

For those students who would be "scientists" of societies, the meliorist impulse and these activist arguments are guaranteed to be schizophrenogenic. Like most men in the middle of a moral contest, the "liberal" student suffers Bateson's "double-bind" (1956). He would seek the truth and tell it, and still find himself on the "right" side,[6] which is usually on the left.

He at once acknowledges the validity of arguments that depreciate his science and undercut his objectivity and yet would hold himself, before his publics, as scientist. One can follow these twists of impulse in the social "scientist" with sympathy, as when Bell (1969) reviews a work on *The Uses of Sociology.* Deference is given the possibility that sociological concepts may be "elitist." Then, to balance this admission, "underdog perspectives" may also be distortions. Yet the reviewer concludes that: People are starving. Cities are being burned. Nuclear war casts its shadow. And sociology—and I mean the *scientific* study of society—has some role to play in helping to solve the world's problems. (P. 422, emphasis in the original)

Granted, the question persists, "What role?" And it will be answered.

But the answer will not allow an easy "out" from the schizoid "bind." The way out cannot be found by "making one's values known" (Myrdal, 1942) or consciously choosing sides (Bell, 1969).

The minimal role to which the term "scientist" might be applied is that of behavioral actuary, an accountant of matters social who can tally what-goes-with-what. This *is* a skill and it tells some truths. But it pleases few urgent students in arts and letters.

One might graduate from this difficult role to another "more scientific." On this plane of knowing, the working assumption is that there is a possibility of explanation from empirical propositions patterned by constructs so that:

Behavior appears rule-ful, so that . . .
Foresight is enhanced, so that . . .
The societal diagnostician can prognosticate: If you do *this,* the chances of
    that happening will be increased, or, what is more likely, so that . . .
The empiricist, following Popper (1957:61), is able to say, from evidence,
    that . . . *such and such a thing cannot happen.*[7]

Either this, or one abandons the pretense of "scientist" of human action and becomes its minister. Either door opens a way out of the bind of being a "scientist-on-the-right-side."

Ministering to societies is what men have long done, with questionable result, and the ultraviolet side of the spectrum of belief in progress through intentional group action hopes that "science can save us" (Lundberg, 1947). Science can save us, it is urged, because what ails us is ignorance, and science we have *defined* as knowledge.

This belief is current among "men of good will." It takes heart from Unamuno who assured us that: Man is evil not so much out of wickedness as out of ignorance.

This is a popular assumption. It is a hope that frequently hides behind tautology: We didn't achieve our objectives because we didn't know how.

A test of faith here is that the man who utters such redundancy can't see its circularity.

To call such beliefs "assumptions" is to question them. The evidence of man's ability to better his worlds by enacting them is slim. No one has scales in which to balance the maleficent against the beneficent consequences of human intention in alleviating the miseries of men. Lacking such measures, the sad history of failed plan — and, worse, of plans that produce more evil than they intend to cure (Fischer, 1956) — this history is ignored,[8] debated, or read as failure from ignorance.

Persistence in the legislative faith is maintained by calling for "more research" or, ideologically, by tainting the motives of the men who would question it.[9] The latter response can be ignored; the former might be defended as a good in itself. "Innocent study" or "pure research" may be defended as art, or the satisfaction of curiosity, or as applicable to one's selected personal and social problems — *depending* upon what one thinks he "knows" from what evidence, and how he applies his imperfect knowledge to the welfare of others.

As one moves to apply his tentative knowledge of human behavior, however, caution is called for — a caution that would protect the purchasers of knowledge against fraud, the beneficiaries from unwanted "benefits," one's colleagues in the search for regularity from implication in the other scholar's applications, and the host of all citizens who pay for the enterprise against unpleasant consequence.

Such caution is required, *a fortiori,* in the light of recent proposals that a National Social Science Foundation be established in the United States to gather data organized as "social indicators" of a nation's welfare (Bauer *et al.,* 1966). Canada, and other nations, are calling for parallel "Human Resources Research." The indicators developed would call attention to sick spots in a nation's economic, physical, psychic, and moral constitution (Olson, 1969). Upon such investigation, it is assumed, appropriate governmental action could be taken, action that, given its information-base, would be wiser than the present pattern of compromise among guesses.

At least these dangers in the founding of a national social "science" can be outlined:

(1) That the professional competence of "scientists" of social behavior be inflated from:

   (a) Technical ability to moral sagacity.

(b) Societal accountancy to societal engineering.
(2) That the inflation of scholarship elevate expectations with such possible consequences as:
(a) The creation of new problems to be solved because hopes have been promoted.
(b) Disappointed reaction against what studies of the social can do.

(1) *The limits of scholarly competence*

(a) There is a literature that holds that morals are made by facts and validated by them. It takes the form of a search for a "rational ethic" and it has led some students to equate efficient means with morality. (Against this, see Nettler, 1950.)

The argument leads readily to an equating of knowing (being correct) with being right. For example, one sociologist asks: If technical competence provides no warrant for making value judgments, then what does? (Gouldner, 1963:37)

This is a surprising question to hear from a student of human relations. It deserves the same reply given the preacher who asked: If there is no God, where do my morals come from?

Both questions betoken an inadequate conception of a moral statement.[10] Both questions disregard the fact that moral sentiments have evolved, that they are transmitted through training, and variously legitimized. "Techniques" and "gods" are justifications and reinforcers of what has been otherwise learned.

The risk from social "scientists" who presume to righteousness as a result of their technical expertise is that *they* will "know" what is "good" for *us*. The person who cannot see the problem here has never been in the hands of an "official helper" or lived with "benevolent" tyranny.

(b) What social "scientists" have learned to do is to count. This is no small feat and it works toward one of the scientific objectives—it enlarges our vision of the world.

The methodology of the behavioral sciences has been skilful in approaching the scientific desideratum of *reliable* observation. There are procedures for replicating what the other man reports. There are ways of measuring the consistency of such repeated observation and of improving upon both the reliability of the observations and the accuracy of reliability-estimation. It is this part of the knowing-problem that has benefited from the operational definition. Reliable counting requires agreed-upon units.

With observations made more reliable, it becomes possible to count associations. Again, scientists of behavior have improved upon common sense in tallying more objectively what-goes-with-what.

It is in this doing that there is a defensible claim to "sciencing" among the students of the social. And it is here that the behavioral scientist may defend himself against his critics.

His efforts have not produced a "Newtonian breakthrough" that would represent some ordering of behavioral axioms never before conceived. The record is nonetheless remarkable when one considers that a science of human behavior would *improve* upon folk knowledge and that the inventory of folk generalization about man is so large as to give novel discovery a low probability.

Nevertheless, there are statements about man—some of solely current interest, others of more perennial concern—that we can make today with greater assurance *because* a stumbling "science" of the social has taken count. To assert this is to arouse humanists to their characteristic cries of "triviality," "elaboration of the obvious," and "redundancy." This is common literary sport, and there are grounds for it but it is played to excess. The game of trivializing "behavior science" proceeds by taking "findings" in the social studies, divesting them of their occult verbiage, translating them into the vernacular, and thus revealing these propositions as either tautologies or banalities. In this spirit, Louch (1966) cites Lazarsfeld to show that . . . the more fire engines that come to a fire, the larger the damage (p. 9), Inkeles to demonstrate that . . . whatever happens in society is a consequence of its state and the personality of its members (p. 11), Homans to prove that . . . a man will do more if he is interested in his work (p. 15), and that . . . people who interact frequently are more like one another in their activities than they are like other persons with whom they interact less frequently (p. 17). And, last, Thorndike's Law of Effect is held to be . . . only a . . . pompous rendering of . . .[the] platitude [that] people will repeat actions with pleasurable consequences (p. 30).

There is a ready reply to men, like Louch, who enjoy this sport of "what do you know that every bright chap didn't know before?" The response can take the form in which Lazarsfeld (1949) answered critics of the studies reported in *The American Soldier* (Stouffer *et al.,* 1950). Lazarsfeld's device was to take some of the findings of these studies and phrase them in obverse form to demonstrate that each proposition also appeared as "obvious" in its false form.

Lazarsfeld's exercise illustrates how some knowledge, held more certainly today by social "scientists" and humanists alike, was less certain, and up for debate, prior to research. The game can be continued by preparing a test that asks questions that can now be answered from empirical evidence, but which could not have been so warranted 50 years ago, or 25. Each man can construct his own test if he finds too much "trivia" in the sample to be presented. But it must be remembered that "trivia," too, is a matter of what does or does not satisfy someone's curiosity.

The point of the suggested sample test is that, if the answers were obvious, the uninformed nonscientists of like I.Q. ("doctored humanists," for example) ought to agree in their answers, and agree on the correct side. The discrepancies within "educated opinion," and between it and behavioral-science data, provide a measure of the contribution of the latter.

A TENTATIVE TEST OF WHAT-GOES-WITH-WHAT
(TIME- AND CULTURE-BOUND)[11]

(1) Do "safe-driving" campaigns work?

(2) Do speed limits reduce automobile accidents?

(3) What is the nature of the relationship between traffic-directing signs and driver behavior?
And on about these "important problems."

(4) Do students learn more from group discussion than they do from lectures?

(5) What is the best way to memorize?

(6) Does class size affect student learning?

(7) Can adult reading ability be changed?

(8) Does a slow learner forget his lessons at a different rate from a fast learner?

(9) Does a human being have to "know what he's doing" or "what he wants" in order for him to be "instrumentally conditioned"?

(10) What is the relationship between the "fixity" of a lesson learned and the training schedule?

(11) Do people classify things without awareness of the principle of classification? Without awareness that a principle is involved?

(12) Do men think differently from women?

(13) Do bright children "burn out"?

(14) Do the "visible" American ethnic groups go to inferior schools from those attended by other children?
And on about similar "important problems."

(15) What is the relationship between the temporal placement of punishment and the change of behavior?

(16) Do prison social workers rehabilitate criminals?

(17) Does ethnicity affect American criminal-sentencing practice?

(18) What is the relationship between the process of ethnic congregation and delinquency rates?

(19) What is the relationship between having laws that may exact life as penalty for murder and murder rates?
And on about these "important problems."

(20) What is the relationship between social distance and moral judgment? Between "moral distance" and moral judgment?

(21) Is liking people the opposite of disliking them?

(22) What is the relationship between economic development and full employment?

(23) What is the relationship between economic growth and rising or falling prices?

(24) What is the relationship between feeling "free" and social structure?

(25) What is the relationship between submitting to psychotherapy and "being cured"?

Behavioral counting is the distinctive competence of those who would be scientists of human action. Yet this skill bears its own troubles:

(i) Counting and correlating are difficult enough:
See the U.S. Census "loss" in 1960 of some estimated few million young, male nonwhite citizens. (Siegel, 1968)
See Morgenstern (1963) on the errors in economics statistics.
See Douglas (1967) on the errors in counting suicides.
Note the discrepancy in a mental health clinic between what comes into the agency and what goes down on the report to government.

(ii) Counting carries its own price in the invasion of privacy.

(iii) Counting carries another price in the exacerbation of problems through their definition:
A problem counted begins to count.
Now that you've told me how sick I am, I feel worse.
Intervention is guided by *what* is counted. By its very nature, sociology

guides certain levels of intervention . . . and has nothing to say about other levels. (Kahn, 1967:629)

(iv) Counting and correlating are deemed unsatisfying because they don't "explain" and don't resolve the moral question that underwrites the definition of a "social problem."

Dissatisfaction with "mere" societal accounting, even among the accountants, tempts such experts to interpret what they've tallied and to move from accountancy to engineering.[12] The movement is already apparent and the threshold of temptation may be expected to lower with the employment of societal accountants as recorders of a nation's sociopsychic ledger.

A chasm of varying dimension separates behaviors or conditions counted and behaviors or conditions explained beyond the experience tables, but students of human action have shown themselves willing performers at leaping this interpretation gap. Illustrations of its tentative hurdling by empathetic explicators have been given in Chapter Three. Whether one leaps with empathy, or without it, the risks of this intellectual sport deserve reminder.

THE INTERPRETATION GAP: ILLUSTRATIONS OF THE LONG-JUMP

Nichols (1966:1314) *on the Coleman Report* (1966): The major findings are imbedded in a mass of trivial detail, and the summary (available as a separate 33-page booklet . . .), which appears to have been guided by a desire to avoid disturbing public opinion, is actually misleading. (P. 1312)

Two additional results of the regression analysis are relevant to the question of the effects of school segregation on student performance. First, the performance of minority children after statistical control for socioeconomic background was better where the proportion of white children in their schools was higher, but this result was attributable to the higher socioeconomic level of the student body in integrated schools rather than to racial balance per se. Second, the performance of minority children (again controlled for socioeconomic background) was more highly related to the socioeconomic level of other children in their schools than was the performance of white children. These two findings lead the authors to say that "if a white pupil from a home that is strongly supportive of education is put in a school where most of the pupils don't come from such homes, his achievement will be little different than if he were in a school composed of others like him. But if a minority pupil from a home without much educational strength is put with schoolmates with strong educational background, his achievement is likely to increase."

This conclusion, which Commissioner of Education Howe appears to have accepted at face value (*Science*, 14 October, 1966, p. 242) is a beautiful example of interpreting correlation as indicating causation. Moreover, the findings on which it is based might also be attributed to inadequate control for the preschool characteristics of the students. Differences in average performance of students attending different schools can be due either to differential effects of schools and associated environmental influences or to differences in initial ability of the students attending the different schools. To study the effects of schools, differences in initial ability must be controlled.

The result of all this is to reinforce the two preceding lines of evidence indicating that the effects of variations in school quality on student achievement are minimal, even less than the authors admit. (P. 1314)

Questionnaires again: The critics versus "Christian beliefs and anti-Semitism" (Glock and Stark, 1966): The respondent who agrees with the statement that "On the average, Jews are wealthier than Christians," is accused of having an image of the Jew as avaricious, even though most available information on religion and social class would suggest merely that the respondent is accurately describing the nature of social reality. (Greeley, 1967:1008)

Consistency of verbal response is *not* an indicator of the validity of a verbal measure. *(Ibid.)*

Redundant scales are "validated" via "verbal agility"; i.e., one scale is used to validate another, where both are measures of the same thing. (Williams, 1967:1006)

Most of the reported correlations are modest. Therefore, . . . if one uses the strong asymmetric relations as per Costner and Leik needed to provide firm plausibility for the causal chain, this study is not confirmed. *(Ibid.)*

van den Haag (1960) *versus Clark* (1954) *on the effects of racial educational segregation* [13]

Clark: Clark administered a projective test to black and white children in elementary schools along the Atlantic seaboard. The test consisted of presenting dolls of different skin colors to children and asking them to show "which is the good doll" and "which one you'd like to play with."

When compared with the choices of white children, black children more frequently preferred dolls with light skin.

Clark's interpretation before the Supreme Court: Racial segregation in schools has been psychically damaging.

van den Haag: van den Haag showed that, if one accepted doll-choice as meaning what Clark read out of it,[14] then a reverse conclusion might be reached since black children in *separated* schools, north or south, tended to prefer dolls of like color *more* frequently than their peers in congregated schools.

It is one thing to count behaviors. It is another to give them meanings, and it is a farther cry to explicate their causes and effects.

The low order of causal connection proved by a science of human behavior, mixed with a "doctor's" degree and moral concern, provides inadequate training for the interpretive long-jump.

(2) *Some likely consequences of the inflation of technical competence*

The dangers of counting lie not solely in the risks of error, nor are they limited to the hazards of the interpretation gap. Governmental foundations of social "science" may promise attention that excites and solutions that cannot be given.

The first possibility is an uncertainty, and yet a consideration if one is to perform *responsibly*[15] in a professional role. The possibility is that of old problems exacerbated and new ones created because attention has promoted hope. With such promise, desire is converted to demand. Demand of services in short supply results in a deterioration of the quality of the service with further complaint that what was promised has not been given.

A second result follows from the likelihood of disappointment with the results of behavior science. If the flattery of expertise prompts scholars to inflate their inexact "science" beyond their carrying capacity, it is probable that they will be caught out. Their operation in the political arena assures it. Disappointment may be expected as:

Societal accountants make errors.

Their interpretations become partisan.

The powers of causal-therapeutic knowledge are oversold.

Policy persists despite such knowledge as may be available.

Policy changes, however well informed, produce "cures" that give more pain than the illness.[16]

With such disappointment in the application of a social "science," it may be expected that the reaction will generalize toward hostility of the intellect. Some students read such anti-intellectual signs now in the devaluation of history, in select politicians' disdain of professors, in select professors' and students' urge to politicize universities,[17] in the public applause of fact-mastery-as-contest and its fear of facts, in youthful disrespect of elders, in escape into "mind-blowing" sensation, arts of the absurd, and the joys of rage.

Our very success in knowing a little may be a cause of dissatisfaction with independent inquiry. Thus the president of a distinguished American university (DuBridge, 1968:1225) writes:

> Despite its faults, our educational system gives more and better opportunities to more young people than any other system in existence — or in the history of civilization. Never, and nowhere, have the opportunities and the fruits of learning been so widely available, so widely utilized, and so widely appreciated.
>
> One must inevitably conclude that the troubles of today are attributable not to the failures of our university system, but to its successes. It has brought higher education to 50 percent of our young people. Why not 100 percent? It has brought scholarly inquiry to bear on a host of areas of human concern. Why not on *all*? Scholarship and research have shed light on many problems which have puzzled the human intellect. Why are some problems still unsolved? Why is it we can understand the structure of the universe and not the structure of human society — or of the human brain or heart?
>
> *Because* higher education has been so successful in so many areas, it is now said to be a colossal failure because success is not yet visible in *every* sphere of human concern. A few hundred years ago no one understood anything about the nature of the universe — and everyone was apparently happy. Today we are overwhelmed with knowledge — and we scream with pain because we don't know everything.
>
> Once our colleagues taught almost nothing except Latin, Greek, philosophy, theology, and jurisprudence — and they were regarded as the pinnacles of civilization. Today they teach everything that the human mind has learned — and are accused of living in the Middle Ages.
>
> Success has thus led only to rising expectations and to mounting accusations of failure. (Emphasis in the original)

All these reactions can receive justification; and they are given such, whether or not one agrees with their reasons. Having taken excessive promise from the powers of knowledge, however, the reaction threatens the exercise of one distinctively human ability: to think about man and his social world without commitment.

The passionate action from ignorance, and the current temptation to translate technique into wisdom, carry their own consequences. The major one of concern here is that such reactions and temptations assure that science will not save us.

WHY SCIENCE WILL NOT SAVE US

There are two ways in which one might answer the hopes of contemporary *encyclopédistes* that scientific knowledge will save us. On the one hand, there is not "enough" science of human behavior; on the other, what ails us is not what facts can cure, although wisdom might palliate the symptoms.

The latter point saves the first from its tautology.

The theme of our exercise bears repetition: That the explanations we give and take are seldom knowledgeable, and that scientific knowledge of human behavior — particularly that which would move beyond counting and correlating to the assignment of causes — is difficult to achieve.

It is expected that this theme will be accepted when one thinks about it, and denied in action. This expectation is supported by the difficult necessity of constantly transmitting our lessons to the young, and by the battle between desire, expectation (the perennial optimism of modern "intellectuals" — Nettler, 1968b:205), and learning (Goldberg, 1968).[18]

We *want* knowledge and plan to succeed. Every organizer for better worlds claims "truth," like God, to be on his side. Successive generations of innocent men, walking fresh onto the stage of history, cry out, "Why won't people behave decently?"

WHY WON'T PEOPLE BEHAVE?

The Revolutionary (Anonymous): Are we creating a New Man, or are we ourselves a reflection of the [obscenity] we hate so much?

The Professor (Etzioni, 1968a:580): What we don't know is how to help the citizens and leaders see where their true interests lie.

The Social Worker (Anonymous), *inhaling deeply of her constant cigarette:* Why can't we get people to do what everyone knows is good for them?

Another Professor (Moore, 1967:408-409): If no one in his right mind really believes that there is any more prospect for a decent society right now than there has been in previous historical epochs, the nagging question remains: why?

> . . . what we are looking for here is an explanation of a recurring histor-
> ical phenomenon: The repeated failure of human societies to come any-
> where near the type of decent society that was perhaps within their reach
> at a given stage of development.

Moore offers answers to his own question about why the world isn't as good
as he thinks it should be or could be. He sees competition as one obstacle
and "good citizens" as another. "Good citizens" have a stake in the prevailing order and hesitate to risk it. So Moore concludes: One might say with
epigrammatic shallowness that the reason we have never had a decent world
is because there have always been too many decent people in it. (*Ibid.*:409)

This may sound like saying, "The world of social relationships is as it is
because people are as they are." This redundancy may be reduced, and the
failure of purposive group action to make the world better "explained," by
describing in outline the natural history of these attempts. If this history
seems accurate, it teaches a lesson: That better worlds, like personal happiness, are by-products, and only rarely the results of intent.

A NATURAL HISTORY OF ORGANIZED GOOD INTENTION:
THE DIALECTIC OF GOODNESS,
OR WHY MORAL SUCCESS IS EVER MOOT

(1) We start from concern. The concerns are various and, potentially, at
war with each other:
> Racism, poverty, war, repression, loneliness, alienation, imprisonment.
> (Zinn, 1967:175)
> The ultimate purpose of social change [is] to enlarge human happiness.
> (*Ibid.*)
> A person like myself . . . regards freedom as the major objective in
> relations among individuals. (Friedman, 1968:7)

And on through any preferred list of "values."

(2) The concerns get defined as moral issues and their failed resolution as
grievances.
   (*a*) Grievance is perceived, not sensed. That means it is attributed, not
   "given."
   (*b*) Grievance is translated as injustice.
   (*c*) The relationship between the intensity with which grievance is felt
   and the absolute deprivation experienced (where that is known) is less

than perfect. "Relative deprivation," that is, perceived grievance, is a function of improvement (Brinton, 1938). It is the perception that wounds and motivates (Runciman, 1966).

(3) Men declaim against injustice and organize to fight it.

(4) The fact of militant organization means that:

(a) Men of multiple motive march under the same banner:

Some are "all good."

Some want to hurt in order to rectify. This ancient feeling-for-justice as the balancing of damages persists.

Some will enjoy receiving the power that they decry in other's hands.

(b) Bureaucracies grow to handle the organization that would fight bureaucracy.

(c) Enemies attacked organize in defense.

(d) Battle is joined and means become separated from ends, although justified by them, so that:

Hatred is evoked as a step toward building a world of love.

Compensatory racism is evoked to end racism.

Killing now is deemed necessary as a means to peace.[19]

Economies are crushed so that poverty may be ended[20] (Lawson, 1969).

Injustice is bred to correct injustice.

Truth is denied in order that truth may prevail.[21]

The needs of combat require that social utility dominate disloyal facts. Some of the truths denied, like economic ones, or military ones, or psychic ones, rebound upon the good movement to make matters worse.[22]

When matters get worse, they are excused.

Blaming the recalcitrant enemy is a first apology. The call-for-sacrifice to ensure a promise is a second. The "pie in the sky bye-and-bye" pledge of the religious reformer has been translated by today's "commissars" as "present pain for future gain."

It seems fair to conclude from such recurring drama that men do not know how to construct "decent societies." The very idea of societal engineering is a novelty and, if not a naïveté, an arrogance.

One source of the naïveté may be linguistic, the failure of English and cognate tongues to distinguish between "knowing how to" and "having knowledge of." The use of one word for disparate referents leads to an easy violation of the canon of singularity or to what Hockett (1968:63) calls . . .

Tarzan thinking: one grabs onto a vine (a word) at one tree (meaning) and leaves it only after it has swung to another tree. The point is simply that the two kinds of "knowing" are not coordinate. Much that we have "knowledge of" gives us no "know how," and much that we "know how to do" we have little "knowledge of."

> A centipede was happy quite,
>   Until a frog in fun
> Said, "Pray, which leg comes after which?"
> This raised her mind to such a pitch,
> She lay distracted in the ditch
>   Considering how to run.   (Author unknown)

The naïveté of confusing "knowledge of" with "knowing how" is transformed into arrogance as students of social behavior assume more science than they have. Encouraged by the successful applications of the physical sciences where some knowledge *did* get translated into "know how," the new men of the social "sciences" are stimulated to move into combat against man's miserable treatment of man. In this ancient arena battle is engaged and the social "scientist," armed with some fragile pieces of "knowledge of," promises heroic deeds from weak generalizations. In the fray the social "scientist" either loses his life and is reborn the ideologist or he retreats with wounds and the recognition that his armament, useful in lesser contests, is inadequate for the moral one.

The innocence of mistaking knowledge for skill and the arrogance of masquerading low orders of information as science are but two of the encouragements given the notion of a societal engineering. A third stimulus is in the questionable ideas about the nature of the social arrangements by which men live together. The architectural view of a social institution sees such a pattern as an instrument of social existence enacted for purposes and subject to change according to plan. It sees dispute about the design as amenable to reasoned discussion and soluble in facts. This is a fresh view, in more than one sense, and a probably incorrect one. In opposition, there is ground for agreeing with Rhees (1947) that social institutions are better described as *forms* of social existence rather than as their instruments, that institutions are crescive rather than enacted, that their reform does not control their development, and that arguments do not solve social conflicts nor experiments decide social issues.

The defective view of social institutions implicit in the promise of a societal engineering rests upon a confusion of decisions with facts and upon a
denial of the "reality" of conflict. The irreducibility of decisions to facts has
been detailed (Chapter Six, note 2). The reality of conflict is guaranteed by
the perennial struggle for values in scarce supply, a guarantee Friedrich
Engels (1934:475) saw in a history in which . . . what each individual wills
is obstructed by everyone else, and what emerges is something that no one
willed. Conflict is further assured as men attempt to maximize more than
one value simultaneously. This attempt is a mathematical impossibility (von
Neumann and Morgenstern, 1947) as well as a sociopsychological one. This
impossibility may be rephrased by saying that men often want something
for nothing, or that they want contradictory things. If this is partly true
within one man, it becomes more true among many men.

AN INVENTORY OF COMPETING VALUES[23]

Value	*Probable cost*
Equality	Freedom (Waelder, 1966)
Freedom to reproduce	Quality of life (Hardin, 1968)
Freedom of physical movement	Urban congestion, ethnic separation
Social mobility	Status inconsistency, discontent, psychic dis-ease
Mass communication: dissemination of "information"	Dissatisfaction, cultural homogenization
Reduced infant and maternal mortality	"Population pressure": famine, hatred, war and revolution, urban ugliness, loss of the pleasures of privacy
Raised material standard of living	Industrial technology: manufacturing "rationalization," commerce, the division of labor ("alienation") and the cash nexus
Affluence	Ennui: the decline of ambition and craftsmanship, dependency, mind-deadening, sensation-seeking, the joys of rage

Mass education	Substitutes for the "thoughtful disciplines" in entertainment, indoctrination, and leisure-time "expression"
Scientific technology	Environmental pollution (Commoner, 1966)
The "politicizing" of "unpolitical" institutions	Academic freedom, scientific inquiry (Simirenko, 1966)
Agricultural policy	Continuing agricultural poverty, rural emigration and urban immigration (Boulding, 1967:885)
Urban renewal	Disorganized community (Ibid.)

We are brought full circle to the relevance of explanation to action, and knowledge to both.

If "knowledge" were deemed to be only what results from a scientific process, it would seem that the preponderance of explanations we offer each other operate with different principles.

We make some things clear by defining the symbols that stand for them. Our definitions are always tentative and torn between their satisfactions. Terms made precise permit the reliable indication of their referents. Such precision, however, omits from communication much that we enjoy. In particular, it dulls the evaluations and emotional tones carried by the abstractions to which our conditioning resonates. As with all ways of making matters clear, what satisfies one purpose in taking thought frustrates another, and the operational definition, useful for some intentions, thwarts others.

It is not always important, then, to define our terms narrowly. The bulk of our explanation, it has been held, is empathetic or ideological. In such explainways, rigorous definition is an enemy. It kills feeling, the ally of empathy and ideology.

There is folk knowledge, of course, and it partakes, un-self-consciously, of many of the principles made conscious in the scientific process—principles such as classification, induction, and generalization. The differences between folk empiricism and scientific constructions are matters of degree, of the formalization of the desiderata of the knowing activity and, under the stress of test, of the kinds of statement and style of validation that will satisfy the questions asked.

Scientific knowledge of human behavior has been shown to be difficult. An approximation toward it is made as men learn to classify actions, count them, and correlate them. Proceeding beyond this orderliness to the assignment of meanings and causes is an effort that thus far has escaped reliable technique.

Given these difficulties, men explain their worlds and themselves by less truthful modes that carry their own consequences. A major one of these is a guarantee that "history will persist," that continuity is more likely than a mutation that will produce the New Man.

Technology changes the setting in which man lives. Physical possibilities are altered. But the "nature" of the human (an idea detested by the meliorist) seems constant. W. C. Field's inference, *What man has done, man can do*, can be projected to: *How man has been, he is likely to be* — a creature who categorizes his world with moral matrices, who seems incapable of loving without hating, of affiliating without discriminating, and who is curious, yet content with little knowledge and dissatisfied as his world expands.

Some conclusions:

(1) The effort to know, simply out of curiosity, is a human constant. It will be challenged by those who need explanations in gratification of other interests. Its working atmosphere may be clouded but, if one may extend pasts into futures, it will persist.

(2) *Knowing* is not an answer to every difficulty, or an emollient to every itch-to-explain. The doctrine that knowledge is omnipotent is a rationalist presumption that confuses technique with wisdom, and the limited expertise of men-of-facts with judgment.

Such presumption tested, fails. Its failure leads to a nausea of knowledge and the therapy of action. This reaction, again, ensures history.

(3) Not all difficulties in living are translatable into "problems" and not all problems are soluble. Hardin (1968) reminds us that there are contests, like the game of tick-tack-toe, that cannot be won if the opponents understand the game.

Life, too, is a struggle in which some difficulties may be converted into problems and some problems resolved under techniques produced by knowledge. These problems are principally, but not solely, physical, and the knowledge, scientific.

Beyond these solutions, the explanations we give ourselves, and each other, in clarification of our actions have not been sturdily built with knowledge. Responding to each other, in the political arenas as in the domestic ones, remains little science, mostly art.

NOTES

[1] It may be suggested that this sentence describes a declining gradient of happiness: from the contentment of the thoughtless through the lesser bliss of the man who would improve himself to the characteristic rancor of the meliorist.

Merely to hypothesize such a gradient is to anger the man who sets himself the task of "helping others." But the hypothesis remains possible, although uncomfortable. Its premise has been variously noted:

Smith (1969): [Rural children] . . . seem quite unaware of their poverty and are generally content with life in Millfield.

Mannheim (1941:110): Speaks of those "programs of opposition" that enjoy . . . the double advantage of having to use reason only in criticizing one's opponents and at the same time, of being able to mobilize without restraint and to one's own profit all the negative emotions of *hatred and resentment* which—according to Simmel's principle of the "negative character of collective behavior"—can unify a large number of people more easily than any positive program. (Emphasis supplied)

[2] "Occasional" rationalists as are we all. The phrase deserves particular application here because current meliorists assume that *they* are reasonable where other men are less so, that *their* reasons are grounded in facts and logically coherent, that their motives rest on these reasons, and that their minds are "open" to change with faults found in these reasons.

The use of the adjective "occasional" questions these assumptions.

[3] America's courts are colonial courts. . . . In America we have Race and Class Justice, pure and simple.

And they have picked off the Panther Leadership and driven it into jail and exile without our burning the [obscenity] country down in retaliation. (Rubin, 1969:27)

[4] *Friedenberg* (1968): I can hardly imagine a worse society than the one we live in.

Student rebel (Center for the Study of Democratic Institutions, 1968:41): I believe there is something fundamentally wrong with this country, and the wrong is caused by the institutions of this country. I sincerely believe that the institutions of this country must be destroyed.

Marcuse (cited by Cranston, 1969:39): The world of the concentration camps was not an exceptionally monstrous society . . . . What we saw there was the image, and in a sense the quintessence, of the infernal society into which we are plunged every day.

[5] It may be difficult to believe, but a graduate student in sociology, a woman upon whom one of the richest nations in history had lavished 17 or 18 years of the best education it could muster, asked: Well, revolutions are bad, but once they're over, don't things get better?

[6] This is asking too much, as the history of the warfare between truth and utility tells us.

No man seems capable of engaging in political contest and accommodating "the whole truth" about what he does. Arendt (1967:68) sees the divorcement of truth and politics as flowing from a harmony of motives in the liar and the politician. . . . the liar is a man of action, the truth-teller . . . most emphatically is not. Politicians and liars are actors by nature. They say

. . . what is not so because [they] want things to be different from what they are — that is, [they] want to change the world.

Similarly, Auden (1962:86) has written . . . in politics, there is a distinction, unknown in science, between Truth and Justice.

[7] Popper reads the *Logic of Scientific Discovery* (1959: Section 15) as relying on "negated existential propositions." He advances such examples as these:

You can't carry water in a sieve.

You cannot introduce agricultural tariffs and at the same time reduce the cost of living.

You cannot have a centrally planned society with a price system that fulfils the main functions of competitive prices.

You cannot introduce a political reform without causing some repercussions which are undesirable from the point of view of the ends aimed at.

You cannot make a revolution without causing a reaction.

You cannot give a man power over other men without tempting him to misuse it.

Vaizey (1968:63) makes Popper's point from a different stance: The great claim of socialism was to be "scientific." So modern socialists have tried to assimilate the findings of the social sciences into their thought. But do the social sciences give positive answers to questions? I think not. I believe that their logic is far more concerned with the disproof of error ("That argument is wrong") than with the establishment of certainty ("If you do X then Y will occur").

[8] Ignoring history is a characteristic of Ortega's "mass-man" (1932). For "mass-man," there are no antecedents.

[9] Need it be said that remarking a human limitation does not constitute its approval?

[10] Arguments about the justification of morals are entwined with debates about definition. The road to research could be paved by the acceptance of such a thoughtful definition of a moral statement as Ladd provides (1957:101-107). Moral statements are distinguished, according to Ladd, by their constituting prescriptions for conduct that claim "superiority" and "legitimacy."

(1) The "superiority" of morals lies in their:

  (a) Autonomy: they are sufficient reasons; they cannot be justified nonmorally.

  (b) Priority: they demand precedence over other lines of conduct.

(2) The "legitimacy" of moral utterances involves:

  (a) The possibility of justification even where none is given.

  (b) Their intersubjective validity; they are binding on oneself and others.

  (c) Their roots in "reality." Ethical systems ". . . (are) in some way derived from man's conception of human nature, or of the world, or of reality in general . . . ." This connection does not lead, in Ladd's conception, to the ". . . so-called 'naturalistic fallacy' (the fallacy of deducing a prescriptive from a nonprescriptive statement)."

Ladd proposes some tests for the identification of ethical discourse. In addition to his suggestions, one might observe to what extent facts in actuality do entail values. One could study, for example, how frequently "logical men" of varying moral persuasion agree on the relevance of "reality" to their ethics and how often, when apprised of the same facts, they arrive at the same moral conclusions. This test compares the relative strength of Ladd's definiens 1a vs. 2c.

If moral judgments are seldom informed (that is, modified) by changes in factual knowledge, they become pragmatically, as well as logically, independent, as Ladd's point 1a predicts.

This issue is relevant to the current thesis insofar as scientists confuse their knowledge with their morals. When they do this, they become susceptible of "selling" their professional competence in defense of their moral preferences. This is one form of intellectual prostitution that can be expected to weaken the repute of scientific endeavor and to do so with greater force among the "soft" (i.e., social) sciences. (Nettler, 1968b:203)

[11] For the professional student, a test such as this can receive a tougher version: Not only must he "guess" correctly, but he must also tell how the answer was learned and, in appropriate cases, describe the nature of the effects achieved.

For any reader who thinks the answers obvious, it bears repeating that many educated men don't know them, and many educated men who "know" them are wrong.

[12] A parallel phenomenon is observed in business where auditors are often moved to assume other managerial functions, including prescribing for design, sales, and personnel.

[13] Inclusion of this debate makes no statement as to the "true" effects of racial segregation upon psyche. It acknowledges that many psychologists and sociologists assume segregation to be damaging (Killian, 1968:53-54), that Negroes in the United States are reported to be disproportionately hospitalized for psychosis but seem less vulnerable than whites to neurosis (Pettigrew, 1964: Chap. 4), and that the allocation of causes to these tentative epidemiological statistics remains in question.

The debate deserves mention, however, as illustration that experts called to influence policy may interpret data as per their preconceptions. Thus some psychiatrists give mixed readings from their assessments (cf. Coles, 1963, and his testimony cited from our preceding page 162), and others can be found to take either side on a variety of issues before the bar (Arens, 1967; Hakeem, 1958; Halleck, 1966; Leifer, 1964, 1967; Szasz, 1963).

[14] "Projection," of which doll-play is one test, is not a singular process (Chapter Two, note 7). Interpretation of the "meaning" of a response is thus liable to loading with the clinician's presumption.

The very hypothesis of projective measurement—that whatever an individual does in response to an ambiguous stimulus reveals something important and persistent about his personality—is resistant to disproof. It dispenses with the possibility of measurement error, a consideration in other attempts to order behaviors, and it overlooks the likelihood that a subject may be "borrowing" his responses (from the mass media, for example) rather than "creating" them (Sechrest, 1968:553).

Further, there is evidence that conflict (Zimmer, 1955) and inhibition of feelings (Feschbach, 1963; Zimbardo, 1964) affect "how one projects," and that clinicians are prone to prefer pathological interpretations where other meanings might have been read from the tests (Cox and Sargent, 1950; Little and Schneidman, 1959).

Given all this, direct measures of psychic functioning would be preferable to those indirect tasks that lure one into the interpretation gap.

[15] To behave "responsibly" is to accept the consequences of one's actions. To behave "irresponsibly" is to ask the other fellow to carry the costs of what one recommends or does.

Since the social "scientist" in government will be part of a "team," a bureaucrat, tracing his advice to its source becomes difficult. Since the costs of his prescriptions are spread over many, and since the "causes" of such costs are difficult to discern, the social "scientist" is himself protected from the impact of his societal doctoring.

Such a situation provides good ground for irresponsible behavior.

[16] One kind of cost, difficult to prove but easy to feel, is a moral price. Citizens, and their representatives in legislatures, argue that the application of social "sciences" beyond their actuarial competence corrodes public morals. Price (1969:27) notes that . . . leading candidates for political office have charged that the Supreme Court's weakness for sociology and statistics is eroding the moral fiber of the nation.

[17] Questioning begins to come out from the university ghetto . . . . The students bring to the struggle their denunciation of culture and values . . . . The faculty is not an independent institution consecrated to the elaboration and transmission of a knowledge for its own sake. A society like ours . . . cannot maintain within itself a zone of free knowledge and free expression . . . . It would be vain to democratize admission to the university if the alienation of the spirit which reigns within its walls were to remain intact. The faculty must become the smithy of tools and works . . . . We must impose institutions and modes of teaching and research that permit critical understanding of reality in all its forms. (Brooks, 1968: 538-540)

[18] Desire and anticipation militate against the keeping of one's predictive score. We are thus prevented from learning lessons that would contradict our wishes. "Learning from experience" (untutored by attempts at controlled public observation) suffers the hazards of hope. Once conditioned to belief, we persist in error. In what is perhaps the most ingenious series of studies of clinical judgment ever carried out, Chapman and Chapman (1967) have demonstrated how prior expectations of the relationships between cues and criteria can lead to faulty observation and inference, even under seemingly excellent conditions for learning. The Chapmans exposed subjects to human figure drawings, each of which was paired with two criterion statements concerning the characteristics of the patients who allegedly drew the figures. Though these training materials were constructed so that there was no relationship between the cues and the criterion statements, most subjects erroneously "learned" the cue-criterion links which they had expected to see. In fact, the "illusory correlation" phenomena demonstrated by the Chapmans was [sic!] such a powerful one that many subjects trained on materials where the cue-criterion relationships were constructed to be the opposite of those expected still persisted in "learning" the erroneous relationships!

The intriguing research of the Chapmans illustrates the ease with which one can "learn" relationships which do not exist. (Goldberg, 1968:493; cf. also Chapman and Chapman, 1969)

[19] Revolutionaries will hardly recognize their kinship with a famous American general of recent vintage who remarked: We will have peace even if we have to fight for it.

[20] The revolutionary program for "a healthy economy" actually means that the people will have it worse ("temporarily" only, of course). And, as a consequence of the real worsening of living conditions, the revolutionary program for a "fuller democracy" actually means that people will have fewer, if any, democratic rights.

This is not theory, but actual practice as formulated by spokesmen of the Old and New Left. The following is from Lenin (Sochineniia, Vol. 31, Moscow, 1951, p. 233): "When we (the Bolsheviks) established the dictatorship of the proletariat the workers became more hungry, and their standard of living went down. The victory of the workers is impossible without sacrifices, without a temporary worsening of their situation."

The same thesis is presented with equally refreshing honesty by Che Guevara, and the passage from his Man and Socialism in Cuba can be found in the recent edition of his collected writings (ed. John Gerassi, pp. 392-3): "The vanguard group is ideologically more advanced than the mass;

the latter is acquainted with the new values, but insufficiently. While in the former a qualitative change takes place which permits them to make sacrifices as a function of their vanguard character, the latter see only by halves and must be subjected to incentives and pressures of some intensity; it is the dictatorship of the proletariat being exercised not only upon the defeated class but also individually upon the victorious class." (O'Brien, 1968:92, emphasis in the original)

[21] In the clash of partisans, one chooses his instances of the foolish results of truth-denial to support his own "wisdom." The further from the event the easier it is to see how blind faith produces failure. We can agree that Hitler got in the way of his generals, to our advantage in World War II. It is more difficult to get students to "see" the errors of Castro and Guevara as bankers, industrialists, and managers of an economy (Draper, 1964; Lawson, 1969).

[22] This is an incomplete list of the paradoxes of social action, of course. These and other contradictions may be expected for particular movements.

A detailed study of one recent set of social movements, those parallel events that might be labeled "student protest," has been conducted by Rubinstein (1969:135-136).

In keeping with the contradictions hypothesized here, Rubinstein notes four "paradoxes of student protest":

Perhaps the most central and prevalent paradox is that in the very effort to uphold their individual freedom the student activists forcibly abridge the freedom of others.

Still another paradox is to be found in the intellectual anti-intellectualism and the dogmatic anti-dogmatism.

A third paradox is that in the rebellion against what the activists see as an authoritarian and unresponsive politicized society they find themselves engaged in all kinds of complex political strategies and tactics.

The last dilemma . . . is difficult to label. It probably comes under the heading of "no matter what you do you can't win!"

Rubinstein describes the fourth paradox as the rebel's yearning for something to confront and his continuing dissatisfaction when a permissive environment yields and leaves no issue to contest.

[23] To offer such an inventory is bound to give offense to someone's urge to achieve *his* value without paying its price. Of course, "prices" too are relative so that one man's bargain may be another man's dear purchase.

The roster of contradictions here suggested refers to reported relationships. Some of these apply to specific programs of current issue; they may be emended. Others are perennial conflicts.

This catalog is purely heuristic, not exhaustive, and subject to each reader's improvement.

BIBLIOGRAPHIC INDEX

Page numbers are shown in brackets at the end of each entry.

Abel, T., 1948. "The operation called *Verstehen*." *American Journal of Sociology*, 54 (November): 211–218. [40, 47]

Abelson, R. P., and M. J. Rosenberg, 1958. "Symbolic psychologic: A model of attitudinal cognition." *Behavior Science*, 3 (January): 1–13. [108]

Ackermann, R., 1966. *Nondeductive Inference*. London: Routledge & Kegan Paul, Ltd. [123]

Adams, H., 1907. *The Education of Henry Adams*. Boston: Houghton Mifflin Company. [56]

Akers, Fred C., 1968. "Negro and white automobile-buying behavior: New evidence." *Journal of Marketing Research*, 5 (August): 283–289. [31]

American Association for the Advancement of Science, Committee, 1957. "Association affairs." *Scientific Monthly* (March): 146–155. [105]

American Psychiatric Association, 1965. *Diagnostic and Statistical Manual for Mental Disorder*. Washington, D.C.: American Psychiatric Association. [83]

American Psychological Association, 1953. *Psychoanalysis as Seen by Analyzed Psychologists*. Washington, D.C.: American Psychological Association. [172]

Arendt, H., 1967. "Reflections: Truth and politics." *The New Yorker*, 43 (25 February): 49–88. [89, 210–211]

Arens, R., 1967. "The Durham rule in action: Judicial psychiatry and psychiatric justice." *Law and Society Review*, 1 (June): 41–80. [212]

Arnold, T., 1937. *The Folklore of Capitalism*. New Haven: Yale University Press. [26–27, 154]

Auden, W. H., 1962. Review of J. Strachey, *The Strangled Cry. Encounter,* 19 (October): 84–88. [105, 211]

Ayer, A. J., 1936. *Language, Truth, and Logic.* New York: Dover Publications, Inc. [65, 188]

Barber, B., 1952. *Science and the Social Order.* Glencoe, Ill.: The Free Press. [88]

Barber, T. X., *et al.,* 1969. "Five attempts to replicate the experimenter bias effect." *Journal of Consulting and Clinical Psychology,* 33 (February): 1–6. [108]

Bartlett, C. J., and C. G. Green, 1966. "Clinical prediction: Does one sometimes know too much?" *Journal of Counseling Psychology,* 13: 267–270. [77]

Bateson, G., *et al.,* 1956. "Toward a theory of schizophrenia." *Behavioral Science,* 1 (October): 251–264. [192]

Bauer, R., *et al.,* 1966. *Social Indicators.* Cambridge: The M.I.T. Press. [194]

Beardslee, D. C., and D. D. O'Dowd, 1961. "The college-student image of the scientist." *Science,* 133 (31 March): 997–1001. [104]

Bell, D., 1960. *The End of Ideology.* New York: The Free Press of Glencoe, Inc. [171]

Bell, D., 1966a. "Sociodicy: A guide to modern usage." *American Scholar,* 35 (Autumn): 696–714. [190]

Bell, D., 1966b. "Comment: Government by commission." *The Public Interest,* 3 (Spring): 3–9. [80]

Bell, W., 1969. Review of P. F. Lazarsfeld *et al., The Uses of Sociology. American Journal of Sociology,* 72 (January): 420–422. [193]

Bem, D. J., 1967. "When saying is believing." *Psychology Today,* 1 (June): 21–27. [66]

Benda, J., 1928. *The Treason of the Intellectuals.* New York: William Morrow & Company, Inc. [171]

Benjamin C., 1955. *Operationism.* Springfield, Ill.: Charles C Thomas, Publisher. [17, 23, 31]

Bennett, Jonathan, 1960. "Moral arguments." *Mind,* 69 (October): 544–549. [188]

Berger, B. M., 1962. "On Talcott Parsons." *Commentary,* 34 (December): 507–513. [134]

Bergin, A. B., 1966. "Some implications of psychotherapy research for therapeutic practice." *Journal of Abnormal Psychology,* 71 (August): 235–246. [172]

Bergmann, G., 1968. "Ideology." Reprinted in M. Brodbeck (ed.), *Readings in the Philosophy of the Social Sciences.* New York: The Macmillan Company. [178, 181, 188]

Berns, W., 1962. "Voting studies." In H. J. Storing (ed.), *Essays on the Scientific Study of Politics.* New York: Holt, Rinehart and Winston, Inc. [81]

Bieri, J., *et. al.,* 1966. *Clinical and Social Judgment.* New York: John Wiley & Sons, Inc. [108]

Blalock, H. M., Jr., and Ann B. Blalock (eds.), 1968. *Methodology in Social Research.* New York: McGraw-Hill Book Company. [22]

Bliven, N., 1969. "Nowhere to go but up." *The New Yorker,* 44 (15 February): 116–122. [81]

Blumer, H., 1962. "Society as symbolic interaction." In A. M. Rose (ed.), *Human Behavior and Social Processes.* Boston: Houghton Mifflin Company. [55]

Bonney, M. E., 1946. "A sociometric study of the relationship of some factors to mutual friend-ships on the elementary, secondary, and college levels." *Sociometry,* 9 (February): 21–47. [78]

Boring, E. G., 1957. "When is human behavior predetermined?" *Scientific Monthly,* 84 (April): 189–196. [106]

Bouissou, R., 1942. *Essai sur l'Abstraction et Son Role dans la Connaissance.* Paris: Librairie Hachette. [110]

Boulding, K., 1967. "Dare we take the social sciences seriously?" *American Psychologist,* 22 (November): 879–887. [208]

Bower, T. G. R., 1966. "The visual world of infants." *Scientific American,* 215 (December): 80–97. [93]

Brain, R., 1950. "The cerebral basis of consciousness." *Brain* 73: 465–479. [110]

Braithwaite, R. B., 1966. "Probability and induction." In C. A. Mace (ed.), *British Philosophy in the Mid-Century.* London: George Allen & Unwin, Ltd. [118, 125]

Bridgman, P. W., 1938. "Operational analysis." *Philosophy of Science,* 5 (January): 115–131. [15]

Bridgman, P. W., 1954. "The present state of operationalism." In P. G. Frank (ed.), *The Validation of Scientific Theories.* Boston: Beacon Press. [14]

Brinton, C., 1938. *The Anatomy of Revolution.* New York: W. W. Norton & Company, Inc. [205]

Brodbeck, M. (ed.), 1968. *Readings in the Philosophy of the Social Sciences.* New York: The Macmillan Company. [46]

Broderick, C. B., 1956. "Predicting friendship behavior: A study of the determinants of friendship selection and maintenance in a college population." Unpublished doctoral dissertation, Cornell University. [78]

Bromley, D. B., 1968. "Conceptual analysis in the study of personality and adjustment." *Bulletin of the British Psychological Society* 21 (July): 155–160. [75]

Brooks, P. (translator), 1968. "Rapport Interdisciplinaire Nanterre, 11 June, 1968." *Partisan Review,* 35 (Fall): 536–541. [192, 213]

Brown, B., and O. Helmer, 1964. "Improving the reliability of estimates obtained from a consensus of experts." Santa Monica, Calif.: The RAND Corporation. Report No. P-2986. [73]

Brown, R., 1959. Review of V. Nabokov, *Lolita. Contemporary Psychology,* 4 (June): 172–174. [83–84]

Bruce, G., 1969. *The Stranglers: The Cult of Thuggee and Its Overthrow in British India.* New York: Harcourt, Brace & World, Inc. [168–169]

Buck, R. C., 1963. "Reflexive predictions." *Philosophy of Science,* 30 (October): 359–369. [111]

Buckley, W. F., Jr., 1969. "On experiencing Gore Vidal." *Esquire,* 72 (August): 108–113, 122–132. [51]

Bunge, M., 1959. *Causality.* Cambridge: Harvard University Press. [172]

Byrne, D., and W. Griffitt, 1966. "A developmental investigation of the law of attraction." *Journal of Personality and Social Psychology,* 4 (December): 699–702. [78]

Byrne, D., *et al.,* 1966. "Effects of economic similarity-dissimilarity on interpersonal attraction." *Journal of Personality and Social Psychology,* 4 (July): 220–224. [78]

Byrne, D., *et al.,* 1969. "Attitude similarity-dissimilarity and attraction: Generality beyond the college sophomore." *Journal of Social Psychology,* 79 (December): 155–161. [78]

Calder, R., 1964. "Common understanding of science." *Impact of Science on Society,* 14: 179–195. [104]

Calhoun, D. W., 1942. Review of R. M. MacIver, *Social Causation. American Sociological Review,* 7 (October): 714–719. [156, 172]

Calvez, J. Y., 1956. *La Penseé de Karl Marx.* Paris: Editions du Seuil. [184]

Campbell, D. T., 1963. "Social attitudes and acquired behavioral dispositions." In S. Koch (ed.), *Psychology: A Study of a Science.* Vol. 6. New York: McGraw-Hill Book Company. [82]

Camus, A., 1948. *The Plague.* New York: Alfred A. Knopf, Inc. [168]

Carney, R. E., 1967. "Environment and criminality." *American Psychologist,* 22 (March): 238. [76]

Cattell, R. B., and F. W. Warburton *et al.,* 1967. *Objective Personality and Motivation Tests: A Theoretical Introduction and Practical Compendium.* Urbana: University of Illinois Press. [111]

Center for the Study of Democratic Institutions, 1968. "Students and society." *Center Occasional Paper,* 1: No. 1. Santa Barbara, Calif. [210]

Chapman, L. J., 1967. "Illusory correlation in observational report." *Journal of Verbal Learning and Verbal Behavior,* 1: 151–155. [213]

Chapman, L. J., and J. P. Chapman, 1967. "Genesis of popular but erroneous psychodiagnostic observations." *Journal of Abnormal Psychology,* 72 (June): 193–204. [213]

Chapman, L. J., and J. P. Chapman, 1969. "Illusory correlation as an obstacle to the use of valid psychodiagnostic signs." *Journal of Abnormal Psychology,* 74 (June): 271–280. [213]

Chase, S., 1938. *The Tyranny of Words.* New York: Harcourt, Brace and Company, Inc. [25]

Cicero, M. T., 1963. *De Divinatione*. Edited by A. S. Pease. Darmstadt: Wissenschaftliche. [123]

Clark, E. L., 1949. "Motivation of Jewish students." *Journal of Social Psychology*, 29 (February): 113–117. [31]

Clark, K. B., 1954. Testimony in Bolling v. Sharpe, 347 U.S. 497; testimony in Brown v. Board of Education, 347 U.S. 483. [200–201]

Coan, R. W., 1968. "Dimensions of psychological theory." *American Psychologist*, 23 (October): 715–722. [28, 75]

Cohen, L. J., 1959. "Are moral arguments always liable to break down?" *Mind*, 68 (October): 530–532. [188]

Cohen, M. R., and E. Nagel, 1934. *An Introduction to Logic and Scientific Method*. New York: Harcourt, Brace and Company, Inc. [89]

Cohn-Bendit, D., *et al.*, 1968. "Why sociologists?" *Partisan Review* (Fall): 543–549. [192]

Coleman, J., *et al.*, 1966. *Equality of Educational Opportunity*. Washington, D.C.: U.S. Government Printing Office. [199]

Coles, R., 1963. "The desegregation of Southern schools: A psychiatric study." Reprinted in H. H. Humphrey (ed.), *School Desegregation: Documents and Commentaries*. New York: Thomas Y. Crowell Company, 1964. [212]

Coles, R., 1967. "Is prejudice against Negroes overrated?" *Trans-Action*, 4 (October): 44–45. [162–163, 212]

Commoner, B., 1966. *Science and Survival*. New York: The Viking Press, Inc. [208]

Coser, L., 1956. *The Functions of Social Conflict*. New York: The Free Press of Glencoe, Ill. [27]

Costner, H. L., 1968. "Theory, deduction, and rules of correspondence." Boston: American Sociological Association. Paper read at 1968 meetings. [32]

Cox, B., and H. Sargent, 1950. "TAT responses of emotionally disturbed and emotionally stable children." *Journal of Projective Techniques*, 14 (March): 60–74. [212]

Cranston, M., 1969. "Herbert Marcuse." *Encounter*, 32 (March): 38–50. [210]

Cressey, D. R., 1953. *Other People's Money*. Glencoe, Ill.: The Free Press. [189]

Cressey, D. R., 1964. "Causes of employee dishonesty." East Lansing: Michigan State University. Paper read at "Top-Management Business Security Seminar," 16 April. [61]

Cronbach, L. J., and G. Gleser, 1953. "Assessing similarity between profiles." *Psychological Bulletin*, 50 (September): 456–473. [113]

Cross, H. J., 1964. "The outcome of psychotherapy: A selected analysis of research findings." *Journal of Consulting Psychology*, 28 (October): 413–417. [172]

Danet, B. N., 1965. "Prediction of mental illness in college students on the basis of 'nonpsychiatric' MMPI profiles." *Journal of Consulting Psychology*, 29 (December): 577–580. [84]

Davis, F., 1960. "Uncertainty in medical prognosis: Clinical and functional." *American Journal of Sociology*, 66 (July): 41–47. [106]

De Charms, R., *et al.*, 1965. "The 'origin-pawn' variable in person perception." *Sociometry*, 28 (September): 241–258. [35, 162]

Decore, A. M., 1966. *Psychological Adjustment and the Perception of Social Reality*. (M. A. dissertation.) Edmonton: The University of Alberta, Department of Sociology. [107]

DeGré, G. L., 1943. *Society and Ideology: An Inquiry into the Sociology of Knowledge*. New York: The Hamilton Press. [108]

Dernburg, T. F., and D. M. McDougall, 1968. *Macroeconomics*. New York: McGraw-Hill Book Company. [70]

De Sola Pool, I. (ed.), 1967. *Contemporary Political Science: Toward Empirical Theory*. New York: McGraw-Hill Book Company. [174]

Deutsch, A., 1950. *The Trouble with Cops*. Boston: Little, Brown and Company. [189]

Deutscher, I., 1966. "Words and deeds: Social science and social policy." *Social Problems*, 13 (Winter): 235–254. [66, 68]

Deutscher, I., 1967. "On adding apples and oranges: Making distinctions and connections in social science." Des Moines, Iowa: Midwest Sociological Society. Paper read at annual meeting, April. [18, 68]

Dodd, S. C., 1943. "Operational definitions operationally defined." *American Journal of Sociology,* 48 (January): 482–489. [14]

Donagan, A., 1966. "The Popper-Hempel theory reconsidered." In W. H. Dray (ed.), *Philosophical Analysis and History.* New York: Harper & Row Publishers. [150–151]

Dooley, D. J., 1959. "Science as cliché, fable, and faith." *Bulletin of Atomic Scientists,* 15 (November): 372–375. [104]

Dostoyevsky, F., 1950. *The Brothers Karamazov.* New York: Modern Library, Inc. [74]

Douglas, J. D., 1967. *The Social Meanings of Suicide.* Princeton: Princeton University Press. [76, 198]

Draper, T., 1964. "Five years of Castro's Cuba." *Commentary,* 37 (January): 25–37. [214]

Dray, W. H. (ed.), 1966. *Philosophical Analysis and History.* New York: Harper & Row, Publishers. [147]

DuBridge, L. A., 1968. "Can success be the cause of failure?" *Science,* 162 (13 December): 1225. [202]

Ducasse, C. J., 1960. "Causality: Critique of Hume's analysis." In E. H. Madden (ed.), *The Structure of Scientific Thought.* Boston: Houghton Mifflin Company. [148, 158]

Durkheim, E., 1963. *Les Régles de la Méthode Sociologique.* (15th ed.) Paris: Alcan and P. U. F. [69]

Dynes, R., and E. L. Quarantelli, 1968. "What looting in civil disturbances really means." *Trans-Action,* 5 (May): 9–14. [52, 53]

Easterbrook, J. A., 1959. "The effect of emotion on cue utilization and the organization of behavior." *Psychological Review,* 66 (May): 183–201. [108]

Edel, Abraham, 1955. *Ethical Judgment: The Use of Science in Ethics.* Chicago: The Free Press of Glencoe, Ill. [188]

Eiduson, B. T., 1962. *Scientists: Their Psychological World.* New York: Basic Books, Inc., Publishers. [90]

Einstein, A., 1934. *The World As I See It.* New York: Covici Friede. [22]

Engels, F., 1934. Letter to Bloch in *Marx-Engels Selected Correspondence,* The Marxist Library, Vol. 29. New York: International Publishers. [207]

Eriksen, C. W., and H. Wechsler, 1955. "Some effects of experimentally induced anxiety upon discrimination behavior." *Journal of Abnormal and Social Psychology,* 51 (November): 458–463. [108]

Eriksen, C. W., 1960. "Discrimination and learning without awareness." *Psychological Review,* 67 (September): 279–300. [57, 66]

Erskine, H. G., 1967–68. "The polls: Demonstrations and race riots." *Public Opinion Quarterly,* 31 (Winter): 655–677. [31]

Etzioni, A., 1968a. Review of K. Boulding, *The Impact of the Social Sciences. Harvard Educational Review,* 38 (Summer): 578–582. [203]

Etzioni, A., 1968b. "Why task-force studies go wrong." *The Wall Street Journal* (9 July): 12 [169, 173]

Evans, B., 1954. *The Spoor of Spooks.* New York: Alfred A. Knopf, Inc. [99]

Evans, J. L., 1968. *Affect and the Attribution of Causation.* (M. A. thesis.) Edmonton: The University of Alberta, Department of Sociology. [1, 35]

Eysenck, H. J., 1964. "Exchange of letters with Miss Kathleen Nott." *Encounter,* 23 (September-December): *passim.* [3–5]

Eysenck, H. J., 1966. *The Effects of Psychotherapy.* New York: International Science Press. [82, 168, 172]

Ezer, M., 1962. "Effect of religion upon children's responses to questions involving physical causality." In J. Rosenblith and W. Allinsmith (eds.), *The Causes of Behavior: Readings in Child Development and Educational Psychology.* (1st ed.) Boston: Allyn and Bacon, Inc. [173]

Fancher, R. E., Jr., 1966. "Explicit personality theories and accuracy in person perception." *Journal of Personality*, 34 (June): 252–261. [84, 132]

Fancher, R. E., Jr., 1967. "Accuracy vs. validity in person perception." *Journal of Consulting Psychology*, 31 (June): 264–269. [32, 84, 132]

Feder, C. Z., 1967. "Relationship of repression-sensitization to adjustment status, social desirability, and acquiescence response set." *Journal of Consulting Psychology*, 31 (August): 401–406. [107]

Feigl, H., 1953. "The scientific outlook: Naturalism and humanism." In H. Feigl and M. Brodbeck (eds.), *Readings in the Philosophy of Science*. New York: Appleton-Century-Crofts, Inc. [98, 99, 100]

Feshbach, S., 1963. "The effects of emotional restraint upon the projection of positive affect." *Journal of Personality*, 31 (December): 471–481. [212]

Festinger, L., *et al.*, 1956. *When Prophecy Fails*. Minneapolis: University of Minnesota Press. [82]

Feuer, L. S., 1963. *The Scientific Intellectual*. New York: Basic Books, Inc., Publishers. [49, 78–79]

Fiedler, F. E., *et al.*, 1952. "Unconscious attitudes as correlates of sociometric choice in a social group." *Journal of Abnormal and Social Psychology*, 47 (October): 790–796. [78]

Finlay, D. J., O. R. Holsti, and R. R. Fagen, 1967. *Enemies in Politics*. Chicago: Rand McNally & Company. [194]

Fischer, J., 1956. "The harm good people do." *Harper's*. 213 (October): 14–20. [194]

Fishbein, M., 1967. "Attitude and the prediction of behavior." In M. Fishbein (ed.), *Readings in Attitude Theory and Measurement*. New York: John Wiley & Sons, Inc. [56, 81]

Fishman, J. A., 1956. "An examination of the process and function of social stereotyping." *Journal of Social Psychology*, 43 (February): 27–64. [30]

Floud, J., 1966. "Karl Mannheim." *New Society*, 8 (29 December): 969–971. [100]

Foot, P., 1958. "Moral arguments." *Mind*, 67 (October): 502–513. [187]

Friedenberg, E. Z., 1960. "Truth: Upper, middle, and lower." *Commentary*, 30 (December): 516–523. [88]

Friedenberg, E. Z., 1968. "Canada 101." Edmonton: CFRN-TV, television broadcast (29 January). [210]

Friedman, Milton, 1968. *Dollars and Deficits*. Englewood Cliffs, N.J.: Prentice-Hall, Inc. [204]

Friedman, Murray, 1969. "Is white racism the problem?" *Commentary*, 47 (January): 61–65. [164]

Gage, N. L., and L. J. Cronbach, 1955. "Conceptual and methodological problems in interpersonal perception." *Psychological Review*, 62 (November): 411–422. [20–21, 32, 50, 84]

Gans, H. J., 1968. "Why did Kennedy die?" *Trans-Action*, 5 (July/August): 5–6. [51, 52]

Gardiner, P. (ed.), 1959. *Theories of History*. New York: The Free Press of Glencoe, Inc. [16]

Gardner, M., 1957. *Fads and Fallacies*. New York: Dover Publications, Inc. [99]

Gardner, M., 1968. "Counting systems and the relationship between numbers and the real world." *Scientific American*, 219 (September): 218–230. [93]

Gerth, H., and C. W. Mills, 1953. *Character and Social Structure: The Psychology of Social Institutions*. New York: Harcourt, Brace and Company, Inc. [60]

Glassen, P., 1959. "The cognitivity of moral judgments." *Mind*, 68 (January): 57–72. [188]

Glazer, N., 1967. "The idological uses of sociology." In P. F. Lazarsfeld *et al.* (eds.), *The Uses of Sociology*. New York: Basic Books, Inc. [108, 166]

Glenn, N. D., 1968. "Social security and income redistribution." *Social Forces*, 46 (June): 538–539. [31]

Glock, C. Y., and R. Stark, 1966. *Christian Beliefs and Anti-Semitism*. New York: Harper & Row, Publishers. [200]

Goldberg, A., and B. Rubin, 1964. "Recovery of patients during periods of supposed neglect." *British Journal of Medical Psychology*, 7 (Pt. 3): 266–272. [172]

Goldberg, L. R., 1965. "Diagnostician vs. diagnostic signs: The diagnosis of psychosis versus neurosis from the MMPI." *Psychological Monographs*. 79: No. 602. [84]

Goldberg, L. R., 1968. "Simple models or simple processes? Some research on clinical judgments." *American Psychologist*, 23 (July): 483–496. [203, 213]

Gordon, T. J., and O. Helmer, 1964. "Report on a long-range forecasting study." Santa Monica, Calif.: The RAND Corporation. Report No. P-2982. [73]

Gottheil, F. M., 1966. *Marx's Economic Predictions*. Evanston, Ill.: Northwestern University Press. [188]

Gouldner, A. W., 1957. "Theoretical requirements of the applied social sciences." *American Sociological Review*, 22 (February): 92–102. [166]

Gouldner, A. W., 1963. "Anti-Minotaur: The myth of a value-free sociology." In M. Stein and A. Vidich (eds.), *Sociology on Trial*. Englewood Cliffs, N.J.: Prentice-Hall, Inc. Reprinted from *Social Problems*, 9 (Winter, 1962): 199–213. [195]

Grebstein, L. C., 1963. "Relative accuracy of actuarial prediction: Experienced clinicians, and graduate students in a clinical judgment task." *Journal of Consulting Psychology*, 27 (April): 127–132. [84]

Greeley, A. M., 1967. Review of C. Glock and R. Stark, *Christian Beliefs and Anti-Semitism*. *American Sociological Review*, 32 (December): 1007–1008. [200]

Green, R. W. (ed.), 1959. *Protestantism and Capitalism: The Weber Thesis and Its Critics*. Boston: D. C. Heath and Company. [49]

Guilford, J. P., 1967. *The Nature of Human Intelligence*. New York: McGraw-Hill Book Company. [115]

Hakeem, M., 1958. "A critique of the psychiatric approach to crime and correction." *Law and Contemporary Problems*, 28 (Autumn): 650–682. [212]

Hakel, M. D., 1968. "How often is often?" *American Psychologist*, 23 (July): 533–534. [31]

Halleck, S. L., 1966. "A critique of current psychiatric roles in the legal process." *Wisconsin Law Review*, 41 (Spring): 379–401. [212]

Halleck, S. L., 1968. "Hypotheses of student unrest." Chicago: American Association for Higher Education, Address, 4 March. [165]

Hardin, G., 1956. "Meaninglessness of the word protoplasm." *Scientific Monthly*, 82 (March): 112–120. [24]

Hardin, G., 1968. "The tragedy of the commons." *Science*, 162 (13 December): 1243–1248. [70, 207, 209]

Hare, R. M., 1952. *The Language of Morals*. London: Clarendon. [188]

Hart, H., 1947. "Factuality and the discussion of values." *Social Forces*, 25 (March): 290–294. [110–111, 189]

Hart, H., et al., 1953. "Toward an operational definition of the term 'operation.'" *American Sociological Review*, 18 (December): 612–617. [14–15]

Hartshorne, H., and M. A. May, 1928. *Studies in the Nature of Character*. Vol. I: *Studies in Deceit*. New York: Macmillan. [66, 82]

Hastings, D. W., 1965. "The psychiatry of presidential assassination." *The Journal-Lancet*, 85 (March, April, May, July): 3–301. [52]

Hayakawa, S. I., 1939. *Language in Action*. New York: Harcourt, Brace and Company, Inc. [25]

Hayek, F. A., 1955. *The Counter-Revolution of Science: Studies on the Abuse of Reason*. Chicago: The Free Press of Glencoe, Ill. [44]

Hayek, F. A., 1967. *Studies in Philosophy, Politics, and Economics*. Chicago: University of Chicago Press. [128]

Hebb, D. O., 1949. *The Organization of Behavior*. New York: John Wiley & Sons, Inc. [93]

Heilbroner, R. L., 1967. "Counter-revolutionary America." *Commentary,* 43 (April): 31–38. [109]

Heilbroner, R. L., 1968. "Putting Marx to work." *The New York Review of Books,* 11 (December 5): 8–12. [133–134]

Helmer, O., and N. Rescher, 1960. "On the epistemology of the inexact sciences." Santa Monica, Calif.: The RAND Corporation, Report R-353. [135–136]

Hempel, C. G., and P. Oppenheim, 1948. "Studies in the logic of explanation." *Philosophy of Science,* 15 (April): 135–175. [135]

Hempel, C. G., 1952. "Fundamentals of concept formation in empirical science." In *International Encyclopedia of Unified Science,* Vol. II. Chicago: University of Chicago Press. [17]

Hempel, C. G., 1965. *Aspects of Scientific Explanation.* New York: The Free Press. [135]

Henderson, L. J., 1932. "An approximate definition of fact." *University of California Studies in Philosophy.* Berkeley: University of California Press. [109]

Hertzberg, A., 1963. "Church, state, and the Jews." *Commentary,* 35 (April): 277–288. [31]

Hiler, E. W., and D. Nesvig, 1965. "An evaluation of criteria used by clinicians to infer pathology from figure drawings." *Journal of Consulting Psychology,* 29 (December): 520–529. [84]

Hillinger, C., 1968. "A generalization of the principle of causality which makes it applicable to evolutionary systems." *Methodology and Science,* 1 (July): 143–147. [147]

Himmelfarb, M., 1965. "How we are." *Commentary,* 39 (January): 69–74. [31]

Himmelfarb, M., 1967. "Are Jews still liberals?" *Commentary,* 43 (April): 67–72. [31]

Hirsch, W., 1956. "The image of the scientist in science fiction: A content analysis." *American Journal of Sociology,* 63 (March): 506–512. [104]

Hirschi, T., and H. C. Selvin, 1966. "False criteria of causality in delinquency research." *Social Problems,* 13 (Winter): 254–268. [148–149, 158, 160, 172]

Hirschi, T., and H. C. Selvin, 1967. *Delinquency Research: An Appraisal of Analytic Methods.* New York: The Free Press. [172]

Hoch, P. H. (ed.), 1948. *Failures in Psychiatric Treatment.* New York: Grune & Stratton, Inc. [172]

Hockett, C. F., 1968. *The State of the Art.* The Hague: Mouton. [105–206]

Hofstaetter, P. R., 1950. "The actuality of questions." *International Journal of Opinion and Attitude Research,* 4 (Spring): 16–26. [82]

Holmes, D. S., 1968. "Dimensions of projection." *Psychological Bulletin,* 69 (April): 248–268. [31]

Homans, G., 1961. *Social Behavior: Its Elementary Forms.* New York: Harcourt, Brace, & World, Inc. [121]

Homans, G., 1964. "Bringing men back in." *American Sociological Review,* 29 (December): 809–818. [69]

Homans, G., 1967. *The Nature of Social Science.* New York: Harcourt, Brace & World, Inc. [69]

Honigmann, J. J., 1954. *Culture and Personality.* New York: Harper & Brothers. [72]

Hook, S., 1957. "Scientific knowledge and philosophic 'knowledge.'" *Partisan Review,* 24 (Spring): 215–234. [86]

Hook, S., (ed.), 1963. *Philosophy and History.* New York: New York University Press. [147]

Hopkins, M., vs. S. M. Hartley, 1967. "Discriminatory statistics?" *Social Forces,* 46 (September): 109–110. [107]

Hoult, T. F., 1968. ". . . Who shall prepare himself to the battle?" *The American Sociologist,* 3 (February): 3–7. [79–80]

Hudson, W. D., 1959. "Moral arguments." *Mind,* 68 (October): 533–534. [188]

Hudson, W. D., 1962. "On the alleged objectivity of moral judgments." *Mind,* 71 (October): 530–534. [188]

Humbert, E. R., 1963. "The 'ought' and the 'is.'" *Mind,* 72 (October): 581–583. [188]

Hume, D., 1874. *A Treatise on Human Nature.* London: Longmans, Green & Co., Ltd. Bk. III, Pt. 1. [187]

Hume, D., 1758. *Enquiry Concerning Human Understanding.* New York: Liberal Arts Press, 1955. [124]

Humphrey, N. D., 1945. "The stereotype and the social types of Mexican-American youths." *Journal of Social Psychology,* 22 (February): 69–78. [30–31]

Hurlock, E. B., 1956. *Child Development.* New York: McGraw-Hill Book Company. [66]

Israel, H. E., 1945. "Two difficulties in operational thinking." *Psychological Review,* 52 (September): 260–261. [15]

Jackson, D. N., and S. Messick (eds.), 1967. *Problems in Human Assessment.* New York: McGraw-Hill Book Company. [84]

James, R. D., 1968. "Genetic blueprints: Horror or hope?" *The Wall Street Journal* (11 November): 12. [106]

James, W., 1890. *The Principles of Psychology.* New York: Henry Holt and Company, Inc. [25–26]

James, W., 1907. *Pragmatism.* London: Longmans, Green & Co., Ltd. [75]

Jaques, E., 1966. "Science and society." *Human Relations,* 19 (May): 125–137. [104]

Jastrow, J., 1962. *Error and Eccentricity in Human Belief.* New York: Dover Publications, Inc. A republication of an original title: *Wish and Wisdom: Episodes in the Vagaries of Belief.* New York: Appleton-Century Company, Inc. 1935. [99, 108]

Kahn, A. J., 1967. "From delinquency treatment to community development." In P. Lazarsfeld *et al.* (eds.), *The Uses of Sociology.* New York: Basic Books, Inc., Publishers. [198–199]

Kahn, H., and A. J. Wiener, 1967. *The Year 2000: A Framework for Speculation on the Next Thirty-Three Years.* New York: The Macmillan Company. [73]

Kaplan, A., 1964. *The Conduct of Inquiry.* San Francisco: Chandler Publishing Company. [8]

Katona, G., 1951. *Psychological Analysis of Economic Behavior.* New York: McGraw-Hill Book Company. [57]

Katona, G., and E. Muller, 1957. *Consumer Expectations, 1953–1956.* Ann Arbor: University of Michigan. [57]

Katona, G., and E. Muller, 1960. *The Powerful Consumer.* New York: McGraw-Hill Book Company. [57]

Kattsoff, L. O., 1947. "Observation and interpretation in science." *Philosophical Review,* 56: 682–689. [109]

Katz, E., and P. F. Lazarsfeld, 1955. *Personal Influence: The Part Played by People in the Flow of Mass Communication.* Chicago: The Free Press of Glencoe, Ill. [170]

Kelly, E. L., 1963. "Consistency of the adult personality." *American Psychologist,* 10 (November): 659–681. [136–137]

Kelsen, H., 1957. *What Is Justice?* Berkeley: University of California Press. [144]

Keniston, K., 1968. "Youth, change and violence." *The American Scholar,* 38 (Spring): 227–245. [165]

Kerner, G. C., 1962. "Approvals, reasons, and moral arguments." *Mind,* 71 (October): 474–486. [188]

Kesey, K., 1964. *One Flew over the Cuckoo's Nest.* New York: Compass. [84]

Killian, L. M., 1968. *The Impossible Revolution?* New York: Random House, Inc. [212]

Kinsey, A., *et al.,* 1948. *Sexual Behavior in the American Male.* Philadelphia: W. B. Saunders Company. [190]

Kleinmuntz, B., 1967. "Sign and seer: Another example." *Journal of Abnormal Psychology,* 72 (April): 163–165. [84]

Koestler, A., 1941. *Darkness at Noon.* New York: The Macmillan Company. [107]

Koestler, A., 1945. *The Yogi and the Commissar.* New York: The Macmillan Company. [192]

Koestler, A., 1967. *The Ghost in the Machine.* London: Hutchinson Publishing Group, Ltd. [26]

Kolenda, K., 1958. "Science and morality." *Mind,* 67 (April): 203–215. [188]

Kopkind, A., 1967. "Soul power." Review of M. L. King, Jr., *Where Do We Go from Here: Chaos or Community? The New York Review of Books* (24 August): 3–6. [52]

Korner, S., 1959. *Conceptual Thinking: A Logical Enquiry.* New York: Dover Publications, Inc. [75]

Krech, D., and R. S. Crutchfield, 1948. *Theory and Problems of Social Psychology.* New York: McGraw-Hill Book Company. [182]

Krech, D., and R. S. Crutchfield, et al., 1962. *Individual in Society.* New York: McGraw-Hill Book Company. [29]

Kristol, I., 1961. "Machiavelli and the profanation of politics." In *The Logic of Personal Knowledge: Essays Presented to Michael Polanyi.* London: Routledge & Kegan Paul, Ltd. [91]

Ladd, J., 1957. *The Structure of a Moral Code.* Cambridge: Harvard University Press. [211]

Laing, R. D., et al., 1966. *Interpersonal Perception.* New York: Springer Publishing Co., Inc. [140]

Lang, P. J., and B. G. Melamed, 1969. "Case report: Avoidance conditioning therapy of an infant with chronic ruminative vomiting." *Journal of Abnormal Psychology,* 74 (February): 1–8. [168]

Langer, S., 1962. *Philosophical Sketches.* Baltimore, Md.: Johns Hopkins Press. [110]

Langer, S., 1967. *Mind: An Essay on Human Feeling.* Baltimore, Md.: Johns Hopkins Press. [56]

LaPiere, R. T., 1930. "The Armenian colony in Fresno County, California: A study in social psychology." Unpublished Ph.D. dissertation, Stanford University. [31]

LaPiere, R. T., 1936. "Type-rationalizations of group antipathy." *Social Forces,* 15 (December): 230–237. [31]

LaPiere, R. T., 1938. *Collective Behavior.* New York: McGraw-Hill Book Company. [163, 165]

Laughlin, W. S., 1966. "Race: A population concept." *Eugenics Quarterly,* 13 (December): 326–340. [113]

Lawrence, N., 1961. "Ethics as mandate." *Mind,* 70 (July): 376–384. [188]

Lawson, H. G., 1969. "Cuba's economy." *The Wall Street Journal,* 80 (7 March): 1 and 14. [205, 214]

Lazarsfeld, P., 1949. "The American soldier: An expository review." *Public Opinion Quarterly,* 13 (Fall): 377–404. [196, 197]

Lefford, A., 1946. "The influence of emotional subject matter on logical reasoning." *Journal of General Psychology,* 34 (April): 127–151. [108, 120, 181]

Leifer, R., 1964. "The psychiatrist and tests of criminal responsibility. *American Psychologist,* 19 (November): 835–830. [1, 34, 142, 161, 212]

Leifer, R., 1967. "Reply to Eckhardt." *American Psychologist,* 22 (August): 676–677. [212]

Lerner, D. (ed.), 1965. *Cause and Effect.* New York: The Free Press. [172]

Levitt, E. E., 1957. "The results of psychotherapy with children: An evaluation." *Journal of Consulting Psychology,* 21 (June): 189–196. [82]

Levonian, D., 1963. "Opinion change in relation to arbitrarily selected personality dimensions." Philadelphia: American Psychological Association. Paper presented at meeting, August. [132]

Levonian, D., 1968. "Interpretation of published results relating personality to opinion change." *Psychological Bulletin,* 69 (June): 388–389. [132–133]

Lichtheim, G., 1967. *The Concept of Ideology.* New York: Random House, Inc. [178, 188]

Light, R. J., 1968. "Report analysis: National Advisory Commission on Civil Disorders." *Harvard Educational Review,* 38 (Fall): 756–767. [162, 164–165, 173–174]

Lindeman, E. C., 1954. "The common man as reader." In J. W. Krutch (ed.), *Is the Common Man Too Common?* Norman: University of Oklahoma Press. [105]

Lindesmith, A. R., and A. L. Strauss, 1956. *Social Psychology.* New York: Holt, Rinehart and Winston, Inc. [45]

Lindzey, G., 1954. *Handbook of Social Psychology.* Reading, Mass.: Addison-Wesley Publishing Company, Inc. [30]

Lindzey, G., 1965. "Seer vs. sign." *Journal of Experimental Research in Personality,* 1 (March): 17–26. [84]

Little, K. B., and E. S. Shneidman, 1955. "The validity of the thematic projective technique interpretations." *Journal of Personality,* 23: 285–294. [212]

Lloyd, T., and J. McLeod (eds.), 1969. *Agenda 1970: Proposals for a Creative Politics.* Toronto: University of Toronto Press. [80]

Locke, D., 1965. Review of Eric D'Arcy, *Human Acts: An Essay in Their Moral Evaluation. Mind,* 74 (January): 138–139. [97]

Louch, A. R., 1966. *Explanation and Human Action.* Oxford: Basil Blackwell. [35, 41, 43, 45, 172, 196]

Luchins, A. S., 1968. "Psychology and the philosophy of science." *Methodology and Science,* 1 (April): 108–113. [135]

Lukes, S., 1968. "Methodological individualism reconsidered." *British Journal of Sociology,* 19 (June): 119–129. [69]

Lundberg, F., 1954. *The Treason of the People.* New York: Harper & Brothers. [189]

Lundberg, G. A., 1941. "Case studies vs. statistical methods: An issue based on misunderstanding." *Sociometry,* 4: 379–383. [131]

Lundberg, G. A., 1947. *Can Science Save Us?* London: Longmans, Green & Co., Ltd. [193]

Mace, C. A., 1965. "Causal explanations in psychology." In C. Banks and P. L. Broadhurst (eds.), *Stephanos: Studies in Psychology.* London: University of London Press. [153–154]

MacIver, R. M., 1942. *Social Causation.* Boston: Ginn and Company. (Rev. 1964.) New York: Harper & Row, Publishers. [156, 172]

Mackie, M. M., 1968. "The accuracy of folk knowledge concerning Alberta Hutterites and North American Indians: An available data stereotype validation technique." Edmonton: The University of Alberta, Department of Sociology. Mimeographed Ph.D. dissertation proposal. [31]

MacNaughton-Smith, P., 1965. *Some Statistical and Other Numerical Techniques for Classifying Individuals.* London: Her Majesty's Stationery Office. [113]

Magid, M., 1963. "The innocence of Tennessee Williams." *Commentary,* 35 (January): 34–43. [140–141]

Mahalanobis, P. C., 1936. "On the generalized distance in statistics." *Proceedings of the National Institute of Science* (India), 12: 49–55. Reprinted in C. R. Rao, *Linear Statistical Inference and Its Applications.* New York: John Wiley & Sons, Inc. (1965). [113]

Mainord, W. A., 1962. "A therapy." *Bulletin of the Division of Mental Health,* 5 (May). State of Washington: Mental Health Research Institute. [168]

Mannheim, K., 1936. *Ideology and Utopia.* New York: Harcourt, Brace and Company, Inc. [179]

Mannheim, K., 1941. *Man and Society in an Age of Reconstruction.* New York: Harcourt, Brace and Company, Inc. [210]

Mao, T., 1967. *Quotations from Chairman Mao Tse-Tung.* New York: Bantam Books. [183]

Marcuse, H., 1969. Cited by M. Cranston, "Herbert Marcuse." *Encounter,* 32 (March): 39. [210]

Marx, K., 1950. *Selected Works of Karl Marx.* Moscow: Foreign Languages Publishing House. [177–178]

Maurer, D. W., 1940. *The Big Con.* Indianapolis: The Bobbs-Merrill Company, Inc. [84]

Mayer, C. W., 1961. "Science, the scientist, and the public." *American Journal of Economics,* 20 (April): 304. [104]

Mayo, B., 1968. "Traces and portents." *Philosophical Quarterly,* 18 (October): 289–298. [127]

Mazur, A., 1968. "The littlest science." *American Sociologist,* 3 (August): 195–200. [172]

McClelland, D. C., 1962. "On the psychodynamics of creative physical scientists." In H. E. Gruber *et al.* (eds.), *Contemporary Approaches to Creative Thinking.* New York: Atherton Press, Inc. [90]

McClosky, H., and J. H. Schaar, 1965. "Psychological dimensions of anomy." *American Sociological Review,* 30 (February): 14–40. [18]

McEvoy, F. P., 1941. "The lie-detector goes into business." *Reader's Digest,* 38: 69–72. [189]

Mead, M., and R. Metraux, 1957. "The image of the scientist among high school students: A pilot study." *Science,* 126 (20 August): 384–390. [104]

Meehan, E. J., 1967. *Contemporary Political Thought: A Critical Study.* Homewood, Ill.: The Dorsey Press. [128]

Meehan, E. J., 1968. *Explanation in Social Science: A System Paradigm.* Homewood, Ill.: The Dorsey Press. [83]

Meehl, P. E., 1954. *Clinical vs. Statistical Prediction.* Minneapolis: University of Minnesota Press. [84, 102]

Meehl, P. E., and A. Rosen, 1955. "Antecedent probability and the efficiency of psychometric signs, patterns, or cutting scores." *Psychological Bulletin,* 52 (May): 194–216. [77]

Meehl, P. E., and A. Rosen, 1965. "Seer over sign: The first good example." *Journal of Experimental Research in Personality,* 1 (March): 27–32. [84]

Megargee, E. I. (ed.), 1966. *Research in Clinical Assessment.* New York: Harper & Row, Publishers. [84]

Mencken, H. L., 1958. *The Bathtub Hoax.* New York: Alfred A. Knopf, Inc. [106]

Menninger, K., 1968. *The Crime of Punishment.* New York: The Viking Press, Inc. [182]

Merritt, C. B., and E. G. Fowler, 1948. "The pecuniary honesty of the public at large." *Journal of Abnormal and Social Psychology,* 43 (January): 90–93. [189]

Merton, R. K., 1949. *Social Theory and Social Structure.* Glencoe, Ill.: The Free Press. [111]

Michael, D. N., 1957. "Scientists through adolescent eyes." *Scientific Monthly,* 84 (March): 135–140. [104]

Michotte, A., 1963. *The Perception of Causality.* New York: Basic Books, Inc., Publishers. [142, 172]

Mill, J. S., 1866. *Auguste Comte and Positivism.* Philadelphia: J. B. Lippincott Company. [123]

Miller, N. E., 1969. "Learning of visceral and glandular responses." *Science,* 163 (31 January): 434–445. [64]

Mills, C. W., 1942. "The professional ideology of social pathologists." *American Journal of Sociology,* 44 (September): 165–180. [160]

Minogue, K. R., 1968. *The Liberal Mind.* New York: Vintage Books (Random House, Inc.). [181]

Molotch, H., 1969. "Sell-out sociology." *The American Sociologist,* 4 (February): 50–51. [188]

Moore, B., Jr., 1967. "The society nobody wants: A look beyond Marxism and liberalism." In K. H. Wolff and B. Moore, Jr., *The Critical Spirit: Essays in Honor of Herbert Marcuse.* Boston: Beacon Press. [203–204]

Moore, W. E., and M. M. Tumin, 1949. "Some social functions of ignorance." *American Sociological Review,* 14 (December): 787–795. [187]

Morgan, D. N., 1958. "Is justification scientifically impossible?" *Ethics,* 69 (October): 19–47. [106]

Morgan, J. J. B., and J. T. Morton, 1944. "The distortion of syllogistic reasoning produced by personal convictions." *Journal of Social Psychology,* 20 (October): 39–59. [108]

Morgenbesser, S., 1958. "Role and status of anthropological theories." *Science* (8 August): 285–288. [67]

Morgenstern, O., 1963. *On the Accuracy of Economic Observations.* Princeton: Princeton University Press. [133, 198]

Moynihan, D. P., 1967. "The urban Negro *is* the 'urban problem.'" *Trans-Action,* 4 (October): 36–38. (Excerpt from testimony before the Ribicoff Senate Subcommittee, hearings on urban problems). [182, 190]

Moynihan, D. P., 1969. *Maximum Feasible Misunderstanding: Community Action in the War on Poverty.* New York: The Free Press. [129–130]

Musil, R., 1953. *The Man Without Qualities.* New York: Coward-McCann, Inc. [105]

Myrdal, G., *et al.,* 1942. *An American Dilemma.* New York: Harper & Brothers. [186, 192, 193]

Myrdal, G., *et al.,* 1968. *Asian Drama.* New York: Pantheon Books. [81]

Nagel, E., 1961. *The Structure of Science: Problems in the Logic of Scientific Explanation.* New York: Harcourt, Brace & World, Inc. [145]

National Advisory Commission on Civil Disorders, 1968. *Report of the National Advisory Commission on Civil Disorders.* New York: E. P. Dutton & Co., Inc. [163–164]

Nettler, G., 1950. "A note on the notion of a 'scientific morality.'" *Journal of Social Psychology,* 32: 115–118. [195]

Nettler, G., 1961. "Good men, bad men, and the perception of reality." *Sociometry,* 24 (September): 279–294. [107]

Nettler, G., 1965. "A further comment on 'anomy.'" *American Sociological Review,* 30 (October): 762–763. [18–19]

Nettler, G., 1967a. "Review essay: On death and dying." *Social Problems,* 14 (Winter): 335–344. [51, 59]

Nettler, G., 1967b. *Social Psychology Syllabus.* Edmonton: The University of Alberta, Department of Sociology. [45]

Nettler, G., 1968a. "The relevance of 'attitude.'" San Francisco: Pacific Sociological Association (April). Mimeographed. [68, 80]

Nettler, G., 1968b. "Using our heads." *American Sociologist,* 3 (August): 200–207. [76, 172, 203, 211–212]

Nettler, G., 1969a. "Moral distance, resentment, and the urge to punish." Edmonton: The University of Alberta, Department of Sociology. Mimeographed. [78]

Nettler, G., 1969b. "Embezzlement without problems: A test of Cressey's thesis." Edmonton: The University of Alberta, Department of Sociology. Mimeographed. [61]

Nichols, R. C., 1966. "Schools and the disadvantaged." *Science,* 154 (9 December): 1312–1314. [199–200]

Nicholson, C., 1960. "Kolenda on science and morality." *Mind,* 69 (April): 259–262. [188]

Nida, A., and W. A. Smalley, 1959. *Introducing Animism.* New York: Friendship Press. [76]

Niebuhr, R., 1932. *Moral Man and Immoral Society.* New York: Charles Scribner's Sons. [70]

Nietzsche, F., 1954. *The Portable Nietzsche.* Translated and edited by Walter Kaufmann. New York: The Viking Press, Inc. [105, 106]

Nisbet, R. A., 1968. "The year 2000 and all that." *Commentary,* 45 (June): 60–66. [73]

Northrop, F. S. C., 1947. *The Logic of the Sciences and the Humanities.* New York: The Macmillan Company. [21–22]

Nott, K., 1964. "Exchange of letters with Professor H. J. Eysenck." *Encounter,* 23 (September–December): *passim.* [3–5]

Oakeshott, M., 1966. "Historical continuity and causal analysis." In W. H. Dray (ed.), *Philosophical Analysis and History.* New York: Harper & Row, Publishers. [150–151, 165]

O'Brien, B., 1968. "Lenin and Guevara." *Encounter,* 31 (October): 92. [213–214]

Offenbacher, D. I., 1968. "Cultures in conflict: Home and school as seen through the eyes of lower-class students." *The Urban Review,* 2 (May): 2–8. [59–60]

Olson, M., 1969. "Toward a social report." Washington, D.C.: U.S. Government Printing Office. [144]

Ortega, Gassett, J., 1932. *The Revolt of the Masses.* New York: W. W. Norton & Company, Inc. [171, 172, 211]

Osgood, C. E., *et al.,* 1957. *The Measurement of Meaning.* Urbana: The University of Illinois Press. [45, 176]

Owens, W. A., 1968. "Toward one discipline of scientific psychology." *American Psychologist,* 23 (November): 782–785. [137]

Pap, A., 1962. *An Introduction to the Philosophy of Science.* New York: The Free Press. [122]

Pareto, V., 1935. *The Mind and Society: A Treatise on General Sociology.* New York: Harcourt, Brace and Company, Inc. [106, 181]

Parmenter, T., 1967. "Breakdown of law and order." *Trans-Action,* 4 (September): 13–15. [53]

Parsons, T., 1937. *The Structure of Social Action.* New York: McGraw-Hill Book Company. [105]

Patterson, C. H., 1948. "Is psychotherapy dependent upon diagnosis?" *American Psychologist,* 3 (May): 155–159. [168]

Peabody, D., 1968. "Group judgments in the Philippines: Evaluative and descriptive aspects." *Journal of Personality and Social Psychology,* 10 (November): 290–300. [176]

Pelcovits, N. A., 1946. "World government now." *Harper's,* 193 (November): 396–403. [27]

Perry, G. L., 1966. *Unemployment, Money Wage Rates and Inflation.* Cambridge: The M.I.T. Press. [116]

Pettigrew, T. F., 1964. *A Profile of the Negro American.* Princeton: D. Van Nostrand Company, Inc. [212]

Phillips, A. W., 1958. "The relation between unemployment and the rate of change of money wage rates in the United Kingdom, 1862–1957." *Economica,* 25 (November): 283–299. [116]

Piaget, J., 1930. *The Child's Conception of Physical Causality.* New York: Harcourt, Brace and Company, Inc. [142, 172]

Pierce, A., 1956. "Empiricism and the social sciences." *American Sociological Review,* 21 (April): 135–137. [72, 83]

Pitts, W., and W. S. McCulloch, 1947. "How we know universals: The perception of auditory and visual forms." *Bulletin of Mathematical Biophysiology,* 9: 127–147. [110]

Polanyi, M., 1965. "On the modern mind." *Encounter,* 24 (May): 12–20. [45]

Pope, A., 1966. "Moral essays." In H. Davis (ed.), *Poetical Works.* London: Oxford University Press. [170]

Popper, K., 1957. *The Poverty of Historicism.* London: Routledge & Kegan Paul, Ltd. [193]

Popper, K., 1959. *The Logic of Scientific Discovery.* Toronto: University of Toronto Press. [19, 126, 150, 211]

Popper, K., 1962. *Conjectures and Refutations.* New York: Basic Books, Inc., Publishers. [70]

Post, R. H., 1962. "Population differences in vision acuity: A review, with speculative notes on selection relaxation." *Eugenics Quarterly,* 9 (December): 189–212. [31]

Postan, M. M., 1968. "A plague of economists?" *Encounter,* 30 (January): 42–47. [133]

Precker, J. A., 1952. "Similarity of valuings as a factor in selection of peers and near-authority figures." *Journal of Abnormal and Social Psychology,* 47 (April): 406–414. [78]

Price, D. K., 1969. "Purists and politicians." *Science,* 163 (3 January): 25–31. [213]

Rahv, P., 1949. "The unfuture of utopia." *Partisan Review,* 16 (July): 743–749. [109]

Rainwater, L., 1967. "Open letter on white justice and the riots." *Trans-Action,* 4 (September): 22–32. [52, 53]

Rainwater, L., and W. L. Yancey, 1967. *The Politics of Controversy.* Cambridge: The M.I.T. Press. [168]

Rawcliffe, D. H., 1959. *Illusions and Delusions of the Supernatural and the Occult.* New York: Dover Publications, Inc. [99]

Reader's Digest, 1941. "Survey of public honesty." *Reader's Digest,* 38 (July, August, September): *passim.* [189]

Reichenbach, H., 1957. *The Rise of Scientific Philosophy.* Berkeley: University of California Press. [86]

Reichstein, K. J., 1965. "Ambulance chasing and the legal profession." *Social Problems,* 13 (Summer): 3–17. [78]

Rhees, R., 1947. "Social engineering." *Mind,* 56 (October): 317–331. [206]

Rice, S. A., 1928. *Quantitative Methods in Politics.* New York: Alfred A. Knopf, Inc. [30]

Richardson, H. M., 1940. "Community of values as a factor in friendships of college and adult women." *Journal of Social Psychology,* 11 (May): 303–312. [78]

Riesman, D., and N. Glazer, 1948–49. "The meaning of opinion." *Public Opinion Quarterly,* 12 (Winter): 633–648. [81]

Robinson, R., 1950. *Definition.* Oxford: Clarendon Press. [11]

Roche, P., 1951. "Truth telling, psychiatric expert testimony, and the impeachment of witnesses." *Pennsylvania Bar Association Quarterly,* 22: 140. [106]

Roe, A., 1963. *The Making of a Scientist.* New York: Dodd, Mead & Company, Inc. [89–90]

Rogers, C. R., 1946. "Significant aspects of client-centered therapy." *American Psychologist,* 1 (October): 415–422. [167]

Rokeach, M., 1968–69. "The role of values in public opinion research." *Public Opinion Quarterly,* 32 (Winter): 547–559. [78]

Rosenthal, R., 1966. *Experimenter Effects in Behavioral Research.* New York: Appleton-Century-Crofts, Inc. [108]

Ross, R., and E. van den Haag, 1957. *The Fabric of Society.* New York: Harcourt, Brace and Company, Inc. [109]

Rovere, R. H., 1968. "Letter from Washington." *The New Yorker,* 44 (15 June): 90–96. [51]

Rovit, E., 1968. "On the contemporary apocalyptic imagination." *The American Scholar,* 38 (Summer): 453–468. [165]

Royster, V., 1968. "The Lysenko syndrome." *The Wall Street Journal* (22 May): 16. [107]

Rubinstein, E. A., 1969. "Paradoxes of student protests." *American Psychologist,* 24 (February): 133–141. [153, 165, 214]

Runciman, W. G., 1966. *Relative Deprivation and Social Justice.* London: Routledge & Kegan Paul, Ltd. [205]

Russell, B., 1955. *Human Society in Ethics and Politics.* New York: Simon & Schuster, Inc. [76]

Ryle, G., 1966. "Ludwig Wittgenstein." In I. M. Copi and R. W. Beard (eds.), *Essays on Wittgenstein's Tractatus.* London: Routledge & Kegan Paul, Ltd. [6]

Sahlman, H., 1959. "Taxes: Evasion and avoidance." *Commentary,* 28 (November): 447–448. [189]

Sampson, E. E., 1967. "Student activism and the decade of protest." *Journal of Social Issues,* 23 (January): 1–33. [165]

San Francisco Sunday Examiner and Chronicle, 1968. "Candidates statements on crime." (3 November): Sec. A, p. B. [129]

Santayana, G., 1963–64. "Spirits in the sanctuary." *American Scholar,* 33 (Winter): 21–26. [106]

Sarbin, T. R., 1944. "The logic of prediction in psychology." *Psychological Review,* 51: 210–228. [131]

Sargant, W., 1964. "Psychiatric treatment: Here and there." *Atlantic,* 214 (July): 88–95. [132]

Savitz, L., and G. Tomasson, 1959. "The identifiability of Jews," *American Journal of Sociology,* 64 (March): 468–475. [77]

Sawyer, J., 1966. "Measurement *and* prediction, clinical *and* statistical." *Psychological Bulletin,* 66 (September): 178–200. [84]

Scheffler, I., 1963. *The Anatomy of Inquiry.* New York: Alfred A. Knopf, Inc. [125]

Scheffler, I., 1967. *Science and Subjectivity.* Indianapolis, Ind.: The Bobbs-Merrill Company, Inc. [94, 100, 101]

Schiffman, H., and R. Wynne, 1963. "Cause and affect." Princeton, N.J.: Educational Testing Service, RM-63-7 (July). [1, 35, 142]

Schimek, J. G., 1968. "Cognitive style and defenses: A longitudinal study of intellectualization and field independence." *Journal of Abnormal Psychology,* 72 (December): 575–580. [75]

Schlesinger, A. M., Jr., 1968. "America 1968: The politics of violence." *Harper's,* 237 (August): 19–24. [52]

Schneider, L., and A. J. Brodbeck, 1955. "Some notes on moral paradoxes in race relations." *Phylon,* 16 (June): 149–158. [163]

Schur, E. M., 1968. "Indecisiveness and evasion." Review of the President's Commission Task Force Report: *Narcotics and Drug Abuse,* in *Law and Society Review,* 2 (May): 483–488. [108]

Schutz, A., 1960. "The social world and the theory of social action." *Social Research,* 27 (Summer): 203–221. [48]

Schwartz, S. H., 1968. "Words, deeds, and the perception of consequences and responsibility in action situations." *Journal of Personality and Social Psychology,* 10 (November): 232–242. [82–83]

Schwitzgebel, R. L., 1967. "Short-term operant conditioning of adolescent offenders on socially relevant variables." *Journal of Abnormal Psychology,* 72 (April): 134–142. [172]

Scriven, M., 1959. "Explanation and prediction in evolutionary theory." *Science,* 130 (28 August): 477–482. [104]

Scriven, M., 1962. "Explanations, predictions, and laws." In H. Feigl and G. Maxwell (eds.), *Minnesota Studies in the Philosophy of Science.* Vol. III. Minneapolis: University of Minnesota Press. [127]

Scriven, M., 1966a. Review of C. G. Hempel, *Aspects of Scientific Explanation and Other Essays. Contemporary Psychology,* 11 (December): 561–562. [15]

Scriven, M., 1966b. "Causes, connections, and conditions in history." In William Dray (ed.), *Philosophical Analysis and History.* New York: Harper & Row, Publishers. [144, 147, 150, 151–152]

Scriven, M., 1968a. "In defense of all causes." Berkeley: University of California, Department of Philosophy. Mimeographed. [143–144]

Scriven, M., 1968b. "Notes on the logic of causes." Berkeley: University of California, Department of Philosophy. Mimeographed. [147, 153, 158–159].

Sechrest, L., 1968. "Testing, measuring, and assessing people." In E. F. Borgatta and W. W. Lambert (eds.), *Handbook of Personality Theory and Research.* Chicago: Rand McNally & Company. [212]

Secord, P. F., and C. W. Backman, 1964. *Social Psychology.* New York: McGraw-Hill Book Company. [29]

Segall, M. H., D. T. Campbell, and M. J. Herskovits, 1966. *The Influence of Culture on Visual Perception.* Indianapolis: The Bobbs-Merrill Company, Inc. [93]

Sevareid, E., 1967. "Politics and the press." Reprinted in part from "The Quill," by the *Wall Street Journal* (25 July): editorial page. [50]

Sherif, M., and H. Cantril, 1947. *The Psychology of Ego-Involvements.* New York: John Wiley & Sons, Inc. [109, 183]

Shonfield, A., 1969. "Thinking about the future." *Encounter,* 32 (February): 15–26. [73]

Shuey, A. M., 1966. *The Testing of Negro Intelligence.* New York: Social Science Press. [30, 31]

Siegel, J. S., 1968. "Completeness of coverage of the nonwhite population in the 1960 census and current estimates, and some implications." In D. M. Heer (ed.), *Social Statistics and the City.* Cambridge: Joint Center for Urban Studies of M.I.T. and Harvard University. [198]

Simirenko, A. (ed.), 1966. *Soviet Sociology.* Chicago: Quadrangle Books. [208]

Simmel, G., 1955. *Conflict.* Chicago: The Free Press of Glencoe, Ill. [27]

Simon, H. A., 1954. "The effect of predictions." *Public Opinion Quarterly,* 18 (Summer): 245–253. [111]

Simon, H. A., 1965. "Causal ordering and identifiability." In D. Lerner (ed.), *Cause and Effect.* New York: The Free Press. [146]

Simon, H. A., 1968. "Causation." In D. L. Sills (ed.), *International Encyclopedia of the Social Sciences.* New York: The Macmillan Company. [146, 156–157, 172–173]

Sines, L. K., 1959. "The relative contribution of four kinds of data to accuracy in personality assessment." *Journal of Consulting Psychology,* 23 (December): 483–492. [77, 84]

Skidmore, W., 1969. *The Relationships of Models of Man to Sociological Explanation in Three Sociological Theories.* Edmonton: The University of Alberta, Department of Sociology. Unpublished Ph.D. dissertation. [121]

Skinner, B. F., 1950. "Are theories of learning necessary?" *Psychological Review,* 57 (July): 193–216. [131]

Skinner, B. F., 1953. *The Science of Behavior.* New York: The Macmillan Company. [144]

Sklare, M., 1968. "The trouble with 'Our Crowd.'" *Commentary,* 45 (January): 57–62. [31]

Smith, J., and R. I. Lanyon, 1968. "Prediction of juvenile probation violators." *Journal of Consulting and Clinical Psychology,* 32 (February): 54–58. [84]

Smith, M. B., 1969. Review of E. E. Baughman and W. G. Dahlstrom, *Negro and White Children. Science,* 163 (31 January): 461–462. [210]

Sokal, R. R., 1966. "Numerical taxonomy." *Scientific American,* 215 (December): 106–116. [113, 114]

Somers, H. M., and A. R. Somers, 1959. "Medical care issues in the United States." Paper read at the National Conference on Social Welfare, San Francisco, 27 May. [167]

Sorokin, P., 1937. *Social and Cultural Dynamics.* New York: American Book Co. [70, 105, 190]

Sorokin, P., 1947. *Society, Culture, and Personality: Their Structure and Dynamics.* New York: Harper & Brothers. [34]

Staats, C. K., and A. W. Staats, 1957. "Meaning established by classical conditioning." *Journal of Experimental Psychology,* 54 (July): 74–80. [42]

Stevenson, C. L., 1963. *Facts and Values.* New Haven: Yale University Press. [188]

Stigen, A., 1960. "Mrs. Foot on moral argument." *Mind,* 69 (January): 76–69. [188]

Stollak, G. E., et al. (eds.), 1966. *Psychotherapy Research.* Chicago: Rand McNally & Company. [172]

Stouffer, S., et al., 1950. *Studies in Social Psychology in World War II.* Princeton: Princeton University Press. 4 vols. [196]

Stricker, G., 1967. "Actuarial, naive clinical, and sophisticated clinical prediction of pathology from figure drawings." *Journal of Consulting Psychology,* 31 (October): 492–494. [84]

Stryker, S., 1957. "Role-taking accuracy and adjustment." *Sociometry,* 20 (December): 286–296. [106]

Sutherland, N. S., 1959. "Motives as explanations." *Mind,* 68 (April): 145–159. [38]

Szasz, T. S., 1963. *Law, Liberty, and Psychiatry.* New York: The Macmillan Company. [212]

Terence, 1888. *Heauton Timoroumenos.* Edited by A. F. West. New York: American Book. Act I, Line 25. [48]

Teuber, H. L., and E. Powers, 1953. "Evaluating therapy in a delinquency prevention program." *Psychiatric Treatment,* 21: 138–147. [82]

Thistlethwaite, D., 1950. "Attitude structure and factors in the distortion of reasoning." *Journal of Abnormal and Social Psychology,* 45 (July): 442–458. [108]

Thomas, W. I., 1923. *The Unadjusted Girl*. Boston: Little, Brown and Company. [44]

Thomas, W. I., and F. Znaniecki, 1918. *The Polish Peasant in Europe and America*. New York: Alfred A. Knopf, Inc. [55, 80–81]

Thouless, R. H., 1959. "The effect of prejudice on reasoning." *British Journal of Psychology*, 50 (November): 289–293. [108]

Thurstone, L. L., 1947. *Multiple Factor Analysis*. Chicago: University of Chicago Press. [102]

Time, 1968. "The hardware store." *Time*, 92 (9 August): 40. [52]

Time, 1969. "The diary of a vandalized car." *Time*, 93 (28 February): 62–65. [189–190]

Tolman, E. C., 1948. "Cognitive maps in rats and men." *Psychological Review* (July): 189–208. [58]

Tomkins, S. S., 1965. "Affect and the psychology of knowledge." In S. S. Tomkins and C. E. Izard (eds.), *Affect, Cognition, and Personality*. New York: Springer Publishing Co., Inc. [58]

Toulmin, S., 1969. "Ludwig Wittgenstein." *Encounter*, 32 (January): 58–71. [188]

Trasler, G., 1962. *The Explanation of Criminality*. London: Routledge & Kegan Paul, Ltd. [48, 76]

Tucker, C. W., 1967. Review of A. K. Cohen, *Deviance and Control*. *Social Forces*, 46 (December): 299. [83]

Tullock, G., 1967. *Toward a Mathematics of Politics*. Ann Arbor: University of Michigan Press. [16]

Turner, R. H., 1968. "Is 'attitude' an obsolete concept?" San Francisco: Pacific Sociological Association. Paper read at annual meeting, April. [69]

Vaizey, J., 1968. "Disenchanted left." *Encounter*, 30 (February): 62–68. [211]

Van den Haag, E., 1960. "Social science testimony in the desegregation cases: A reply to Professor Kenneth Clark." *Villanova Law Review*, 6 (Fall): 69–79. [200–201]

Van den Haag, E., 1968. "On deterrence and the death penalty." *Ethics*, 78 (July): 280–288. [155]

Von Mises, R., 1956. *Positivism*. New York: George Braziller, Inc. [6, 188]

Von Neumann, J., and O. Morgenstern, 1947. *Theory of Games and Economic Behavior*. Princeton: Princeton University Press. [207]

Waelder, R., 1966. "The concept of justice and the quest for an absolutely just society." *Journal of Criminal Law, Criminology, and Police Science*, 58 (March): 1–6. [207]

Waelder, R., 1966. "A reply to Professor Morris' statement of dissent." *University of Pennsylvania Law Review*, 115 (November): 17–21. [207]

Wainwright, L., 1968. "The Kennedy's." *Life*, (Spec. ed.). Undated, p. 73. [83]

Walsh, R. P., 1961. "A generation of skeptics." *American Psychologist*, 16 (November): 712–713. [172]

Walsh, W. H., 1951. *An Introduction to the Philosophy of History*. London: Hutchinson. [13]

Walsh, W. H., 1959. "'Meaning' in history." In P. Gardiner (ed.), *Theories of History*. New York: The Free Press of Glencoe, Inc. [47]

Ward, J. H., and M. E. Hook, 1963. "Application of an hierarchical grouping procedure to a problem of grouping profiles." *Educational and Psychological Measurement*, 23 (Spring): 69–81. [113]

Warriner, C. K., 1958. "The nature and functions of official morality." *American Sociological Review*, 64 (September): 165–168. [67]

Webb, E. J., *et al.*, 1966. *Unobtrusive Measures: Nonreactive Research in the Social Sciences*. Chicago: Rand McNally & Company. [82]

Weber, M., 1947. *Gesammelte Aüfsatze zur Wissenschaftslehre*. Tübingen: Siebeck. Portions reprinted in A. M. Henderson and T. Parsons (eds.), *Max Weber: The Theory of Social and Economic Organization*. New York: Oxford University Press, 1947. [39, 40]

Webster-Merriam, 1923. *New International Dictionary of the English Language*. Springfield, Mass.: G. & C. Merriam Company. [86]

Weitzman, B., 1967. "Behavior therapy and psychotherapy." *Psychological Review,* 72 (July): 300–317. [172]

Wheeler, J. A., 1968. "Maria Sklodowska Curie: Copernicus of the world of the small." *Science,* 160 (14 June): 1197–1200. [111]

Whitla, D. K. (ed.), 1968. *Handbook of Measurement and Assessment in Behavioral Sciences.* Reading, Mass. Addison-Wesley Publishing Company, Inc. [84]

Wiener, N., 1961. *Cybernetics.* Cambridge: The M.I.T. Press. [90]

Wilkins, L. T., and A. Chandler, 1965. "Confidence and competence in decision making." *British Journal of Criminology,* 5 (January): 22–35. [77]

Wilkins, M., 1965. "The effects of information and cognitive complexity upon interpersonal perception." Boulder: University of Colorado, Institute of Behavioral Science. Report No. 70 (Fall). [78]

Will, F. L., 1947. "Will the future be like the past?" *Mind,* 56 (October): 332–347. [125]

Williams, R., 1967. Review of C. Glock and R. Stark, *Christian Beliefs and Anti-Semitism. American Sociological Review,* 32 (December): 1004–1006. [200]

Wilson, G. D., and J. R. Patterson, 1968. "A new measure of conservatism." *British Journal of Social and Clinical Psychology,* 7 (December): 264–269. [81]

Winch, P., 1958. *The Idea of a Social Science.* London: Routledge & Kegan Paul, Ltd. [41–43]

Winslow, C. N., 1937. "A study of the extent of agreement between friends' opinions and their ability to estimate the opinions of each other." *Journal of Social Psychology,* 8 (November): 433–442. [78]

Wirth, L., 1936. "Preface" to Karl Mannheim, *Ideology and Utopia.* New York: Harcourt, Brace and Company, Inc. [106]

Withey, S. B., 1959. "Public opinion and science and scientists." *Public Opinion Quarterly,* 23 (Fall): 382–388. [104]

Witkin, H., *et al.,* 1962. *Psychological Differentiation.* New York: John Wiley & Sons, Inc. [75]

Wittgenstein, L., 1922. *Tractatus Logico-Philosophicus.* London: Kegan Paul, Trench, Trubner. [6]

Wittgenstein, L., 1958. *The Blue and Brown Books.* New York: Harper & Row, Publishers. [41, 55]

Wolpe, J., 1966. *Behavior Therapy.* Oxford: Pergamon Press. [168]

Woodmansee, J. J., and S. W. Cook, 1967. "Dimensions of verbal racial attitudes." *Journal of Personality and Social Psychology,* 7 (November): 240–250. [56]

Wootton, B., 1965. "Crime and its rewards." *New Society,* 2 (23 September): 17–19. [77]

Wright, Q., 1964. *A Study of War.* (Revised) Chicago: The University of Chicago Press. [190]

Yinger, J. M., 1968. "Recent developments in minority and race relations." *Annals of the American Academy of Political and Social Science,* 378 (July): 130–145. [164]

Zarnowitz, V., 1967. *An Appraisal of Short-Term Economic Forecasts.* New York: Columbia University Press. [133]

Zegers, R. A., 1968. "Expectancy and the effects of confirmation and disconfirmation." *Journal of Personality and Social Psychology,* 9 (May): 67–71. [108]

Zimbardo, P. G., 1964. "Relationship between projective and direct measures of fear arousal." *Journal of Abnormal and Social Psychology,* 69 (March): 196–199. [212]

Zimbardo, P. G., 1969. "Diary of a vandalized car." Summary of his research reported in *Time* (28 February): 62–65. [189–190]

Zimmer, H., 1955. "The roles of conflict and internalized demands in projection." *Journal of Abnormal and Social Psychology,* 50 (March): 188–192. [212]

Zinn, H., 1967. "History as private enterprise." In K. H. Wolff and B. Moore (eds.), *The Critical Spirit: Essays in Honor of Herbert Marcuse.* Boston: Beacon Press. [180, 188, 204]

Zonis, M., 1969. Review of I. de Sola Pool (ed.), "Contemporary political science." *American Journal of Sociology,* 74 (January): 427–428. [174]

SUBJECT INDEX

Footnote numbers are shown in parentheses following their page numbers.

235